# UNLEASHING THE REBEL WITHIN

How to Break Free from the Hidden Programming That Shapes Your Life: A MANIFESTO FOR THE NEW ERA

**Lane Keller**

Introduction by
**Jane Donovan**

Copyright © 2025 by Lane Keller

eBook ISBN: 978-1-941117-18-7

Paperback ISBN: 978-1-941117-17-0

All rights reserved.

No part of this book may be reproduced in any form or by any electronic or mechanical means, including information storage and retrieval systems, without written permission from the author, with the exception of brief quotations in book reviews.

*This book is dedicated to my parents, Joyce and Jack Keller, the original free-thinkers who never stopped questioning and seeking truth. Thank you for passing your rebellious spirit on to me.*

### Author's Note

*Since this book was written, my mother, Joyce Keller, has passed. Readers will encounter her throughout these pages as a living influence. Joyce was a pioneer in every sense of the word. Long before "conscious media" existed as a concept, she stepped into public arenas hostile to intuition and met skepticism head-on—with humor, precision, and fearless clarity. She proved, repeatedly and publicly, that discernment and intuition are not opposites, but allies.*

*For more than three decades, she and my father, Jack Keller, hosted The Joyce Keller Show, creating a platform that welcomed inquiry and curiosity rather than dogma. She refused mystification, rejected ego-driven spirituality, and modeled a form of intuitive intelligence that withstood scrutiny without losing its humanity.*

*Much of what I challenge in this book—false authority, guru culture, manufactured mystique—I learned to recognize because I watched her navigate those waters without compromise. If this work has a backbone, it is because she taught me how to stand upright in truth, even when it wasn't popular, profitable, or safe.*

*This book is, in many ways, a continuation of that relationship.*

# Acknowledgments

Writing acknowledgments for a book such as this is challenging because the work has blossomed from wisdom gained over a lifetime. How does one pinpoint the influences in his or her life?

I gratefully acknowledge my parents, the original free-thinking souls whose endless quest for truth and wisdom ignited my own inner questioning.

I most gratefully acknowledge the highest teachers of all, God, or Yahweh, and Yeshua—also known as Jesus, the Planetary Logos, or "Brother," as he said he prefers—who exemplify the ultimate defiance of limitation through unconditional love and wisdom.

I gratefully acknowledge the master teachers who continuously illuminate humanity, including those whom I've been fortunate to spiritually connect with: Edgar Cayce, Paramahansa Yogananda, Nikola Tesla, my own father in spirit, and the countless others who collectively challenge humanity's perception as "The Collective."

Toward this purpose, I gratefully acknowledge the Arcturians and the diverse community of interdimensional guides who share their expansive insights, including Running Bear and others from indigenous nations, who inspire a deeper questioning of perceived reality.

I gratefully acknowledge the teachers whose rebellious ideas first inspired me in my youth and early adulthood, such as Ruth Montgomery, Dr. Raymond Moody, Brian Weiss, Baird Spalding, Kahlil Gibran, Delores Cannon, Alex Collier, David Icke, and numerous others. It's impossible to fully measure how profoundly these sources have influenced my path; all have contributed to shaping a transformative paradigm that I'm grateful and honored to take part in.

Finally, I gratefully acknowledge Jane Donovan, who serves as an interviewer in this book, and whose insightful, motivational strength embodies the spirit of fearless inquiry.

# Contents

| | |
|---|---|
| Preface | ix |
| Introduction | xxi |
| A Note to the Reader | xxiii |
| Phase I: Rebel Alchemy | 1 |
| 1. Where Rebellion Begins | 3 |
| 2. Lighting the Fuse | 20 |
| 3. MindFlips | 31 |
| 4. Magnetic Manifestation | 42 |
| 5. Soul Partners | 54 |
| 6. Reality Pivots | 75 |
| 7. States of Beingness | 95 |
| 8. Frequency Jumping | 107 |
| Phase II: Cracks in the Illusion | 125 |
| A Note Before You Begin | 127 |
| 9. Awakening in the Physical World | 128 |
| 10. Unmasking the Machine | 134 |
| 11. Puncturing the Cabal Veil | 143 |
| 12. Body Wars | 156 |
| 13. Raising Lions | 163 |
| 14. Breaking the Code | 170 |
| Phase III: The Rebel Path | 181 |
| 15. Signal vs. Static | 182 |
| 16. Staying Ignited | 194 |
| 17. Electromagnetic Reality | 205 |
| 18. Meeting the Monster | 214 |
| 19. The War for Your Heart | 221 |
| 20. The Consent Loophole | 231 |
| Phase IV: Crystalline Rebel | 239 |
| 21. Love in the Time of Ascension | 240 |
| 22. Timeline Outlaws | 249 |
| 23. Skyrocketing Through 5D | 259 |
| 24. Mastery or Bust | 266 |

| | |
|---|---|
| 25. Your Superpower | 273 |
| 26. Being Untouchable | 281 |
| Appendix: The Exit Sequence | 287 |
| Gate I: Escaping the Theater of Control | 291 |
| Gate II: Exit the Currency Trap | 299 |
| Gate III: Reclaiming the Body | 307 |
| Gate IV: Sovereign Toolkit | 319 |
| Glossary Of Terms | 329 |
| Afterword | 347 |
| I Hope You Enjoyed This | 349 |
| About the Author | 351 |
| Other Works by Lane Keller | 353 |

# Preface

You could call me a rebel. I don't really listen to anyone. I listen to my (psychic) mom from time to time, but even that is debatable. There is a small handful of people on social media who provide good information whom I give credence to sometimes. I definitely do not listen to anyone positioning themselves as knowing it all, who charge for "ascension" techniques, who charge high prices for psychic readings, or to any so-called "gurus." You can keep your golden thrones, your secret handshakes, and your seven easy payments for enlightenment —I'll pass, thanks.

I didn't listen in school, and I don't listen to schools of thought, particularly when it comes to spirituality. I have reasons for this and I'll share them as we go on. I don't attend spirituality classes and have not taken a course in ascension or manifesting—unless of course you count the time my mother enrolled me in Shelly Dumas' spirituality class in her basement in Syosset, NY when I was 12. Do I have the benefit of having been born to two incredible truth-seeker parents? Yes, I do.

They were on a trajectory of learning which I benefitted from. Their desire for information centered on spiritual growth and

## Preface

personal health. Through trial and error, they came to look to the teachings of Edgar Cayce, Paramahansa Yogananda, the mystery schools revealed by Astara, *Masters of the Far East* by Spalding, and many pertinent others as the basis of their blossoming spiritual understanding.

My parents had no limits on their quest to understand the spiritual universe and our parts in it. The exception to this was anything fake, a deliberate ploy for money, anything unnecessarily "mysterious," or which had at its basis ego. There was their story of one well-known Spirit Guru and his channeler, whose "cult" has continued to multiply to this day, whose amazing information would be bestowed upon you once you forked over thousands of dollars. This was back in the 70's. The initial session was so rife with mind control programming that people were pulling out their checkbooks before session's end, except of course for my parents, who sniffed this sort of stuff out like suspicious bloodhounds.

There were psychic fairs, yoga camps, spiritual camps like Silverbell and Lilydale, and visits with every psychic within a 1500-mile radius of our home on Long Island. This foray into the supernatural taught me the immense value of discernment and of keeping your mind open—because the highest and most trustworthy info came from the most unlikely sources. A brilliant psychic named Irwin, for instance, whose skill at pulling out brilliant tidbits from the ethers was matched only by his very unpsychic family's gluttonous attachment to my mom's cooking. When Irwin first saw the Twin Towers being built some 28 years before their demise, he stuck out two fingers and lowered them with a whistle. "Down they come," he said, mimicking their eventual fall. The psychic adventures taught me the difference between light and dark. As young children my brother and I knew who was working in the dark and who was in the light. Emily, for one, a powerful psychic who excelled at giving bad news, who ranked high on our "we don't like her" list. We may not have always been able to put the reason into words, but we knew who not to trust. We didn't trust the dark ones, or actually anybody except our own

## Preface

mom. For her powers were formidable, helping hundreds if not thousands of people find loved ones, connect with the departed, get married, or become pregnant. Of course, her powers were mysteriously off when it came to us. "I see you becoming a biochemist," she said as I ran off to study drama at NYU. Well, maybe she didn't say that exactly, but you get the picture.

My parents questioned everything, as I do, and I question even their philosophies. I question the masters not because their wisdom is faulty but because the needs and understanding of humanity is evolving while our ability to assimilate and utilize information declines. We on this planet are going in many trajectories at once. Dangers are magnifying. We are in the midst of an all-out war between light and dark, a war some may not even be aware we are in. Know it or not, we are engaged in the fight of our lives.

At this point, some might suggest I calm down, perhaps read a little Thoreau by the lake and contemplate peace. Instead, I resonate more with what other great teachers warned us about. Cayce spoke of a sleeping humanity. Tesla knew the universe was vibration and frequency—and that most people were being manipulated by forces they couldn't see. Yogananda spoke to the necessity of soul realization. Dolores Cannon mapped out the hypnotic layers of soul programming, while David Icke exposed how tightly the illusion is managed.

This book is not to spread fear. The more you know the better actions you can take. The more you heal your inner and outer worlds, the further you will go in helping to win this war. The fact that we are all here now is because on some level we chose to partake in the most epic battle ever waged, in which humanity, goodness, and the side of God, the Source wins.

Everything I have relayed in this book, all techniques, fixes, short cuts, wisdoms, and truths come from direct experience. I take no one's word as law and neither should you. If Alex Collier were here, he might utter something about the Andromedans watching closely, and remind you that sovereignty begins with asking better questions.

# Preface

Every bit of information must be sifted and held to the light for examination. To understand it, you need to feel it, and use it.

Let me repeat that, as it is a vital part of this book. To understand it, you need to feel it, and use it.

Words are cheap, as they say. What counts is whether or not something works, and whether it works for you.

You won't find any arbitrary repeating of concepts, truths or laws here, only methods that work that I have uncovered through real life experience and personal discovery. My guides, who stand by with answers, have helped assemble and define the ideas contained here. They are also the ones who urged me to write this book. A few months prior to writing this they made it clear I was to release a book clarifying spiritual concepts and to help people transform into their highest, best selves. The time had come, and I was to deliver this book in a clear, easy to follow, no nonsense way. Wait, I said, how on earth am I supposed to do this in—what? a couple of months you say?

My previous writings had taken far longer to complete. Some took years. My guides said not to worry, and sure enough it came together in the time frame they stipulated.

Sometimes my beautiful guides provide a straight downpour of information. I can get this to occur by asking a question then walking around the lake near my home with my dog and recorder. Words fly out as I dictate the answer.

Other times, like when I'm running a meeting, in conversation with someone, or as often happens, in the semi-dream state, my guides deliver concepts through a single word. If this happens when I'm sleeping, I will bolt upright in bed and write it down. It's up to me then to discover the meaning behind the word and to expand on it. If I'm in a meeting and share a word or name I've just received, the people around me know to take this word seriously. Without fail, it will expand or accurately redirect whatever we're talking about.

I love that my guides join meetings with us. They know I love language and so this is sometimes a fun game that we play, as a

# Preface

completely unthought of word pops into my head at exactly the right time or in answer to this or that problem. It is always perfect.

You would recognize the names of some of these guides, but they prefer not to be named and instead call themselves the Collective. The Arcturians also prefer not to use individual names. The reasons for this have to do with humility and because they are part of unity consciousness. Ego requires names. Delivering profound information that helps humanity does not.

As you now know, my background might be considered different, if not a bit peculiar. I stand as an iconoclast, although I have chosen at times to blend in. The reasons for this are similar to that of the Collective's. Information, vibration, truth—your brand of personal authenticity—are more readily accepted when you meet others at their level.

I am different in other ways as well. I can't be told something for I will not absorb or accept it. Instead, I have to feel it. At first, I thought this was due to stubbornness, but as I matured, I became grateful for this tool that was soon integrated into my process. By feeling into a conceptual thought, you can utilize it without effort. It is what I call assimilation: the absorption of information that becomes integral to your being. In other words, through feeling, concepts become part of your nature. This is not to put down analysis. As a writer/researcher I put great store in intellect and research. That said, when learning a new concept, it is always best to feel it, in my opinion.

Everything found in this book comes from my own process, every single thing. It is the result of years of effort and integration, as well as distillation of complex ideas into simple truths. I use "effort" loosely because much of it flowed as I pushed forward in my pursuit of truth. I never knowingly embarked on the path of ascension, yet I have been on it since birth.

What I thought I was on was the perpetual quest for truth and authenticity. This was my driving force, coupled with the intense outrage I felt over injustice and harm done to innocents and good hearts. I dislike injustice in all its forms. I won't use the word "hate"

# Preface

because everything, absolutely everything has a spiritual, or let's say "unknown," purpose that you can uncover if you look hard enough.

This acceptance of the unknown order of things eventually integrates into your personality. This holds true for the other concepts shared here as well, such as how to embody humor, love, lightness, and joy. These are abstract concepts and cannot be pursued on their own, nor should they be. They are instead the benefits of the path that drives you. Let me repeat that. Instead of pursuing "happiness," for example, pursuing the path of personal integrity and authenticity will provide happiness as a byproduct.

Is your path a quest for truth? Is it a path for justice? Maybe it is a path of self-betterment. Maybe you are motivated by the desire to eradicate the dark. You will find your motivational force as you move forward, if you haven't already.

The way this book is written differs from others. It is not meant to be a highly organized and strict How-To. It flows and meshes and instead follows a river of knowing. It is a fun river I hope, as the ideas, some of which are repeated and presented in different ways, take hold.

As this occurs, what changes do they bring within? What bells go off as you land upon something that resonates with you? That resonance, when it comes, should be isolated and cherished. That is a leaping off point.

Read this book not as a primer or a textbook, but as a discussion. From time to time my interviewer, Jane Donovan's voice pops in, because many of these ideas needed to be solidified and isolated. Until such times as Jane helped bring them out there were hidden aspects of my being that I did not in myself recognize, for I had so integrated them into my personality they were difficult to pinpoint. In other words, my quest for truth, justice and authenticity had generated self-development shortcuts that I did not myself always perceive until the beautiful being of Jane pointed them out to me. An impressive and insightful intuitive in her own right, Jane graciously stepped into the role of guide and reflector—drawing out the deeper

# Preface

themes, clarifying complex ideas, and helping to consolidate the core truths of this work. Her presence allowed for a dynamic unfolding as a masterful facilitator whose clarity sharpened the edges of every revelation.

That being said, my quest has been a painful process at times, encompassing the dark night of the soul, that enormous wall of despair that threatens to engulf you until you come out on the other side. The most difficult moments spent with my twin flame combined with the discovery of the worst, most hidden, dark secrets of the shadow world created a tsunami of grief which marked a major turning point for me, or what I consider my true point of embarkation. In other words, this is where my journey really began.

As I travelled down to the pits of child trafficking, Luciferian worship, and demonic behaviors that entailed untold tortures of our most innocent, I wondered how the world could ever pull itself back up. I knew it would not do so without our help—all of our help. Instead of taking me down, it quadrupled my conviction. I became indomitable. I refocused my direction into bringing awareness to these things. It has taken years of pouring effort into these ends. Some wrong turns—let's not say wrong, but detours—ended in what appeared to be dead ends. During this time, I produced 60+ *Lane Explains* videos which were all taken down by the YouTube bots, *The Arcturians* and *Talking Galactic* with my mom, documentaries on child trafficking (*Alice in Pedoland, Parts I & II*) and FDA cover ups, created a network of truth-bearing documentary producers, and much more. I have worked with various "humanitarian" groups who were as ostensibly set on creating the new media as I was, or funding the same. These groups did not turn out to be fruitful and some were downright harmful. I will say at least one was demonic, because the subterfuges the alleged leaders used could only point to dark forces out to subvert those trying to do good for humanity.

Eventually, and probably because of these episodes, I knew I had to stop relying on others, because that was what it was doing. I was aligning myself with those whom I wrongly believed had more to say

## Preface

or better ways of saying things than I did. Many of these individuals turned out to be very dark despite appearances to the contrary. This recognition was also part of my growth process. When I broke free of the last of these groups, I knew I would never put my energy behind someone else again, but instead would forge forth, solely, if I had to, using my own voice and garnering whatever energies I could muster into the force for positive change.

At that time of breaking free several stalwart souls surged forward with me. They knew as I did that the time for change had come, and that we had the knowledge, tools and passion to help it transpire. The media endeavor, LifeSource was created, and multiple trajectories shot off from there.

There is another faction that must be identified here, the Arcturians.

"You've got to choose," they say, meaning you've got to choose the side of ascension. Do you? Do you choose to live an authentic life that is free of harm to others or yourself? Yes? Then that is a choice.

For we create our own paradise, a world we were meant to have all along, a world that is right side up. The longer we are in a higher vibration, the more we get to associate with people vibrating at the same frequency, or in other words who are like us. The idea of experiencing love and peace all the time probably sounds boring. Yet ascension is merely a way of being that eliminates strife and unhappiness. It can be as exciting as you make it.

I've never yearned for peace on earth, exactly. I've yearned for truth and for people to awaken from this dream reality and to see who's creating the wars and divisions. To be over on the other side or in an elevated state, means you don't have to participate in the carnage but sometimes you still have to watch it.

Getting to more on how this book came about, in 2015 the Arcturians started delivering plans for a new world that included a new media, and a new way of being. Remembering that for them time is fluid and boundless, they told me that soon it would be time to develop that blueprint as the world enters the new paradigm.

# Preface

Before this could occur, however, the related philosophies and knowledge had to come out. This was to be the framework for the book.

What did I want the world to know? Jane then asked me, having heard the story. I said I didn't have a clue. "Yes, you do," said Jane.

I have the kind of brain that puts things into organizational patterns. Only I didn't want to have to adhere to a limiting formal structure. So, I invited the Collective to speak. To help this along, Jane asked questions. From there things opened up.

It hit me that Phase I of this book wouldn't be about following steps, reciting affirmations, or politely waiting for someone else's permission slip to heal. No—Rebel Alchemy starts inside, where you grab your trauma by the scruff and drag it out into the daylight. This is your awakening to programming, trauma, and self-deception. You confront the roles you've inherited, the beliefs you've swallowed, and begin the radical act of self-inquiry. Here, the hidden programming and self-sabotage lose their power because you're finally looking them in the eye and laughing. That's the spark.

Phase II: Cracks in the Illusion means it's time to tear off the blinders. You begin to see through media deceptions, social engineering, fear-based programming, and the manipulation of your mind, emotions, and biology. I'm not here to gently suggest you notice the world is upside down; I'm here to pry open the shutters, let the sunlight in, and toss you a pair of X-ray glasses. This phase may be difficult to read, and you are invited to skip over it if you do not wish to go down the rabbit hole right now. Should you wish to tackle it, know that it's about refusing to play along with the trance that's kept humanity sleepwalking, about poking holes in every inherited belief until you see daylight pouring through, and offering solutions along the way.

Phase III: The Rebel Path returns to dive into the heart of inner liberation, guiding the reader through a piercing unraveling of false identities, inherited programs, and energetic distortions. It challenges the illusions we've absorbed from culture, authority, and trauma—

## Preface

shining a light on the internal mechanisms that keep us bound. As the journey deepens this is where the rebel becomes a seer, stripping away static, confronting the deeper architecture of darkness, and reclaiming emotional sovereignty from systems that have fed off unconscious consent. Rather than offering surface empowerment, these chapters supply the means of a total energetic reset—one that dismantles the lies within and without, anchoring the reader into unshakable clarity, radical responsibility, and the raw frequency of truth.

Then comes Phase IV: Crystalline Rebel. This is where theory becomes transmission. You're not just awake—you're activated. Your thoughts manifest faster. Your intuition sharpens. Your pineal comes online. You begin to walk this earth like the rebel-seer you were meant to be—anchored, discerning, and free. You stop playing the role you were handed, and instead radiate the frequency of who you truly are.

These phases aren't a checklist or ladder—they're a spiral path of remembering, each one deepening your clarity, expanding your freedom, and anchoring you more fully in your truth.

I'd like to share something interesting about Hermes, the ancient Egyptian who created the Emerald Tablets, the sacred texts written on green stone. He talked about the alchemical process, which some take to be about gold, but translator Dr. Matthew Barnes said, no, what the process really referred to was the alchemy within.

The alchemy within being the wild, unsupervised science of spinning the mess you were handed—old programming, guilt, trauma, inherited fear—into something that actually shines. Forget waiting for some wise robed elder to pass you the secret formula. The real transformation happens when you're willing to take the ugly, tangled stuff and spin it into gold by staring it down, day after day, until it gives way. You start seeing through the old illusions, tuning your senses, and spotting where your ego tries to play king of the hill.

Answers don't always show up on command, neatly packaged. They reveal themselves sideways—in the split-second gut punches,

# Preface

the stubborn laughs that bubble up when old patterns try to drag you back, the sudden yes! that pulses through your whole system when you know, absolutely, you're done playing small. That's how collective change starts: not from consensus, but from the handful of us willing to torch the script and write something true.

After that, the alchemy explodes outward. This is the part where you stop asking for permission to live beyond yourself. You start seeing through the world's costume party—relationship roles, business scripts, all the inherited posturing. The old paradigms start to look ridiculous. You don't just "awaken," you catch the hidden strings, step off the puppet stage, and get real.

If all this ever starts to feel heavy or strange, let me drop the act for a second: it's supposed to. The best medicine isn't always sweet. This book works like classical homeopathy—the undiluted, high-frequency stuff. Just let the words buzz around in your psyche. You don't need to take notes, build a vision board, or stress over technique. Let the vibration do the heavy lifting. Sleep with the book under your pillow if you like—sometimes rebellion is a matter of osmosis.

If you've gotten this far, let's be honest: you've already proven you're not one for groupthink or guru-worship. You've got the immune system of a philosophical honey badger. If Emerson were here, he'd toast your nerve; if Nietzsche could text, he'd send a fire emoji.

Hold tight. You're not here to fit in—you're here to wake up. The world you're about to step into is bigger, wilder, and more alive than the one you were told to settle for.

See you on the other side of conformity.

With Lots of Love,
    Lane


Thank you for taking the time to read this book. When you're ready, please take a few minutes to write a quick and honest review on

## Preface

Amazon. I read every review and use the feedback to improve the book and future writings.

If you haven't already please subscribe to my newsletter at https://lanekeller.substack.com/ or https://lanekeller.com/ where you can join a community of like-thinkers as well as receive free books and other goodies.

Hold on tight now as you are soon to enter new realms and the fulfilling life you in your deepest being know is possible.

# Introduction

by Jane Donovan

When I first met Lane, we immediately knew who the other was. Some would say it's that 'soul sisters' feeling, however it was more than that. We appeared to be a mirror to each other and as our time spent together grew, the synchronicities between our decades of living became greater and greater. While not being doppelgängers, we still to this day are incredulous at the similarities.

During this time, I had the pleasure of being on dozens if not hundreds of Zoom calls with Lane and the various production and project teams related to LifeSource. It was during these meetings that I started to see the differences between Lane and myself. I'll start by saying that often these meetings became passionate, sometimes triggering, argumentative and philosophical as they are filled with richly spiritual humanitarians. Many of them are the real doers of this world who are in a hurry to get stuff done. Others are philosophers or visionaries, some networkers, and others gentle earth angels. This melting pot of extreme personality types and passion can often be a recipe for chaos.

# Introduction

Lane directed these sometimes 3-hour long meetings with the consistent mastery of many qualities I admire and that are much needed in this world at this time. She navigated potentially tricky situations with grace, leadership, support, inspiration, solutions, and wisdom while holding a consistent high vibration. That's not an easy feat to achieve. Not once did I feel her being triggered. The woman appeared to have superpowers I didn't, and I wanted to know how she had developed these skills.

I have been fascinated by emotional intelligence since the age of 10 and I wanted to know how Lane became so masterful. I soon realized she had a combination of an unusual childhood raised by two very conscious parents, and the ability to quantum leap spiritual lessons. It would be easy to suggest that Lane had spiritually bypassed some lessons however as you will discover in the reading of this book, she hasn't.

My voice is minimal in the book however it appears where Lane has potentially made an assumption that her quantum leap is a doable thing for us all. I interject where I feel needed to gain greater clarity about the 'how' in some situations and I hope like me, you are fascinated by Lane's journey and wisdom that we all, I know, wish an abundance of in the world for us all today.

Happy reading, Jane xx

# A Note to the Reader

This book is not written to persuade, convert, or reassure. It does not offer a single belief system, political stance, or spiritual doctrine to adopt. Instead, it invites reflection, discernment, and personal responsibility.

*Unleashing the Rebel Within* is best approached slowly, thoughtfully, and with a willingness to question both external systems and internal assumptions. Take what resonates. Leave what doesn't. The work belongs to you.

# Phase I: Rebel Alchemy

"The only way to deal with an unfree world is to become so absolutely free that your very existence is an act of rebellion."
—Albert Camus

## Chapter 1
# Where Rebellion Begins

Talk of "ascendence" or higher vibration fills bookshelves and soundbites—but the truth is sharper than most will admit. As seers before now have warned, the world is rising, yes—but through fire.

Despite the noise, the chaos, and the illusion of regression, we are being pulled—sometimes dragged—into a higher state of awareness. Slowly, painfully, the frequency is shifting. It's not optional. For ascendence isn't a trend—it's a revolt. A rising frequency is tearing through illusion, not tiptoeing around it. The world is shifting, even if most are too programmed to see it. Despite the noise, despite the fear, despite the grip of control systems, consciousness is rising. Not politely. Not quietly. Instead, with fire. You're either riding the wave —or getting dragged under.

I didn't write this book to play nice with the old paradigm. Ascendence isn't a soft glow or a spiritual daydream—it's a full-blown uprising of consciousness. We are ascending, yes—but not the way most imagine. It's messy. It's uncomfortable. It rips through illusion like wildfire. Despite the propaganda, despite the control structures clinging for dear life, the vibration of this planet is rising. I've seen it. I've lived it. I'm here to help you ride the current.

What does ascendancy actually mean—and why should it matter to you now, in this moment?

Because in a high-vibrational state of existence, you stop begging the world to give you what you already have. You start radiating what's real. That changes everything.

You become the frequency that rewrites your reality. You draw in what aligns, and you repel what doesn't. People either rise to meet you or fall away without a fight. You're no longer hustling uphill toward some external success model. You're doing what sets your soul on fire—because you're finally in tune with your purpose, not the program.

You wake up charged. Not dragging through obligation, but pulled toward something luminous, something yours. As you walk this new path, something wild happens: You start breaking other people free, just by being who you are.

This isn't about "being happy." That's the candy coating they sell you. This is about liberation. From the lies. From the conditioning. From the quiet soul-death that comes from playing small in a world that trained you to forget who you are.

When you start vibrating at a higher frequency, darkness can't stick. The static clears. You don't have to fight the low energy anymore—it just falls off. Your soul family starts showing up, one by one, like they've been waiting for you to wake up. The fake connections dissolve. The real ones root.

You feel the connection between all things—not as a soft, preachy slogan—but as a pulsing, undeniable truth. You become the kind of human being who stands tall without stepping on others, who sets boundaries without guilt, who uplifts without depleting yourself. You don't need validation because you've claimed your own knowing.

You no longer need to forgive—because you've transmuted it all into thankfulness. Even the pain. Even the detours. Especially those. Your body gets the memo too: shedding stress, softening, strengthening. You glow, but not because you're trying. Because you're living true.

Family becomes sacred again—not because they match your expectations, but because you let go of needing them to. You're open, grateful, present.

Money? That shows up when you're aligned. You don't chase. You magnetize. Source—the Infinite Force, the Creator, Yahweh, God, Goddess, call it what you will—starts flowing through your life like a glowing river. You meet it with clarity, not clutching.

Love? Absolutely. You love yourself. You love others. If your sacred partner is meant for you, they will appear. If not—if you've outgrown what was—then you'll walk forward, alone but not lonely, until your match meets you in the mirror. Sacred union begins within. Everything else flows from that.

Joy stops being an accident. It becomes your default setting. You find yourself smiling in moments that used to flatten you. You witness the beauty in absurd places. You laugh louder. You love bigger. You stop apologizing for being awake in a world still half-asleep.

You start to realize: this was never out of reach. You were just taught to look the other way.

## **Rebellion Starts Here**

There are countless books and courses that claim to show you how to bring more light, power, and purpose into your life. Many of them are beautiful. Even so, let's be honest: many are buried in workbooks, mantras, mystified language, or twelve-step processes that take years to master—if you make it that far.

This book is different.

There are no gates to pass, no gurus to impress, no certification to hang on your wall. Instead, what I offer you here are real-world strategies—some downloaded from realms beyond this one, others born through sheer necessity in the heat of life. They're methods I've actually lived, often without even knowing they were methods at the time. What turned everything around for me wasn't some epic ritual. It was often a simple mind flip. A shift in perception so potent, it cracked the false ceiling wide open.

These tools didn't come to me alone. I thank my incredible spirit guides, and I thank Jane Donovan—my bold, brilliant interviewer and co-conspirator in this quest for truth. Jane has a knack for pulling the gold out of a passing sentence. You'll hear her voice throughout this book, chiming in just when you need a mirror, a nudge, or a dose of straight-up clarity. She's the one who often stopped me mid-story with, "Wait, stop there, Darling. That is surprisingly unique. Do you realize how unusual that is?"

So, here we are.

This book isn't just a guide. It's a spotlight on the truths that have been buried and the power you forgot you had.

## Choose Your Frequency

Looking back, I can tell you—this entire journey begins with a choice. Not a dramatic one. Not a ritual. Just a quiet, internal "yes." A decision you may never say out loud. Yet make no mistake: it's a threshold.

The problem is, most people think they've made this choice when they haven't. They speak the words, wear the shirts, light the candles—but deep down, they're still plugged into the very system they claim to reject.

The choice I'm talking about is this:

Will you align yourself with the light—truly, wholly, no turning back?

Because the alternative is not neutral.

The "dark" path isn't always gothic or obviously evil. It's subtle. It's the slow hypnosis of conformity. It's the boxed-in thinking that keeps you working for systems that drain you. It's the obedient body in the doctor's office, trusting pills over intuition. It's blind faith in politicians, dogma, or scripted history. It's the belief that you are small, powerless, or broken.

This is the trap of *The Matrix*—what the Wachowski Brothers, Sophia Stewart, Alex Collier, David Icke, and others have named in different ways. It's the veil. The simulation. The invisible fence that feeds off your disempowerment and calls it normal.

Most people don't even realize they're living in it.

Conditioning makes them stagnant. Fear of change keeps them frozen. Eventually—as Plato warned—we begin to love our chains.

## A Radical Shift

Choosing the light doesn't mean moral superiority or spiritual bypassing. It means full-spectrum alignment with the real: with Source, with truth, with the infinite creative intelligence that pulses through everything.

It means opting into a code that is both ancient and revolutionary:
- Never stop becoming who you truly are (check)
- Never stop shedding the lies you were sold (check)
- Never stop raising others up as you rise (check)
- Never stop seeking truth, even when it burns (check)
- Never stop doing the work, even when it's quiet (check)

If you feel that in your bones, then you've already chosen ascension. You just haven't claimed it fully yet.

Ascension is not some esoteric ladder to the stars. It's a radical shift in how you see, feel, live, and walk in this world. It begins inside —and then it rewrites your external life at warp speed. At first, the changes trickle. Then they rush. Soon you won't remember what it felt like to be stuck, drained, unseen, or small.

Because those were illusions.

Now you're authoring your reality. Not surviving. Not waiting. Creating.

You're about to turn your world right side up. Trust me, it's going to feel like rebellion.

Are you ready?

## The Inner Mirror

How do we flip our inner world 180° when it feels like we've been living upside down for decades? What do we do with the triggers, the traumas, and the hidden conditioning that keeps hijacking our joy?

Let's start with the ancient truth bomb from Socrates:

"The unexamined life is not worth living."

He said that before being sentenced to death—for teaching the youth to think for themselves.

No, this isn't a cute self-help slogan. It's the cornerstone of your liberation.

Self-examination is not a phase. It's not a weekend workshop or a healing retreat in Bali. It's a way of being. A frequency. A lens you never take off. The longer you live this way, the clearer it gets:

You can undo almost anything.

That trigger? Track it to the emotional root. That pain in your body? Follow it back to the unresolved energy it's holding. That fake smile you wear in front of certain people? Ask why. What are you hiding? What are you afraid of?

This is how the real healing begins. Not by pretending. Not by bypassing. Instead, by relentlessly choosing truth over comfort.

Because if you don't? You get runaway ego. Chronic illness. False stories that calcify into "identity." You get trapped in a character that was never the real you to begin with.

Self-examination is how we become authentic. Without authenticity, there is no power.

## Burn the Pedestals

# UNLEASHING THE REBEL WITHIN

Let's talk about gurus. Experts. Authors—including me (yes, I see the irony).

If you ever start believing your message is bigger, better, or more sacred than someone else's, prepare to be humbled. This universe has a very specific way of correcting ego inflation. It's not subtle.

Right now, we're in a planetary wave where Spirit is choosing to work through many people. Not just the flashy ones. Not just the verified ones. You may be one of them. You may be the very frequency the world is waiting for. No one's going to hand you a microphone. You've got to claim your voice.

Here's what you need to know:

All channeled information, all insights, all teachings are filtered through the ego of the receiver. No matter how clear the message, it's still coming through a human vessel—shaped by biases, beliefs, and personal wounds.

That's why I'll always say this:

Don't just take my word for it. Learn to do it yourself.

Because when the wisdom comes from your own higher knowing, it's unshakable. It doesn't need a platform or a cult following. It just is.

## The Raw You, No Filters

Living an examined life means you interrogate everything. Your habits. Your reactions. Your fears. Your beliefs. You don't get to coast on autopilot anymore. You don't get to hide behind trauma, conditioning, or the idea that "this is just who I am."

Because here's the hard truth:

Most of what you think is "you" isn't actually you.

It's programming. It's defense mechanisms. It's survival patterns passed down through generations or etched into your nervous system by early experiences. It's ego dressing itself up as personality.

Authenticity is what remains when you strip all that away.

It asks hard questions:

- What in my actions or thoughts is rooted in fear?
- What am I doing to be liked, instead of to be true?
- Where am I lying—either to myself or others—just to avoid discomfort?

There are people who lie all day, every day. Not because they're malicious, but because it's easier. It keeps them in control. It helps them maintain the story they've sold themselves about who they are.

The thing is, you? You're not here for that.

You're here for truth. Integrity. Realness.

You're here to live a life so cleanly aligned with who you really are that the lies burn off on contact. That includes the lie that you need external validation to matter. Or that you're only as worthy as your productivity, your beauty, or your success.

Authenticity means showing up unmasked—while still having the discernment to protect your energetic boundaries. It means knowing who you are, while staying humble enough to grow.

## Self-Realization: Meet the Real You

Self-realization isn't some esoteric spiritual prize at the end of a long path. It's the path itself. If you're doing this right, it never ends.

You might heal your marriage, get your body back in alignment, build your dream life... and still, the work continues. Because the moment you stop examining, the moment you believe you've "arrived," ego creeps back in and seduces you with comfort and illusion.

Plato, student of Socrates, called it "mere waste"—a life without examination or realization. He said we must develop our sixth sense, that intuitive inner knowing, in order to reach our highest state of being.

Then there's Paramahansa Yogananda, who laid it out beautifully: "Self-realization is the knowing—in body, mind, and soul—that you are now in possession of the kingdom of God... that God's omnipresence is your omnipresence."

## UNLEASHING THE REBEL WITHIN

That's power. That's what happens when you stop living reactively and start living consciously. When you stop outsourcing your decisions to fear. When you stop being a victim of your own inner story.

This is about awareness.

It's about taking ownership of every trigger, every emotional reaction, every pattern you play out on repeat. It's about catching yourself before you spiral. It's about asking the deeper questions.

Why did I react that way?

What part of me still believes I'm not enough?

Whose voice is that in my head—and is it even mine?

When you do this enough, your life stops being a series of dramas and starts becoming a sacred unfolding. You magnetize the right people, experiences, opportunities—not because you're lucky, but because you're in alignment with your truth.

When you get there?

You don't need to preach love. You radiate it.

You don't chase success. You embody it.

You don't have to prove your worth. You remember it.

Because now, finally, you're not operating from wounding. You're operating from knowing.

## Scripted Love

A lot of people appear loving. They smile, say the right things, do kind acts—especially when someone's watching. Yet beneath the surface, it's performative. Conditional. Programmed.

They're loving because the "good book" told them to. Or because their religion rewards them for it. Or because they're terrified of otherworldly punishment. Others try to convince themselves they're good by convincing others first.

Now let's be clear:

That's not real love.

Real love doesn't need a witness. It doesn't tally points or wait for applause. It doesn't come from obligation or fear. It rises from the heart like sunlight—warm, constant, and impossible to fake.

You're not here to fake it.

You're here to evolve past the charade. To tap into the kind of love that exists when no one's looking. To become the kind of person who picks up the trash no one saw you drop, who blesses the soul that just cursed you out, who forgives because it sets you free—not because it makes you look spiritual.

That's real evolution. That's unconditional love.

It doesn't mean rolling over or tolerating abuse. It does mean choosing to act from alignment—even toward the so-called "bad guys." Especially them.

If you can't love them, then wrap them in a big pink heart bubble, place them in Source's hands, and send them off to Planet Lala where they can't do any more harm. Don't let them poison your frequency. Don't let them shrink your capacity to radiate.

Because love isn't weakness. Love is rebellion against the machine. The matrix wants you resentful. Angry. Divided. Vengeful.

Real love breaks the whole damn system.

## Connected Distance

We toss around phrases like "We're all connected." The thing is: do we actually know what that means?

Can you feel it? Do you understand it on a cellular, soul-deep level? Can you sense that the pain in someone else's chest echoes your own from another timeline, another lifetime, another layer of the spiral?

That's energetic reality.

Yet there's a razor-thin line here—especially for empaths. Feeling someone's pain is not the same as taking it on. Too many sensitive souls drown in compassion without remembering to breathe.

Time for the rebellion: feel deeply—but do not bleed.

Empathy without boundaries is martyrdom. The martyr complex

is one of the most seductive traps in the spiritual matrix. It flatters your ego and drains your life force.

That's not the path.

True connection requires distance. Not coldness—but self-determination. The ability to stand beside someone in anguish, to witness their struggle, to radiate calm presence and love—without collapsing into it.

This is the tightrope we're all learning to walk.

The planetary field is demanding it. As crises ramp up—illness, loss, reckoning—we're being asked to hold both love and detachment. To stay open without becoming entangled. To care deeply, without carrying what's not ours.

For death, even illness, even tragedy—is chosen on some level. It is chosen on a karmic, soul-based, multidimensional level. You don't have to understand it to honor it. Instead, you have to stop trying to control it. The soul knows what it's doing.

Sometimes, the most loving thing you can do... is witness, without rescuing.

The true revolution isn't just about waking up—it's about learning how to stay awake and sane, while the world unravels around you. That's what real connection requires.

**Your Vibrational Fire**

Next, you need to examine your vibration.

Not constantly. Not obsessively. But at key moments—especially the moments that feel... off.

When people act standoffish, hostile, or avoidant—it might not be them. It might be you. Or rather, it might be your frequency. You're always transmitting something. The question is, what?

Are you down in the dumps? Numb? Cynical? Depressed?

Don't slap a smiley face on it. Don't bypass it with love-and-light platitudes. Be honest. Be raw. Just don't stay there. The low states aren't a sin, but they're not your home either.

Your vibration doesn't lie. It tells the truth you've been hiding from yourself.

Are you torn? Feeling neglected, unseen, or betrayed? Good. That means there's something ready to be looked at. Don't offload it onto others. Don't weaponize it. It's not their burden to carry.

Work through it. Own it. Transform it.

Because every unresolved emotion you suppress becomes a radio tower broadcasting static. That static repels the very harmony you crave.

Vibration is the pulse of your becoming. It shapes who and what shows up in your life. If you want peace, emit peace. If you want respect, radiate it. If you want soul-level love, become its match.

When you catch yourself spiraling? Pause. Breathe. Recalibrate. You're not at the mercy of your moods. You are the sacred architect of your frequency.

Let me repeat that. You, and only you, are the sacred architect of your frequency.

That's the first major rebellion. It's a quiet one.


**Guard the Charge**

Ask yourself—in every room, every conversation, every exchange—am I giving energy or taking it?

This is about integrity. About presence. About frequency hygiene.

Are you shedding light and clarity—or are you sucking others dry with unconscious need? Are you genuinely connecting—or are you performing to get something in return?

Because every word you speak, every glance, every sigh carries a charge. It ripples outward. Your vibration is not private. It's viral. It affects people.

Be the light you wish to see. Be the clarity you wish others had. Be the calm in the room—not the storm.

This doesn't mean being fake. Or hiding your struggles. Yet it does mean owning your energy before you unleash it on the world.

Think about what the other person needs—not just what you want. What would uplift them? Even in silence. Even in stillness.

This isn't about people-pleasing, but about energetic responsibility.

Raise the vibration of every space you enter. That's true power.

Because the alternative? The energetic vampire path? It's real. Most people are doing it and have no idea. They leave others confused, irritable, drained. They think it's charisma or charm. It's not. It's extraction.

Refuse to be that.

Yes, sometimes this requires brutal honesty with yourself. Sometimes it means shutting up when you want to vent. Sometimes it means walking away until your energy is clean.

You're here to radiate, not leech.

That's how you know you're on the path. That's how you light the fire in others—without even trying.

## Real World Discussion: Ego

Let's talk about ego. Not the cartoon villain version. Not the "you should be humble" trope. I mean the real, everyday ego that subtly warps how we move through the world.

Self-esteem says, "I'm important. I'm valuable. I have something to give."

It's right. You are. Own that.

On the other hand, ego? Ego whispers, "I'm more important than the person next to me." It pits you against others in an invisible contest you never agreed to enter. It doesn't just believe you're smart—it believes you're the smartest in the room, and that others need to know it.

You may be brilliant. You may be powerful. That's not the point.

Because the person next to you—your neighbor, the local barista, a disruptive child—might be a Gandhi in the making. He might be carrying a piece of the divine puzzle you'll never unlock on your own. She might be the teacher you didn't know you needed.

Your job isn't to win.

Your job is to wake others up to their own power. To fan the flame of recognition. To lift the veil, not drop a curtain on their light.

If you're truly standing in your worth, there's no need to dominate. There's no impulse to one-up. There's no hunger to be seen as superior.

In contrast, when ego runs the show, you become the main character in a play nobody else wants to see.

When you set ego aside—without shrinking—you become part of something vast. You start asking:

What am I here to offer?

What frequency am I broadcasting?

What truth wants to come through me, unfiltered?

This doesn't mean becoming submissive or self-sacrificing. It means operating from a clear center. A place of strength, not scarcity.

You're not here to compete. You're here to contribute.

That shift alone can change everything.


**Genius Tip: Seeing Vibration and Frequency**

Here's a perspective hack most people never consider: Frequency is external. Vibration is internal.

Frequency is what's sent or received—like a radio signal. Vibration is what you carry at your core. It's the hum of your essence. The magnetism of your state of being.

You might be able to fake frequency. You cannot fake vibration.

Now imagine—just imagine—if everyone could see energy the way we see color or shape.

The world would be unrecognizable.

If you could see auras—actual frequency fields, rippling in motion—you'd know instantly when someone's words didn't match their energy. You'd feel the dissonance of manipulation, the sting of sarcasm disguised as humor, the rot under false kindness.

You'd also recognize truth. Feel purity. Sense resonance.

Conversations would become transmissions. Interactions would become sacred. Intentions would purify themselves. Body language would realign.

Start now.

Train your inner sight.

Visualize the waves people give off. The colors, the pulses, the sparks or shadows. Sense how yours land, how theirs affect you.

Feel it.

When something dark tries to latch on—anger, envy, manipulation—see it clearly. Then deflect it. Not with fear. Not with hate. With power. With clarity. With sovereign detachment.

You are not required to absorb what is not yours.

When you truly perceive energy, you can no longer unsee the damage that unconsciousness causes.

A raised voice becomes a projectile. A cruel word becomes a toxin. An unresolved emotion becomes a storm in another person's field.

That? That is why you commit—fully—to vibrational integrity.

Because once you see energy, you'll never again choose to harm a living creature. Not just because it's wrong—but because you know what it does.

## This Is Where You Rise

This work, this rebellion of self-awakening, isn't a one-time epiphany. It's a lived revolution. It begins the moment you stop performing for the world and start living from the center of your truth.

There is no final boss to defeat, no mountaintop where it all clicks and you float away in permanent bliss. What you get instead is something far more powerful—clarity. Presence. Discernment. The ability to feel the difference between what lifts you and what leeches from you.

You begin to sense the distortions in the system. The falseness in a smile. The static in someone's words. You don't need to argue with it. You just know.

This knowing is your compass now.

It's what lets you move through the chaos without getting infected by it. It's what sharpens your yes, strengthens your no, and clears the fog from every room you walk into.

It's not always easy. You will lose people. You will irritate the matrix. You will start to feel like a glitch in the system—because you are.

The trade-off is this: you regain yourself.

You return to that centered, high-vibrational self that creates from alignment rather than fear. You become the person you were always meant to be—before the conditioning, before the shame, before the silent agreements you made just to survive.

You start to experience real joy—not the counterfeit kind handed out by advertisements and algorithms, but the kind that rises unprovoked when you're doing exactly what you came here to do.

You begin to love people not out of obligation, but because it's your nature to radiate. Your frequency becomes medicine for others. Not because you're trying, but because you're finally being.

This journey does not promise perfection. It demands presence.

It does not guarantee you won't fall. It guarantees you'll get up—faster, clearer, fiercer—each time.

This is where it begins.

Right here, in the middle of your life, in the chaos of a collapsing system, in the friction between who you've been and who you're becoming.

It begins with a refusal:

- To sleepwalk
- To obey blindly

## UNLEASHING THE REBEL WITHIN

- To forget who you are

It begins with a vow:

- To see clearly
- To stand in integrity
- To radiate what's real

This is the turning point, not out there in some distant future.
Here. Now. With you.
So begins the journey.

## Chapter 2
# Lighting the Fuse

For me, it's comes down to one thing, one magical way of looking at things that changes everything and lifts your vibration. It's something that never fails and just —well it just works.

What is it?

You laugh. Yes, laugh.

You laugh at sleeping in and missing the train or that the car is not starting again even though it's raining and you just had it fixed. You laugh at tripping and bruising your tailbone, because you didn't break something, at least. Murphy's law is funny. This is about perceiving the irony in things. It's about things turning out the opposite of how you've planned.

You know what happens when we make plans, right?

God laughs. The Universe generally has other things in store for us. In fact, the Universe and our spiritual helpers have a great sense of humor.

Train yourself to see irony. Irony is funny. The alternative is being pissed off or angry or stressed, and there goes your vibration: way down. This vibration brings more bad things to you.

## UNLEASHING THE REBEL WITHIN

So, laugh instead, dammit, and mean it.

It's been laughter for me my whole life. Why? Because I want to lighten the load on not just myself but on others. Always. How do I do that? Use humor, as best I can.

Sometimes I'm not as funny as I want to be, but I'm always trying. I try to lighten whatever it is.

If I'm in a car and I've just flown off the road and down a hill, which happened to me, as soon as you come out of the shock you make a joke or funny comment. It's because you're thinking about the other person's experience and the vibration you're transmitting.

Enter Jane.

Jane: Okay, wait, you've taken a quantum leap that most people haven't. So, I want to ask you, how did you get to the point of caring so much about other people without being a people pleaser? Because that's a key point. Most people can't do that and we can't make the assumption that it's an easy thing for people to do.

Lane: That's part of the inner alchemy. Let's go back to examining. I've just slid down a hill and this happened to me when I first moved to Maryland with my then husband and the kids. It was a snowy Sunday morning, and I was off to meet them for holiday photos. I was probably rushing or not paying complete attention, and as I come out of a hairpin turn, I suddenly find myself flying over black ice. I went into a 360-degree spin and my car flew down an embankment sideways, landing exactly between two tall pine trees.

There was not an inch to spare on either side. I slid between them like a letter into an envelope, an exact fit.

So, first is silent shock. Then a man appears out of nowhere. An angel, I believe, and raps on my window, asking, Are you okay? He adds as I roll down the window, "Because a jeep with four teenagers went down that same hill a few months ago and three of the boys died."

## Lane Keller

I nodded to indicate that I was okay and said, "But something terrible happened. I spilled my coffee."

Because the coffee I had prepared for myself that morning had splashed all over the dashboard and messed up my car. For some reason, I found that hilarious. Maybe I didn't want to think about those poor kids and what could have happened to me.

I know I'll be more conscious of turns and black ice in the future, but at a moment like this you need to laugh, and that's because I wanted to put the man at ease. I was thinking of him.

Afterwards, you have to examine it. Why did I fly down that hill? Perhaps that was my grandmother or one of my guides saying, Laney, you've got to slow down. Why did I land between two trees? Because I was not meant to leave the planet at this time and my guides and angels are working to protect me. The irony is that the only thing I could think of in that moment was the spilled coffee.

So, examination is essential. Why did this happen? Why am I not dead? Thank you, God, is the thought. So is being thankful.

Jane: Is gratitude a big part of your life?

Lane: I'm sorry to say that I really dislike that word. I dislike it because it's on every mug, pillow, cute little plaque, and painted rock from here to Australia.

Gratitude, gratitude, gratitude. I dislike cliches in general because they lessen the impact of what the words mean. I imagine some fat cat globalist elitists behind the gratitude agenda pushing complacency on us instead of encouraging us to be all we can be. It sounds cynical, but I'm very aware of agendas. That does not mean I'm not highly, highly grateful, however, but that comes from me and not from a piece of crockery.

Jane: Okay, I get it. I totally agree. However, it does have a place as a valid tool in assisting people who are lower on the emotional ladder to climb up to a better feeling place.

So, maybe gratitude is useful as long as one doesn't stay in gratitude and continues to reach for a higher vibration of way of being.

Lane: I say instead, examine your life, examine every moment, and be thankful for the lesson. Thank God, thank the Universe! Ask yourself, why did this happen? And don't forget to laugh.

## Radical Karma

In looking for the reasons behind our experiences, we've got karmic life lessons being learned at every point. I took a big leap early on when I realized something radical: we could probably control the karma we experience. I asked my guides—straight up—what if I learned my lesson right there on the spot? Wouldn't that eliminate karma?

So, in my youth, I started ascertaining the reasons behind my experiences and never stopped. I don't like creating karma, and I definitely don't like experiences that become increasingly difficult until you've "received the message." The process of karma has my healthy respect, which is why I do everything I can to outwit it, reroute it, and evolve beyond it. Realizing this was a key moment in my life—a jailbreak of the mind.

Another epiphany I had sometime later was about fear. I stopped fear within a day—done and over. No drama. Just flipped the switch. I'll explain that a bit further on.

Back to using karma to your advantage. At the exact moment I was dictating this passage, I dropped my groceries and decimated a dozen and a half eggs—and my dented cans rolled down the driveway like rebellious runaways.

Why did that happen? Maybe my guides were delaying me for some reason. Maybe I just missed getting hit by a car.

So, thank you, Universe. I'm very appreciative that you just saved me from something, whatever it was.

Maybe I was simply meant to learn that I am not supposed to be doing too many things at once. Or maybe those eggs were bad. I take that onboard. Message received.

. . .

## Universal Synchronicity

There are many stories of people wondering whether something is a coincidence or some form of sign. I don't believe in coincidences. Period. As soon as you say you don't believe in coincidences, the whole grid shifts. Everything changes.

Here's an overused axiom I dislike: "Everything happens for a reason." Yet—darn it—it's true. I've said it to my own kids a million times. I even dislike my own voice saying it. Yet truth has a way of coming back around.

What's another way of putting it? Universal synchronicity.

There are reasons for everything—including things you can't see and haven't been taught to look for. Once you know there's an entire world beyond what we perceive, then you know there's also a whole lot of invisible traffic in motion. Angelic guides. Spirit helpers. Interplanetary beings. Unseen alliances. Multiversal nudges.

Many are reaching out to you at this very moment—if you're unplugged enough to notice.

Jane joins the conversation.

Jane: A professor from Harvard School of Consciousness said maybe 20 years ago that if the Empire State Building represents everything that we know to exist, how much of the building do you think we are actually physically able to see?

So, students guessed, oh, half of it, a quarter, etc. He answered that it was one grain of sand at the base of the entire building. That's what we physically can see versus what we know exists that we cannot see.

Lane: I don't know how that professor could possibly reduce human knowledge down to one grain of sand, because in fact, he has no idea of what we don't know.

Maybe it's a tenth of a grain of sand that we perceive. What I can say is that there is a tremendous world around us in very close proximity that is constantly interacting with us. It's not about seeing ghosts or detecting whether your deceased grandfather is in the room. Rather, it's about understanding the moments of connection and delivery of information. These things expand once you recognize them.

Their information is right at our fingertips. There's a couple of rules before getting there. First is to transform your thinking to accept that there are things we cannot see. Then moving forward, there is a sure footedness in saying, yes, I can make mistakes.

Jane: We all make mistakes. I don't make as many mistakes as I did before my dark night of the soul challenges. However, I strive to be as consciously aware of every move I make with dedication to come from love and not from fear.

Lane: I feel that it's important to acknowledge the path of least resistance. I'm not saying to avoid challenges or to take no for an answer. Nonetheless, when you are hit with obstacle after obstacle, it's wise to take a step back and ask, okay, why isn't this working? What you are doing is probably not the best way forward.

If it's clear sailing all the way through and you're in the flow of giving and receiving, it's marvelous. You're flowing in the stream. The energy is rising. You're inspired. You've got new doorways opening up and new ideas budding. You're feeling great. That's how you know the way is right. You're feeling your way through it.

## The Rebel's Compass

What if your soul came equipped with a precision guidance system—always broadcasting, always calibrated to truth? It does. You just haven't been taught to listen.

Emotions are not random. They're not "too much." They're not a weakness. They're intel.

Your emotions are the barometer of your soul—a sacred internal compass that lets you know, in real time, whether you're aligned with truth or entangled in illusion.

This compass doesn't lie.

It doesn't care about your resume.

It doesn't care what your friends think.

It doesn't care what your spiritual teacher, Instagram algorithm, or inner critic says.

It feels the truth.

When you're in alignment—when your choices, words, and direction harmonize with your deepest self—you feel it. There's a lightness. A quiet joy. A grounded clarity. That's your soul saying: yes, more of this.

When you're not in alignment, your body knows before your brain catches up. There's anxiety. Resistance. Dullness. That quiet tug in your chest. That clench in your gut. That rising sense of dread when you're about to say "yes" to something that screams "no" inside.

What appears to be a negative response is actually feedback.

The system works if you don't override it. Yet, you've been trained to ignore it

From childhood, we're taught to override our inner compass. We're told to be polite instead of honest. To be agreeable instead of authentic. To put others first—even when it betrays our own truth. We're told our feelings are inconvenient. Dramatic. Untrustworthy.

As a result, we tune our innermost guidance out. We hand the wheel to logic, social rules, external authorities. Before we know it, we're off-course—saying yes when we mean no, staying when we need to go, playing small when our soul is screaming to expand.

Now, here's the truth.

Tuning back in to your inner compass is one of the most radical acts of rebellion you can take.

Because it means you no longer need permission. You no longer ask others to confirm what you already know. You move from internal authority, not external validation.

You say:

"I don't need proof. I feel it."

"This path might not make sense to others, but it lights me up."

"That deal looks good on paper, but something feels off—and that's enough."

"I'm not waiting for permission to trust myself."

# UNLEASHING THE REBEL WITHIN

This is the compass that doesn't point north. It points true.

## Rebellion Starts in the Silence

Start simple. Next time you're about to make a decision—small or large—ask:

How does this feel in my body?
- Expansive or constrictive?
- Light or heavy?
- Alive or dull?
- Like truth—or like strategy?

Then trust the answer. Even if you don't act on it immediately, acknowledge it. That's how you recalibrate.

Over time, your barometer gets louder, clearer, faster. It becomes second nature. You'll no longer ask others to read your map. You'll be reading energy in real time. You'll be walking in sync with your own internal terrain—and nothing is more magnetic than that.

The bottom line: Emotion is direction.

When your inner compass says yes, lean in.

When it says no, listen.

That subtle tug of misalignment you feel? That's the warning light before the storm.

The rebel within you isn't impulsive. She's attuned.

She knows the truth—not because she thinks it.

Because she feels it.

## The Chains of Ego

Let's clarify something further. Self-esteem is not ego.

They might look similar on the surface—but they come from entirely different places. One sets you free. The other keeps you chained.

Self-esteem is the quiet, powerful, grounded sense that you are enough—right now, right here, no applause necessary.

Ego is the loud, restless voice inside your head that needs more—more validation, more status, more people to think you're winning, even if you're falling apart inside.

Self-esteem is built from truth—inner truth.

It comes from knowing your gifts, honoring your growth, recognizing your value even when no one is clapping.

It says:

"I am who I am, and I don't need to prove it."

"I have work to do, but I am already whole."

"My worth isn't up for debate."

Ego, by contrast, is built on fear.

Fear of not being good enough. Fear of being invisible. Fear of being exposed as inadequate. Ego will do anything to avoid that fear—including tearing someone else down just to feel a little higher.

## Ego Traps

You've seen it. You've probably done it. We all have.

Let's say you're feeling bad about yourself. Maybe you've put on weight, or fallen behind, or feel like you're not measuring up. Then you spot someone doing worse—and instantly, your ego perks up.

"Well, at least I'm not that bad. They've been trying forever and still can't get it right."

That tiny jab feels good for a moment. Yet it's not real.

You didn't rise. You just pulled someone else down.

That's ego posturing as confidence.

It's counterfeit currency for the soul.

There's something that ego won't tell you: every time you use it to boost yourself at someone else's expense, you reinforce the core wound that says you're not enough.

Every time you seek validation outside yourself, you disempower the rebel within.

You hand over the keys to your worth. You place your self-perception in someone else's hands.

This is how the matrix keeps you compliant.

It makes you feel like you need permission to love yourself.

It makes you depend on others to confirm what your soul already knows.

**Your Real Power**

Self-esteem isn't noisy. It doesn't beg. It doesn't compare.

It's the voice that whispers:

"You're not perfect. You're powerful."

"You're still growing. You're already worthy."

"You can shine without dimming anyone else."

When you stand in that kind of self-knowing, something wild happens.

You stop needing praise.

You stop fearing criticism.

You stop playing small just to fit in with people who don't even see you.

You start lifting others up—not because it gets you anywhere, but because you have the bandwidth to do it.

That's beautiful magnetism.

Just imagine for a second:

What if you never needed another compliment to feel valid?

What if you no longer got high off someone else's failure?

What if you walked into a room without shrinking, competing, or pretending?

What would you create?

What would you free yourself to become?

Because here's the rebel's truth: the world doesn't need more self-importance.

It needs more self-knowing.

More people anchored in their own sacred value who are unafraid to see it in others, too.

. . .

## Lane Keller

**Your Mirror Check**

Say it. Out loud. In the mirror. Right now.

"I am enough. I am worthy. I am already whole."

This isn't fluff. It's rewiring. It's reclamation. It's rebellion.

Once you stop outsourcing your worth, no one—not a parent, not a partner, not a culture—can ever take it from you again.

That's soul authority.

That's freedom.

That's how you unleash the rebel within.

## Chapter 3
# MindFlips

MindFlips are quick revolutions for the sovereign soul. They are simple shifts that crack the programming.

MindFlips are not fluffy affirmations. They are soul-honed reboots—truth reversals that dismantle the lies you've been living under. Flip them once, and they'll land like lightning. Flip them often, and they'll rewire your life.

For best results, read these in a relaxed state. Lie down. Let go. Let your subconscious take the wheel for a while. If you fall asleep while reading, don't worry—you're not zoning out. You're plugging in. These flips work on multiple layers.

When you wake up, read a few more. These are keys. Let them unlock you.

**MindFlip 1: Be the Magnet**

The Universe—let's also call it the universal energy field—doesn't simply listen to what you say. It responds to what you radiate.

Energy is everything, and yours is magnetic. Your moods, your thoughts, even your silent assumptions are picked up by others and mirrored back by the energetic field. Whether you're aware of it or not, you are constantly broadcasting a frequency—and life sends you matching signals.

If you're transmitting worry, scarcity, or desperation, don't be surprised when more of it shows up. Flip the script. Tune your channel.

Radiate joy. Radiate helpfulness. Radiate abundance.

Even if you don't fully feel it yet—act as if. You'll begin to.

The Universe listens. The field responds. The return signal?

Tenfold.

## MindFlip 2: It Isn't Always You

That crystal-clear insight? That phrase that popped into your head out of nowhere? That instinct that saved you from disaster?

You didn't invent it.

You received it.

You are not alone—and you never were. Every human being on this planet is walking with an invisible team. Call them spirit guides, angels, higher selves, galactic allies, ancestors, or the Collective—whatever name you give them, they are real, and they are trying to reach you.

Even those who scoff at the spirit world have been visited in dreams or nudged by insight they couldn't explain. In contrast, if you believe in it, you open the line wider. You become a more active receiver.

Truth: You are being contacted. Right now. Through whispers, nudges, images, songs, and flashes of knowing.

You don't have to earn it. You just have to listen and acknowledge.

## MindFlip 3: Darkness, Begone

Let's cut through the noise:

There is darkness.

It doesn't play fair.

If you're receiving evil, distorted, chaotic information—or if your space feels off—you're picking up interference. Dark forces thrive on low vibration. They feed off fear, depression, addiction, anger, self-loathing, and apathy. They attach to energy patterns—not just people.

What opens the door?
- Ouija boards
- Drugs and alcohol
- Environments of decay (bars, haunted spaces, trauma-filled homes)
- Negativity and rage
- Chronic dissatisfaction or hopelessness

They sense it. They follow it. They amplify it.

In contrast, here's what they hate: your self-mastery.

Clean your space. All of it—physically, mentally, emotionally, spiritually. Eliminate what isn't of the Light. Speak with authority. This is one of the most powerful tools in your arsenal:

Thrust your arm out, palm facing outward, fingers upward, and command:

"I do not consent. Darkness, BEGONE."

Do it until the energy clears. Say it inwardly if you must. Eventually, you won't even need to speak it—your very vibration will repel interference.

You are not prey. You are power.

## MindFlip 4: Laugh Instead

You're about to scream. Or cry. Or spiral.

Flip it.

Humor is a disruption code. It breaks the frequency of despair and replaces it with levity—one of the Universe's favorite frequencies.

How? When something triggers a reaction—anger, shame, fear—notice it. Then ask:

"How can I laugh at this?"

At first, it may feel forced. That's okay. You're rewriting the groove in your brain. New reaction. New pathway. New power.

I use the Monty Python method and say to myself, "I scoff in your general direction." (I mean it.)

Try it. Nothing throws the dark off like someone who laughs in its face.

Remember this: Dark forces are only strong when you forget who you are.

That said, when you laugh? You remember.


## MindFlip 5: Fear? BOOM. Get Rid of It

Picture two balloons. One white. One black.

Every time you feel fear—boom—the black one grows. The white one shrinks.

Guess which one feeds the matrix?

Guess which one feeds the Light?

This isn't metaphor. Loosh—the energetic substance of human suffering—is the fuel of control systems. Fear feeds wars. Fear fuels media. Fear fattens the pockets of those who engineer disasters.

I say, don't feed them. Don't inflate the black balloon.

Every time fear creeps in—a bill, a threat, a worry—STOP.

Say: "Nope. Not happening."

Then flip it.

"Ha! I scoff at this bill. God's got it."

You don't have to believe it perfectly—just long enough to shift the channel. The white balloon inflates. The good side gets stronger. You just reclaimed a piece of your power.


## MindFlip 6: Still Got Fear? Look Deeper

Fear is sticky. Sometimes it hides beneath logic.

"What if I can't pay the rent?"

"What if the diagnosis is true?"

Is this fear real—or is it a memory, a projection, a lie?

If a doctor gives you three months to live—ask yourself:

Who made them God?

Have they factored in spontaneous healing? Emotional cleansing? Spiritual upgrades? Natural cures or dietary changes? No? Then their prediction is flawed.

What they don't know, or tell you, is that many people have defied all odds—not because they followed protocol, but because they believed they could. The knew it in all parts of their being.

They tuned in. They reached higher. They stopped feeding fear.

When fear hits, flip it and say: "All my needs are taken care of."

This isn't blind optimism. It's cosmic alignment. It's declaring your vibration louder than the fear signal.

Even in a dark alley with a pursuer closing in on you, fear won't help. Calm clarity will. Fear leads to panic. Panic leads to bad decisions.

Choose your response.

Choose your frequency.

Choose your authority.

Enter Jane.

Jane: What we're talking about here is a false truth running the fear narrative.

Lane: When it happens you need to examine that and turn it into a true truth. Take out fear, and hold it up to the light. What do you see? Where did it come from? Who started this lack of belief in the abundance of your life?

Tell yourself, this fear is unreasonable. Fear will accomplish nothing, except bring more stress into your life. Fear is a hotbed for negativity, a petri dish full of premature aging and disease. It creates a pall of negativity that affects your well-being and that of others. Do you want this? I don't think so.

Instead say goodbye fear, then go deal with the problem in a calm, productive, and empowered frame of mind.

**MindFlip 7: Say Yes! to the Flow**

Picture this: You're clenching a crystal wine glass in your fist, muscles tight with tension. What's going to happen? Shatter. Instead, hold it gently between two fingers, and it balances with ease, letting you savor every sip. This is the Law of Flow in action.

The same principle applies to energy, money, time, and love. The tighter you grip out of fear—fear of lack, fear of failure, fear of falling behind—the more likely you are to fracture the very thing you're trying to hold. Flow is what happens when you stop controlling. When you stop micromanaging. When you trust the higher currents.

Let's take something real. You open a bill and instantly your gut clenches. You feel that ancestral fear kick in—maybe from parents who lived paycheck to paycheck, or from the memory of sleeping in your car. That fear? It stops the flow cold.

It's time to remember that there's another way. Pause. Breathe. Say a prayer—not one of begging, but one of co-creation. Invite your angels, your higher guides, or Source to assist you. Then release it. Don't stew in the problem. Move your energy. Go sing a song. Take a walk. Watch a hawk circle overhead. Laugh with a child. Trust that life responds not to panic, but to presence.

Congratulations—you've just reentered the flow.

**MindFlip 8: Money Is Energy**

You've been lied to. Money isn't real—not in the way we were trained to believe. It's not safety. It's not success. It's not even real. What's in your account is a series of digital digits. Fiat currency is paper backed by nothing but collective belief and centralized manipulation. The whole system is a sleight of hand.

Yet... money moves things. It feeds your pets, buys your tires, and pays the guy to fix your deck. Then what is it really?

Energy.

When energy flows, so does money. When you share it with generosity, it circulates. When you hoard it in fear, it stagnates. When you curse it, it resists you. When you bless it, it becomes a conduit.

That $300 you gave your handyman? It wasn't you paying what you couldn't afford. It was a ripple—feeding his family, fueling a day's worth of service, and multiplying through your generosity. Because energy obeys universal law, it comes back—sometimes as unexpected kindness, sometimes as extended payment plans, sometimes as miracles dressed up as customer service reps.

To stay in flow let go of the grip. Stop worshipping numbers and start moving energy. Money isn't your master. It's your mirror.

## MindFlip 9: Call On Your Spirit Helpers

As I've said, you are not alone. Not ever. Not even for a second. Now take things further.

There are benevolent intelligences—interdimensional allies, angelic guides, ancestral spirits, members of the Collective—who are here to assist you. The thing is, they cannot override your free will. They need permission. They need an invitation.

So, invite them. Call them in. Surround yourself in pure white light—the highest Source light—and consciously open the line. Say, "Show me what I need to know. Surround me with truth. Walk with me through this."

A note of caution: beware the fakes. Not every entity wearing spiritual garb is working in your favor. Anyone who tells you something laced with fear—like your partner is leaving you or your life is doomed unless you buy their potion—is either working through ego or channeling something distorted. Real spirit guidance is clean. It uplifts. It empowers. It gives clear nudges, not dire threats.

If you don't get an answer right away, that's okay. The silence can be a message too: either "not yet," "not that," or "trust yourself."

Never forget: you have a spiritual support team on call, 24/7. Use them. That's what they're there for.

Jane: Do you want to talk a little bit about that? Because I think it's something that people need to know.

Lane: There has never ever been a dark prediction issued by the other side by your guides. If they do it's a malevolent force coming in or you're with an inexperienced practitioner who's misinterpreting. What the guides would say is, be more aware when you drive, or, you're driving too quickly. Make sure to wear that safety belt and you should also check your brakes.

They would never say you're going to get in a car accident next week. It's not the way the universal energy field works. They're not allowed to interfere with karma, and the guides are never going to give you a negative pronouncement.

## MindFlip 10: The Most Important Thing You May Ever Hear

This isn't just a MindFlip. It's the entire game.

There are no absolutes. None. That means: Nothing is set in stone. No outcome is predetermined. No prophecy is ironclad. No pattern is unbreakable. You—yes, you—have the capacity to rewrite the script at any moment. Why? Because you have free will. Free will overrides fate. Every time.

This has been one of my deepest truths and favorite laws to live by.

Yet not everyone agrees. My mother and I have danced around this for years. She's highly intuitive, a natural channel, and she's often prompted—by guides, by energy, by producers and audiences—to offer predictions. It's become a part of her public persona. She might say, "Here's what I'm seeing," and then immediately qualify it with, "Of course, it can change." This is absolutely true. I respond,

"Then why say it at all? Why set people on a projected course, even lightly, when the most important message is that you can change anything?"

See, predictions are what the media wants. They can be dazzling. Spot on accurate. That said, they also have the potential to implant subconscious beliefs that subtly strip people of their power. It's a kind of programming—benevolent in appearance, but still shaping the field.

This doesn't sit right with me. Why? Because I've seen too many people live inside someone else's idea of their future. They internalize a message like: "Your soulmate is five years away," or "This illness will get worse before it gets better," or "You'll struggle financially until your Saturn return ends." Then they build their life around that forecast—as if the script can't be burned, rewritten, or upgraded.

But the script can be rewritten. It always can. Conscientious psychics like my mother do say this.

Predictions, psychic readings and astrological horoscopes, at their core, are just trajectories—possibilities based on the current energy field. What appear to be heavenly mandates are in fact mere weather reports. If the spiritual practitioner or intuitive doesn't remind you of that—if they don't emphasize your ability to change the outcome of *anything*—then they are missing the whole point.

Because here's the rebel truth most won't tell you:

You are not here to obey predictions, but to override them.

Not with wishful thinking. With choice. With will. With the conscious, rebellious act of declaring: "Nope. That's not my story."

That declaration? That's where the magic begins.

Jane: I've had a situation where I was getting guidance for a client. I just received a message of: your brother would really be a lot happier if you reconnected and spent some time with him soon. It turned out that the brother died not long after.

I share that as an example because they're not going to directly tell me something horrible. Oh, your brother's about to die. They're not going to instill the fear. But what they're going to do is put love in, which is go and spend some time with your brother. She was given the gift of guidance to do so. When her brother did cross, she was very grateful that they'd had that time together.

Lane: Beautiful. Psychic readings are in the hands of the interpreter. Information is only as good as the reader and most everyone is highly influenced by their own thoughts and opinions. It's a rare individual who can put aside their thoughts and be a true channel.

Even then—even when the messages come wrapped in shimmering love-and-light packaging—channeling is suspect.

This became glaringly obvious during one of the most disillusioning chapters of the New Age movement, which I will dub here, "the Great Channeling Debacle." It was a time when droves of hopeful seekers tuned in to seemingly benevolent frequencies, only to find themselves misled, manipulated, and dulled into passivity. False light infiltrated the stream. People bought it.

Not all channelers were naive. Unfortunately, too many failed to question the source. Too many trusted the honeyed tone of the message, assuming anything that "felt" high-vibe must be pure. That's exactly how the deception worked: it didn't come as a growling demon. It came as a smiling master, purring about "unity" and "ascension," while slowly diverting humanity away from discernment and into spiritual sedation.

Thankfully, some woke up.

A number of channelers began to realize the infiltration. They tightened their filters. They started interrogating the source, demanding clarity, setting spiritual safeguards. They stopped allowing anything into their field that didn't resonate with absolute sovereignty and truth.

That's the key.

Channeling isn't inherently bad. It is however, open-source spiritual software, and if you don't guard your ports, incoming energy can hijack the signal.

This brings us back to predictions of any kind.

## UNLEASHING THE REBEL WITHIN

If you receive them—whether from a spirit guide, a doctor, a scientist, a dream, or a psychic reading—take them as energetic trends, not verdicts. Ask: What is this pattern asking me to notice? Where is this momentum heading—and what can I do to change it, if I choose to?

When COVID hit, I asked my mother how long it would last.

"Three years," she said without hesitation.

My gut recoiled. "No way," I said. "We're going to be done in six months."

Deep down, I sensed the truth in her words. Sure enough, humanity's collective submission to fear, control, and mass programming allowed the timeline to stretch out nearly exactly three years. Not because it had to, but because that's the reality most people accepted. The script played out as written—because no one tore it up.

That's what our guides, spirit helpers, and higher selves can offer us: a preview of probable reality, based on the energies in motion. Not to lock us into fate. Instead, it's to give us a chance to choose differently.

If you don't like what's predicted? Flip it. Override it. Rebel.

Because the greatest prophecy is the one you rewrite. With fire. With clarity. With the unwavering knowing that you create your own reality.

## Chapter 4
# Magnetic Manifestation

It's liberating—electrifying, even—to step into the flow of magnetic manifestation. To realize that you don't need to chase things down, claw your way up, or beg the world to give you scraps. You are here to magnetize. To emit a signal so clear and strong that your field begins pulling the right people, ideas, synchronicities, and quantum openings directly to you.

Let's get one thing straight: information is energy. Thoughts are energy. Desire is energy. Every intention, emotion, and action you send into the field creates a ripple. As Nikola Tesla—one of the most prophetic and misunderstood minds in history—reminded us:

"If you want to find the secrets of the universe, think in terms of energy, frequency, and vibration."

That's just the beginning.

Tesla wasn't merely talking about mechanical oscillations or radio waves. He saw the entire cosmos as a living symphony of frequencies. He believed that what we perceive as matter is simply energy slowed down into form—vibrating at a rate that makes it visible and tangible.

Tesla also said: "All perceptible matter comes from a primary substance, or tenuity beyond conception, filling all space—the akasha or luminiferous ether—which is acted upon by the life-giving Prana or creative force, calling into existence, in never-ending cycles, all things and phenomena."

This is metaphysics. He was pointing to what ancient mystics also knew: that the world you see is not the whole story.

Tesla believed that human beings are conductors and transmitters of frequency. He intuitively understood what quantum theorists and consciousness explorers are only beginning to map—that we are in a constant dance with unseen forces, translating energy into form through the lens of our beliefs, thoughts, and emotional charge.

To go further, when you tune your thoughts to despair, to fear, to bitterness—you're broadcasting low frequencies that entangle with similar patterns. On the other hand, when you align with clarity, courage, and coherence, you become a kind of frequency tuner—emitting signals that restructure your experience.

Tesla's work with wireless power and zero-point energy wasn't just about lighting cities. It was about tapping into the limitless energy field that animates everything.

Now for the twist: he believed that the moment we fully understood frequency, we could heal disease, alter reality, and access boundless creative power.

The next time you hear that quote, don't just nod along. Ask yourself:

What am I vibrating?

What am I broadcasting?

What am I unconsciously tuning into?

Because the universal energy field? It doesn't speak English.

It speaks vibration.

You are the signal.

That's what this chapter is about. Not just thinking in those terms—but living in them.

How does energy work? More importantly, how do you harness it to serve your awakening rather than your enslavement?

You begin with one critical skill: discernment.

. . .

### **Instant Energy Reading**

Your body already knows how to do this. When something is good for you—really aligned, not just shiny—you feel lifted. Your vibration rises. Your chest opens. You lean in. You sense that you're being guided forward into something that wants you back.

On the flip side, when something hits your field and you feel drained, tight, anxious, or suddenly cynical—that's not you being "realistic." That's programming. That's a signature of interference.

Most people don't recognize it, but there's an entire invisible battlefield around us made of frequencies. Every word you read, every broadcast you hear, every voice note or meme or tweet—it's all coded with energetic intent. Some of it is designed to feed you, empower you, wake you up.

Nonetheless, a lot of it?

It's designed to fracture your clarity, scramble your nervous system, and keep you emotionally hijacked.


### **Recognizing Weaponized Information**

Let's talk about news. Information. Internet scroll. "Well-meaning" friends.

If something you're hearing brings on dread, fear, guilt, or a sense of hopeless collapse, you're not just dealing with an unpleasant truth. You're dealing with an intentional energy weapon. It's fear by design.

In media terms, we call this fear porn. Not just because it's shocking or disturbing, but because it stimulates a compulsive, addictive reaction in the brain. It's not meant to inform you, but instead, to disempower you. To make you feel helpless, paralyzed, and more easily controlled. And at its core? It's addictive.

There's something else to keep in mind: fear porn doesn't only come from sources like CNN. It can come through well-meaning friends, alleged authorities, online bots, and urgent TikTockers. If their delivery shuts you down or fills your mind with dread, it's not truth. It's a trap.

At the opposite end of the spectrum? Beware the sugar-coated twin of fear porn: hopium.

Hopium feeds you a sweet, numbing lie. It tells you "Don't worry," someone else will fix it. The aliens. The military. The secret plan. The next politician. Your doctor.

While it's true that there are benevolent forces working behind the scenes, hopium lets you abdicate your power. It puts you to sleep under a weighted blanket of spiritual sedatives. The dark side loves that.

Because either way—fear or fantasy—you're not creating your reality. You're just reacting to someone else's version of it.

## **Real Light Feeds You**

How do you know when it's the real thing?

Truth—the pure, aligned kind—comes through effortlessly. It doesn't lurch into your field like a bulldozer. It doesn't give you anxiety attacks or dopamine highs. It lands clean. You'll feel a subtle click in your chest. You'll feel your spine align. You'll have a quiet sense of knowing.

That's real light. It feeds you.

Sometimes it's an answer to a question you've been carrying for days. Sometimes it's a thought that feels familiar, like you knew it already and just needed to hear it again.

I see this every time I'm with my mother. Maybe we're out eating dinner or in her living room with a friend. The moment I sit beside her, my field shifts. Her vibration lifts the room—and the channels open. It's like the truth is waiting there, just beyond the veil, and the second she grounds the frequency, the whole stream pours through.

The funny thing is, it doesn't come with fireworks. It sometimes comes with tears.

When I tap into a divine source—when I receive pure, high-frequency love from the other side—I cry. I don't mean sobbing. I mean that unmistakable wave that hits your heart and leaks out your eyes. It happens every time. It's a frequency of such authenticity, such remembering, that my human form can't help but respond.

That's how I know.

Jane: I know when I'm delivered information that I get the goosebumps.

Lane: Yes, to add to the goosebumps, there's a flash of electricity. It's like you just got a little jolt. Yes, a good jolt.

Jane: All tingly.

Lane: The other thing I want to add is that whenever I manifest something a bit crazy, like something I really want and it happens, it just moves me up one more pin on the ladder toward the whole thing coming together.

Jane: What whole thing is that?

Lane: It's an infinite connection between all things, all experiences, and all knowing. It's so large that I can only just put my finger on it. With every manifestation and confirmation, I get a little bit closer to understanding how large this whole thing is. It's huge. I can feel it and it is sublime.

Jane: When I share my thoughts about things I'd like to have happen, most people say, you're kidding, there's no way you can manifest that. I'll say, I just did. I did it by talking about it as though it's here.

I giggle like I'm five years old when I manifest something special. It's hilarious. I'll get a phone call saying, hey, here's this opportunity for you, blah, blah, blah. I just break into giggles. It's a playful joyfulness. I think a lot of the time we've lost that pixie fun, cheeky, playful energy. It feels like you're playing with the Universe and winning.

The more you recognize synchronicities and responses to your manifestations, the more they will come. Why? Because we're operating in the law of flow. It's just... flowing.

## UNLEASHING THE REBEL WITHIN

I don't get the giggles when they arrive—not like some people do. What I get is something quieter and extremely potent: complete confirmation that something much larger than us exists.

Not only that it exists, but that it's intelligent. That there's a higher power—benevolent, conscious, and loving—and it's not off in the distance. It's right here. With you.

Sometimes a synchronicity will seem small. You could brush it off if you wanted to. Yet, if you're listening? If you're tuned in? It's them saying, yes, we're working on the bigger stuff, but it's not time yet.

Maybe it's not quite right for you yet. Maybe it needs some tuning. Or maybe... maybe that person you're manifesting? He doesn't exist yet. We have to create him. We're on it. Trust.

That brings me to the dog story. It's not one of the massive manifestations—but it hit hard. It reminded me to step back and chill out about the bigger asks I'd been pushing into the field. Because the message was clear: they're working on it.

My previous dog—my soul protector—was a little white Maltese named Spartacus. He was ten. He weighed exactly 10.4 pounds. He fit in my purse. I could take him everywhere. I did—especially in Manhattan, into places which were not particularly dog friendly. We traveled all over the country together. We walked everywhere. We had this psychic communication that ran so deep I can still feel it.

Then he got sick. He hung on longer than he needed to—probably one or two years past what his little body could take. When he passed, it wrecked me. I asked my holistic vet what to do differently next time. Spartacus hadn't lived long. Even though he'd carried a ton of energy for me, some of it was also genetic—just too much inbreeding.

My vet told me three things: First, find a dog who hasn't been vaccinated yet. Second, put him on a raw diet. Third, no purebreds. Let nature do its thing.

I put it out to the Universe. I said: "Please send me a pup who's strong and hardy, but I need him to be the same size. I need to carry him the way I carried Spartacus."

## Lane Keller

I searched for months. I was combing Craigslist one night when I found this little terrier mix puppy. The woman showed me his DNA—he was part Yorkie, part Jack Russell, part Pomeranian, even a bit of pit. I convinced her to let me take him before he'd been vaccinated. I promised to take him straight to my vet, and I did.

A year later, he hit full growth. His weight?

10.4 pounds.

Exactly the same as Spartacus.

He's all black. Spartacus was all white. Every time I look at him, I lift a little. Because I know—

He is a divine gift.

Jane: That's so beautiful. That's spot on. There's just no mistaking it. Shall I say my favorite manifestation story?

It didn't happen to me. It happened to a friend of mine, a beautiful woman who's on the other side. Now, many years ago, she wanted to open up a healing center and she had many courses. She taught inner child therapy and energetic healers, all sorts of things. She was a wonderful indigenous Australian woman, and she needed at the time 15,000 Australian dollars to open up her center.

And it wasn't happening. She was just not getting the money together and she became really annoyed and frustrated at the Universe. She said, if you really want me to do this, I demand this money now. A short time after she gets her bank statement and there's 15,000 in her bank. She laughed at the Universe and said, okay, I get it. Thanks very much. That's not my money, but I do get your sign. Thank you for that.

So, she goes to the bank, which was one of Australia's largest and said, look, there's been a mistake. There's 15 grand that's been put in my bank and it's not mine. They said, okay, leave it with us. She then gets a phone call and they said, "Look, we can see that this money isn't your money, but we can't see where it came from. Our rules prevent us from taking that money out of your bank account unless we know where it came from. So, it's your money."

She said, well, "look, that's all well and good, but I don't want you coming back to me in three years' time saying, 'oh, we found where the money goes and you owe us 15 grand." They said, "no, we've actually really researched this. We cannot work out where it came from." They gave her a letter that said it was her money. She got her 15 grand and opened up a healing center. She's helped thousands of people over the years. I think that's one of the most beautiful stories of getting out of the way of the how.

Lane: Oh, that's wonderful. We think that we want something and then we've got to look at the steps to take to get there. It's important to take actions that maintain the vibration to be a match for manifestation. That was a great example of getting out of the how it's going to happen phase.

Everything was in alignment. She was obviously meant to do that, or it was in her blueprint, if you want to say a soul blueprint, where she was supposed to have that center. But it was her doing. She asked for it. It was her free will. The timing was right, and everything fell into place.

Because I do think timing is a big part of manifestation. It just doesn't always happen exactly when you want it to happen, or in the manner that you expect it to happen. The other thing I want to say about manifestation is, it seems like when you say it in a very clear and concise, and almost offhand manner, oh, I love having a little dog who's exactly the same size as Sparty, it works better than any other way.

It needs to be very clear, very concise, very easy instructions to follow. I didn't write it on a note and stick it in my wallet. I didn't do a mantra every day. I may have said it three times. I'm not putting down mantras, but I think that often when people are manifesting, they actually get attached to the idea of not having it, meaning they are so used to not having it that lack begins to feel as comfortable as your favorite bathrobe.

Yearning doesn't work either, because that's more not having. What you want is grateful acknowledgement that it is already done, even in an offhand way. Detach from the results before fear or doubt kicks in, and block thoughts like: what if it doesn't happen? Or, I really need this to happen.

Jane: That's where if you detach, as you said, you very simply said thank you for what you're getting and detached and went about life. If you're holding the glass, you're holding the glass too tightly. Say, I'm grateful for this, not that I would need this.

Lane: Perfect. I hope most people know by now you have to get rid of the words need or want, and that neither belong in your vocabulary.

It's telling the universal energy field that you don't have something. I learned early on in my youth to banish those words and the phrases, no, I can't do this. I can't imagine this. I can't have this. They don't belong.

Get rid of them and get rid of the word no when it's directed at the self, as in no, you can't have that. No, you're not worthy, or, no, that isn't for me.

There are a million reasons for no. There's only one necessary for yes, and it's bigger than all the no's combined. As you evolve, you'll never again say, I want or I need. Instead, say I like, I appreciate. I want is selfish, and I need creates a lack that the Universe will respond to by increasing that lack.

Jane: You're putting it into the present tense. Of course, the I AM in capital letters is a pretty powerful big statement too.

Lane: Yes, I also like past tense. Thank you for sending that blah blah blah.

Jane: That's very powerful. Yes. Then you relax and let go and realize it's already done. It's happened. You just don't know the timing.

Lane: It's here. Move on. Thank the Universe. Then the Universe will fill in the gap. That's the law of flow and giving the request space to occur. Chances are it will come. Chances are it will come when you least expect it or, funny enough, when you don't need or want it anymore. Then you're like, um, thank you. They were waiting for you to evolve to a point where you didn't need it.

## UNLEASHING THE REBEL WITHIN

. . .

**Interdimensional Humor**

I sometimes wonder if the delay in manifestation is some kind of universal prank. A cosmic wink. A celestial elbow in the ribs. Hilarious.

You have to understand—Jesus, Source, the Universe... they're all funny. Truly. They have a wicked sense of humor. The Arcturians too. It may not always mirror our brand of humor, but they absolutely get the joke. Humor is a universal language, even if their dialect is interstellar.

I remember trying to get an Arcturian I was in communication with to share his name. He hesitated. He said there was no way for me to pronounce it.

If you know me, you already know what I said next: "Try me."

Challenge accepted.

What came through was an utterly unpronounceable sequence of sound. No syllables. No vowels. No human mouth could form it. We don't even have the letters to attempt a transcription. I laughed so hard. They laughed too—or whatever their version of laughter is. He gave it to me anyway. Because they're good sports.

Jane: I think you're onto something incredible with this humor. I'm not really sure where or how it fits yet, but I'm fully on board. I've never heard anyone talk about it quite this way—well, maybe Esther Hicks years ago. She touched on the healing power of humor and how it relates to diseases like cancer.

Lane: Humor is woven into me—but I wouldn't say it's a character trait. What is a character trait is my deep desire to put people at ease. That's where the humor arises. That, and the reverence I hold for its power when used in writing or public speaking.

Because humor doesn't just lift the vibration—it levels the field. It's the great equalizer. Rich or poor, broken or mighty, rigid or raw—humor invites everyone to the same table.

It opens doors. It slips the mind into alpha state—quieting resistance, increasing receptivity. It's like a password. A secret knock that tells the nervous system, "Relax. This isn't war. This is play."

If you can disarm someone with laughter, you can reach them with truth. You can say the hard things. You can pull back the veil. Humor allows us to tell the truth without triggering every defense mechanism in the room.

Honestly? It's just more fun. When people sense humor, they soften. The inner shields come down.

They think, oh, okay, we're going to enjoy this.

Or, phew, I thought this was going to be heavy.

Then the alpha waves roll in, and they're open. Available. Ready.

Jane: You describing it that way... I can feel the energy of it. It's something I've honestly never encountered before—not in this way. I think you're really onto something here, because it's accessible. Anyone can relate to it. Everyone wants it.

Lane: Yet people are so serious. Myself included. I mean, if someone opens the door to a deep conversation, I'll go there. I'm not afraid of shadow. I'll excavate it all the way down. But sometimes we forget to laugh at how upside-down things are.

Jane: It's great, though. You're opening a pathway. You're clarifying this thing we take for granted.

Lane: To me, it all comes down to irony. If you look up the definition, it says:

> The expression of one's meaning by using language that normally signifies the opposite—typically for humorous effect.

Still, it's not sarcasm. Not even close.

Jane: Right. Sarcasm feels sharp. Kind of cruel.

Lane: Exactly. I generally dislike sarcasm, although when I get with my New York friends it can fly in a hilarious way. Sarcasm has a bite to it. A residue. Irony is gentler. It's not a jab—it's an observation. It's noticing the incongruity of a situation, the absurdity baked into reality.

## UNLEASHING THE REBEL WITHIN

It's not "Haha, I just lost control of my car and slid down a hill almost killing myself and a couple of trees."

It's "I lost control of my car and spilled my coffee. Now that's tragic."

It's noticing that we live in an upside-down world where logic collapses and chaos reigns—and laughing at it, because if we don't, we'll drown in it.

Irony helps us survive the contradiction.

It reminds us that this place is wild, beautiful, and very much not what it appears to be.

# Chapter 5
# Soul Partners

I once brought up the concept of the divine feminine to a millennial friend, and she blinked at me, confused. "What's that?" she asked. Her question stopped me in my tracks. It wasn't just that she didn't resonate with it—she'd never even heard the term. It hit me then: for many young people, especially in Westernized, postmodern culture, there is no working framework for what it truly means to be female—let alone what it means to embody the highest aspect of that energy.

Since that moment, the confusion has deepened. The sacred energies of both the elevated feminine and elevated masculine have been buried beneath layer after layer of distortion. Words like "woman," "man," "masculine," and "feminine" have become loaded with politically charged subtext. Identity politics pushed us further into a war of definitions—one that fractures us from our spiritual archetypes. While individual journeys around gender are valid and deeply personal, there's also no denying the broader agenda at play.

Much of this confusion is not accidental. It has been seeded and cultivated by psychological and social engineering programs like those developed by Tavistock and other think tanks. Their goal? To disrupt the family unit, disorient the masses, and sever our connection from Source energies. This isn't conspiracy—it's a strategy. It's working. You'll find deeper exploration of these mechanisms later in the book, but suffice to say, the blurring of gender archetypes is not simply an evolution—it's a calculated dismantling.

This doesn't mean we should dismiss the lived experiences of those navigating gender identity. Quite the opposite. Many people feel disconnected from their physical form because they are carrying the essence of another lifetime—a soul imprint that transcends biological sex. If you were female in a past life and now find yourself in a male body, you may be carrying feminine energy that doesn't match the societal mold. That dissonance isn't a flaw—it's a calling to explore.

In truth, we are all hybrids—multidimensional mixtures of masculine and feminine, past and present, soul and body. The indigenous world has understood this. In many ancient cultures, those who carried a blend of genders were revered, not erased. They were seen as bridges—holding the wisdom of both polarities, embodying integration.

## The Divine Feminine

What is the divine feminine, really? It's not a trend, not a self-help buzzword, and definitely not a commercialized archetype wrapped in moon water and Snapchat filters. The divine feminine is the purest expression of feminine energy in its most exalted form—timeless, ancient, and encoded into the very fabric of life itself.

She is the force of creation. She is fertility, yes—but not just biological. She births ideas, art, healing, connection, intuition, and compassion. She is the pulse of the cosmos that whispers, you are safe, you are loved, you are more than what you produce. She is nonlinear, right-brain dominant, emotionally intelligent, and soul-deep.

She is present in all of us.

Divine feminine energy isn't exclusive to women, just as divine masculine energy isn't exclusive to men. As I said, we're hybrid beings. When a man embraces his feminine energy—his ability to feel, to receive, to nurture, to intuit—he becomes more whole, not less masculine.

In fact, the most powerful beings on this planet are those who've learned to harmonize both polarities within themselves. That's the real evolution—not gender confusion, but sacred integration.

Now let's be clear: the highest form of feminine is not weakness. She is not submissive by default. She is not a pushover. She is fierce in her softness. Boundaried in her compassion. Unshakeable in her capacity to love without condition. She is what the modern world fears most: a woman (or a man) who knows how to love fully and say no. Who can hold space without self-abandoning. Who nurtures without losing herself.

In her distorted, toxic form, the feminine becomes needy, manipulative, overly emotional, martyr-like, codependent. This isn't divine. It's the wounded echo of powerlessness. It's the version of femininity the system often prefers—because it's easier to control.

To reclaim the divine feminine is to dismantle centuries of programming. It's to stand in a place of both open-hearted love and unshakable self-determination. She sees through illusion. She knows when something is off. She feels it in her bones. When she rises—when we rise with her—everything changes.

## The Divine Masculine

Just as the divine feminine embodies the sacred power of love, intuition, and life-giving energy, the divine masculine represents its perfectly balanced counterpart: the energy of strength, clarity, direction, and unwavering presence. When fully activated, this, the highest form of masculine does not dominate—it grounds. It does not conquer—it protects. It is the steady mountain to the river's flow.

The divine masculine at its highest frequency is not afraid to act

—but it does so from a place of conscious intent, not reactive impulse. It is the part of us that builds structures, maintains order, offers stability, and initiates right action. It's logical, focused, and strategic. More than anything, the divine masculine is safe. It makes others feel protected—not because it overpowers, but because it holds space with honor.

This is where many get confused. Our culture has long mistaken brute force and domination for masculine strength. True masculinity is never rooted in fear, control, or competition. Those are distortions —wounded expressions of a masculinity that has lost its sacred center. When masculine energy turns toxic, it becomes cold, power-hungry, dismissive, or destructive. It seeks control because it has lost connection.

Yet, the healed masculine? He listens deeply. He does not need to prove. He knows when to step forward and when to hold back. He is the sword and the silence. He leads—but never to self-aggrandize. He leads because he must, because others are safer when he does. He disciplines not to punish, but to create integrity.

We are now living through a pivotal rebalancing—a collective initiation. The divine feminine is reawakening, yes. However, she is not meant to rise alone. She is calling for her masculine counterpart— not to suppress her, but to stand beside her.

As the world slowly shifts from the ruthless, exploitative hierarchies of the old patriarchal paradigm into something more heart-centered, the divine masculine has a crucial role to play. His steadiness is needed. His focus, his sense of justice, his integrity, his protection of the innocent—all are essential in this unfolding.

We are not moving toward a feminine-dominant world. We are moving toward balance. Toward the sacred reunion of both forces. The feminine shows us how to feel. The masculine shows us how to act from those feelings without losing our center.

That's the future worth building: one where love and logic, intuition and action, heart and will—walk hand in hand.

. . .

## Manifesting Partners

Can you manifest your divine partner? Absolutely—but not by parroting someone else's list or envisioning a Hollywood script. The true manifestation of a soul partner is less about conjuring a "perfect match" and more about calling in the being who reflects, activates, and expands the truest version of you.

Yes, part of that process involves clarity. When you get clear about what you want—crystal clear—you begin to send coherent signals into the quantum field. Still, here's the catch: the clarity must come not from ego or wounding, but from soul-level discernment.

This is where it gets real. You can't skip the self-work and expect a divine partner to show up fully formed, ready to "fix" your life. That's not how it works. Your partner will meet you at the frequency you're currently emitting. When you decide to manifest love, the first step is always the same: clean your own frequency first.

Years ago, I thought I had done that. I entered a relationship with someone who, on paper, matched many of the things I believed I needed—depth, passion, intelligence, spiritual alignment. What I hadn't accounted for was how unresolved trauma can still wear a mask of spiritual magnetism. What followed was a painful entanglement that nearly destroyed me. Yet—I emerged.

That relationship, as difficult as it was, became the crucible that forged deeper clarity. I had to look at every line on that list of mine and ask: Was this a soul truth or a subconscious program? Because if your list is built on fear, control, fantasy, or societal conditioning, you'll attract someone who reflects those exact frequencies back to you.

The real question isn't can you manifest your divine partner? It's: Can you tell the difference between what your soul needs and what your wounded parts crave?

You refine the list as you grow. Not out of cynicism, but wisdom. Over time, you'll find the traits you once saw as essential begin to fall away—until all that's left are the non-negotiables rooted in deep self-knowing.

## UNLEASHING THE REBEL WITHIN

This process is not a formula. It's a living, evolving dialogue between your inner being and the greater field of life. When you finally understand that your true partner is not here to complete you, but to walk beside you as an equal—when you stop trying to manifest "perfection" and start manifesting resonance—everything changes.

You don't call them in with desperation. You call them in with alignment.

They come.

Lane: When you think about manifestation, it isn't a bad idea to make a list and write out exactly what you need, and to be very specific.

When manifesting who and what you desire, you have to hone in on the exact qualities you need. I zeroed in on this through the years, especially after I went through that destructive relationship.

His controlling behavior nearly brought me down, but instead I emerged stronger. When I met him, I thought he embodied all I desired in a mate. Apparently, I forgot a few things on the list. As you grow, you need to refine your requirements further and further, until isolating those things that are not just essential to your happiness, but essential to a fulfilling partnership with another being.

Jane: In the beginning, it was a long list.

Lane: You told me one day; you've got to change some of that. I kept looking it over and said, I can't, I can't. He has to be taller than me, for instance. I simply cannot make love to a man or lie in his arms who's physically shorter than me. I don't like it. Everything else was mandatory. He has to be funny, he has to be intelligent, or I will not feel challenged. His heart needs to be huge and his emotional baggage mostly healed. I don't want it to be a tutoring session where he's my student either. Instead, he tutors me as much as I tutor him.

In other words, questing and growing together. To me, that is essential. He needs a passion for life and for our relationship. He needs to enjoy giving as much as receiving. You'd be surprised how many men perform sex perfunctorily or as a conquest and not as an intimate connection, and most simply do not reciprocate. This was vital as well.

He needed to be more athletic than me so he could help get me out of my hermit like writing mode every once in a while. It went on and on and on. Oh right, and one last thing, he needed to be out of the matrix.

Jane: That one's almost impossible.

Lane: I know, it is! At last, I said, okay, okay. I'm not going to presume what he looks like. Any preconception on my type, I let go. At one point I thought I wanted a guitarist with dark hair. Then I decided that's just not important. I said, Universe, send him. Then he came.

Jane: There's a big thing in there when you said it's not important what he looks like.

Lane: Black, white, gray, brown, short hair, long hair, no hair. I said, Universe, surprise me. You know what? It did.

Jane: Can I tell you that 99. 9999 percent of women could not say that. When I said you need to examine that list and reduce it, you reduced it by 99.9999 percent on that one thing. You went for what is important versus what you perceive to be important. This ties in with many of the topics we've spoken of, which is that you have a unique way of looking at things that differs vastly from others, even those in this field.

Lane: This is a program where specific looks have been fed to us as to what is attractive. It's why so many have body dysmorphia. It's impossible to measure up.

Jane: Advertising's been telling us 20 million times per second every single day what should matter. The programming goes into who we should and shouldn't be attracted to, and yet you have to let go of dozens and dozens of programs in that one statement.

Therefore, you opened up a massive door of who could walk into your life because the thing that the elite, the controlling programmers want to have happen is for us to run programs that make it hard for us to connect with our soulmate or partner or whatever term you want to give it. In essence, they have stopped the masculine and feminine divine from uniting and doing their dance together.

Lane: When doing that dance, you become infinitely more powerful. Being with a divine partner causes our ability to manifest to explode. That is the very last thing they want us to know. The program has run very deep to make sure that meeting your true partner doesn't happen in life.

Jane: Yet, you've just thrown away that program that has the greatest success for them in one smart move.

Lane: Okay. Then the rule is, don't define appearance because love defines everything.

**Secrets to Soul Partner Manifestation**

When you set out to define the characteristics of your ideal partner, it all comes down to one thing: self-knowledge. You must know yourself deeply enough to recognize the difference between what your soul craves and what the world has conditioned you to want.

You have to strip away every programmed expectation, every projection, every fantasy you've absorbed about what a "good partner" should be. What remains must be soul-level truth—non-negotiable, deeply felt, utterly authentic.

I couldn't have done this work in my twenties. Back then, I was looking for someone who'd make a good father and a stable provider. That wasn't shallow—it was biological. Women, especially in earlier stages of life, are evolutionarily wired to seek stability for child-rearing. I was no different. Laughter and intelligence mattered, of course, but there was something else beneath it all—an unconscious checklist of how our match would look to others. Did he embody my ideal of what I wanted to marry? Did he reflect something that would validate me?

It's startling to consider how much of our attraction can be shaped by what we think we're supposed to want. I now believe that part of what allowed me to fall in love was the fact that he fit the script. That realization marked a turning point—a reckoning with all the programming I'd unknowingly swallowed. I don't regret those choices, but I do believe they deserve examination.

Wherever you are in your journey, whether you're just beginning or several lifetimes deep, the question is the same:

What can you absolutely not live without in a partner?

Drill down. Get specific. Then get brutal. Peel away the illusions and the placeholders.

One of the big things I let go of? Money. In the early stages, it mattered—again, because of that child-rearing instinct. Eventually, I realized I didn't need someone wealthy. I needed someone self-realized. Someone who wouldn't cling to me for financial or emotional security, and who I wouldn't need to financially rescue. Mutual sovereignty became the new non-negotiable.

Because financial dependence—on either side—can rot a relationship from the inside. It's disempowering. It breeds resentment. Self-sufficiency isn't just a bonus; it's emotional hygiene.

From there, the list refines even more. Maybe you're a woman who longs for a partner embodying the divine masculine—not in a cliché sense, but someone who stands fully in his own being, someone whose selfhood is intact. That's called presence. It's inner stability.

If you're a man seeking a partner who will nurture and feed you and take care of your physical needs like your mom once did... then what you're seeking is a mother, not a soulmate. Time to dig deeper. Divine partnership is not codependency with better lighting.

This kind of soul search reveals where your maturity level actually is—not where you pretend it is. You have to ask: What am I actually looking for in a relationship? Is it power? Is it someone I can fix or mold into what I need? Is he or she a trophy to display to my friends? If so, you're not looking for a partner. You're looking for control or outside validation.

True partnership does not thrive in imbalance. You can't call in someone strong and independent if what you really want is someone pliable and weak. Or who simply looks good on your arm.

With regard to control, there are moments in love when one person takes the lead and the other follows. That's part of the dance. The grace comes in knowing when to step forward, and when to step back. That's mastery.

## The Divine Partnership

There's a kind of confusion permeating our current culture—especially among men—about how to show up in relationships. No wonder. The cultural pendulum has swung so far in both directions, it's easy to see why so many men today are paralyzed by hesitation.

Yes, there was a time when toxic masculinity dominated. Men took what they wanted without consequence. The patriarchy reigned, and women paid the price. We've overcorrected in some ways, replacing one distortion with another. Now, in many circles, masculinity itself is treated as a threat. Feminism—originally intended to uplift—has been hijacked by dogma. Somewhere in the chaos, true polarity was lost.

When a man offers to help me assemble my bike and asks if I'm "one of those women who feels she has to do everything herself," I don't bristle. I gratefully hand him the screwdriver.

Because here's the truth: I don't want to be the man. I can be, if needed—I have strength, logic, and leadership in spades. I'm good with a screwdriver. I don't need to perform masculinity to prove my capability. My feminine essence is not weakness. It's power in a different form.

Yes, men can cook and women can fix cars. Those surface roles aren't the point. Emotions versus logic isn't the point either. What matters is balance. Sacred union means finding someone who doesn't compete with you but complements you. You bring out the full spectrum of each other's divine energies. You don't cancel each other out—you expand each other.

This is what makes a divine partnership sacred. Two whole

beings, each capable in their own right, coming together to form something even greater.

**Sacred Sex**

Now let's talk about sex. Because our modern culture sure doesn't know how to.

We've been conditioned to see it either as dirty and taboo—or as a meaningless pleasure fix. Either way, it's been stripped of its deeper essence.

In truth, sex is neither profane nor purely carnal. In the context of divine partnership, it is holy. It is transformative. It is the original portal.

When two emotionally connected souls engage in physical intimacy, it transcends the body. It becomes a spiritual transmission. It lifts, expands, and awakens. It feeds you on every level—physical, emotional, energetic, and soul.

Nothing about this is shameful. There's no right way to do it, as long as it's consensual and rooted in love or deep respect. What you explore together is sacred if it honors the wholeness of each person involved.

When it is sacred—when the love is true and the energy aligned—sex becomes a form of interdimensional travel. That's not a metaphor. You can leave your body. You can astral project. You can touch realms most people only glimpse in altered states. The most powerful, mind-expanding substance on earth isn't a plant or a pill—it's sexual union with your divine counterpart.

That's what they don't want you to know. That's why the sexual frequency has been hijacked, distorted, and diminished. Because when we reclaim it—not for power or performance, but for union—we become unstoppable.

**Your Divine Partner**

## UNLEASHING THE REBEL WITHIN

Your divine partner is somebody with whom you immediately share connection. This is because they were either sent to you, or you've been with them before—across lifetimes, realms, or soul contracts. There is a familiar ease, a natural resonance between you that defies logic or timeline. It's not a jolt of adrenaline or a scripted romance. It's a knowing. A remembrance. A subtle, steady homecoming. You feel met. Seen. Safe. There is no power struggle. No diminishment. Instead, there is support. Deep, unwavering support.

Jane: What else?

Lane: Obviously truth, deep truth. This is the basis of intimacy, also chemistry, where there's sexual intensity and connection. You want to physically be with them. They could look like a troll from under the bridge, but to you, they're beautiful, because you see their inner being. To me, my twin flame was physically beautiful, although others didn't think so.

This is because beauty isn't surface-level—it is soul-deep. In divine partnership, you see beyond form. You perceive their essence. Their light. You don't love them because they check boxes. You love them because you recognize something eternal in them, even if they challenge you. Especially if they challenge you.

Divine partnership is seeing straight through to each other's inner being, and not just seeing it, but treasuring what you find there. It's knowing their shadows and still choosing them. It's wanting their growth as much as your own. Yes—sexual attraction remains. It deepens. It doesn't fade with age or routine, because the magnetism is soul-based. It's not about novelty or conquest. It's about union.

Does their head swivel when a 19-year-old with perky breasts pops by? Well, if the tongue falls out and the eyes bulge, you've got the wrong guy.

Couples who say they're allowed to look or have sex with partners outside their relationship are not in divine partnerships. If they are, they haven't discovered it yet and are tossing it away.

Jane: So, how do you define divine partnership?

Lane: It's an elevation. A resonance so complete that you don't need constant words, but when you do speak, you speak forever. You can sit on a bench and watch clouds and not be bored. You don't feel restless or distracted. You're not scanning the horizon for someone else. You're home.

That goes for insouciant breasts or bulging biceps. It's okay to admire beauty, but not to lust after it. If that happens, it's a sign you are in the wrong relationship. Either that, or you need to define how you really, on the most deeply intimate level, feel about each other.

Jane: When you're home alone by yourself, at your ugliest, who is the person that can sit next to you and support you in your journey to be the best version of yourself, especially when you're at your worst? When my partner fails to do something the way I wish it was done, and I want to show him how fabulous I am and how not fabulous he is, that's not a good situation to be creating.

Observe when this happens and then acknowledge it. Say, I didn't like how I showed up that day. I don't like how I felt. You tell him, I don't like the way I treated you, then you admit what your real fear is. Maybe you don't want to be in control of everything, and when he can't do something as well as you, it sends you into fear.

This can launch into a real deep beautiful conversation of vulnerability, which from there leads to a very uplifting conversation of him wanting the best for you and you wanting the best for him. So, the divine partner is the person who sits next to you when you are at your absolute worst and still wants the best for you and helps you to get through that and you do exactly the same for them.

Lane: Exactly. That's the soul contract—the sacred mirror. Not a mirror of perfection, but one of truth. Of grace. The divine partner holds space for your breakdowns and still sees your brilliance. They don't fix you. They don't enable you. They simply hold the vision of who you truly are—until you can remember again. You do the same for them.

That is a soul agreement. When it's real, nothing else compares.

. . .

## Are You With the Right Partner?

Lane: Many people who are evolving are suddenly finding themselves on a different timeline or let's say headspace from their current partner.

Jane: The easy answer to this would be to consciously uncouple and move on. As hard as that might be in a 3D world, it's actually the easy answer.

Lane: There could be a better answer or a higher answer. Separating doesn't necessarily mean it's the right answer.

Jane: I think it's very important that a higher answer doesn't mean better or right. It just means a different way. What is unconditional love? Can you do it?

Lane: Let's hold on to that for a second. That would be the best outcome. If you have unconditional love for each other and you're prepared to help bring that person with you on your journey.

Yet what happens if you discover that the person you're with is in essence your handler, or somebody who is dead set on holding you back? He or she may not even realize it. It's them being so mired in a 3D mindset, that you feel there is no other way forward than pulling out. Is it selfish to go onward and to leave, especially when you've pledged a lifetime together?

Jane: I'm not a fan of that lifetime pledge at all. I don't think that we have any right to promise anything of any length to anyone. I think the promise is that we show up and commit to do our best to support each other, to be the best versions of ourselves.

I can promise to love my husband for the rest of my life, and that is absolutely my intention and still is my intention, but I can't control him. What if he turns around tomorrow and says, I never expected this to happen. You know, I love you, but I've met somebody who I just can't stop thinking about. I can't control that. So, I don't get to make a promise that I can't necessarily keep.

Lane: Right. What if he's turned to violence? I mean, am I meant to still love this guy and hang around?

Jane: I think the pledge is a program to control and manipulate us.

Lane: To give another twist to that, in coming to terms with leaving my own marriage, because I also thought that when I was marrying, I was pledging for a lifetime, I had no idea that our, let's say, timelines were going to diverge so severely.

When they did, there was no going back. He was on a completely different level, and I'm not saying that in an egotistical way, but he was hell bent on staying in the box he created for himself. There was just no getting around it. The realization I came to over the years since we were together is that we may not have just one partner in this lifetime.

We are evolving so quickly and in such divergent ways. How can one person fulfill you for a lifetime? I've probably reinvented myself six times over the past 30 years. Probably more. After my marriage, I fell into the twin flame relationship that took me to heaven and hell and back again.

It sped up my evolvement so fast, it took years to break down all I had learned. I'm still breaking it down in some senses.

Jane: I think you better define twin flame. When defining twin flames and differentiating the term from soulmates and sacred partners, I feel like we need to throw all of these labels out and find new terms.

Lane: Yes, but as soon as we find a new term, the Deep State would place a sign on it. For example, there's a show produced by the mainstream called Twin Flames.

Jane: It's been twisted, just like anything pure has been twisted. They would twist it to make sure that we look like idiots, because we are the most powerful on the planet, and we are the biggest threat to them.

Lane: Not only do they twist it, they use it as a way of blocking the truth. So now, if I as a normal person who hasn't done a lot of deep research, go searching for information on twin flames, I'm going to continually get led to the Netflix show, instead of to the real info that I'm looking for.

There are search techniques to get around this, but most don't know them. This happens time and again when there's an important concept or information out there. They simply block it by putting something else out there using the same terminology.

Jane: They'll twist the meaning, implying there's something dark and sinister about it, and then they will, as you say, block it in search engines, so it becomes suppressed, distorted, and hidden.

Lane: Yes. They will invert and hide it. We need new terms and new ways of looking at things. So, we attract and choose partners and there are no mistakes.

Jane: Every relationship is divine. Every relationship is with a soulmate.

Lane: I would say every relationship is with someone from your soul group. Every relationship has moments of being a twin flame. Every relationship has moments of being a soul sister or brother.

Jane: We're all soul sisters and brothers, and well said, I agree, that's it.

Lane: I will say that the twin flame term, though we need to get rid of these labels, is not necessarily the relationship that's going to last the longest in your life. The really important aspect to the relationship with this person, is that it is a humongous mirror.

Now, everyone is a mirror because everyone's going to mirror back what's functional and dysfunctional about you. However, a twin flame is going to do it in an extreme way, and sometimes in such a hypersonic way that the person could be in and out of your life in a heartbeat, a few years, or maybe it'll last forever.

The traditional explanation of a twin flame is someone with whom you experience almost instant unexplainable attraction. If it's a love relationship you share immense passion and deep feeling. On the other side of that is great distress, for it's a hugely polar relationship. For mirroring all the good and wonderfulness are dark and difficult times that come with it.

The reason for this is that this individual has been thrown into your path to help you advance quickly, to make things happen at an accelerated rate. It may burn itself out and may not last, but that's not what's important. What is important is taking the ride.

As difficult as it may be, it's important to thank the Universe for the experience.

Jane, when you and I came together, holy moly, we were like opposites of the same coin. We were from opposite sides of the world. We didn't even have to use words.

Jane: That was such a special moment of instant deep knowing of each other. Just more proof of design synchronicity in action. It's also the growing of our ability to connect with our tribe easily and effortlessly.

What I love about this, and a lot of people started to experience this in their own way of by virtual signaling during COVID. You'd go into a supermarket for instance, and you've got 99 percent of the people there masked. Then you turn down an aisle or walk into another shop and there's somebody else who's also unmasked.

You glance at each other and there's a knowing. I was in a bakery in a country town and this guy walked in and took one look at me then walked up and hugged me. I said, "Oh, hello stranger." He said, "Hello family." We had glimpses of it then. Another time I'd be dodging the QR check-in code to get into a shop, and someone else would be doing the same thing, and we'd just share that knowing sideways look.

Lots of people have been experiencing things like this. Sometimes we have the experience of just meeting somebody and then you look into their eyes and there's a knowing. I really appreciate it most when that happens with somebody who, in our 3D societal structure, you would not normally find commonality with, like a middle-aged woman and a 20-year-old punk rocker covered in tats.

In other words, between those who seem completely opposite to one another physically in age, socioeconomic position. But when your eyes meet, you get that special little nod of acknowledgement from one to the other. You know you've just crossed paths with another member of our soul family.

Lane: Perhaps the question is, what is a relationship? And what is it that people want from a relationship?

Jane: Being with somebody who isn't growing at the same rate as you may be difficult, but there may be other aspects that you find valuable.

This is where it gets really complex in relationships, and to be able to guide on this is a very individual thing. I guess where I come from in having been a matchmaker, and particularly with people in their 30s, 40s and beyond, many come to me post long-term relationship separation. What I saw was an awful lot of people who ended a relationship thinking the grass is greener.

In other words, they thought their happiness was external, not having done the internal work. So, we've got two different groups. One group is, have you done the work? If you haven't done the work, then you stay with that person that you're with until you've done the work.

Then you can consciously decide if that person's right for you or not for the next chapter of evolution of your life. But if you have done the work, then you're going to have a different answer.

Lane: What if you can't do the work while you're in that particular situation?

Jane: I think you can do the work wherever you are.

There's always going to be exceptions. That's the problem that we have though, when the majority of people believe that they are the exception, what we've got then is self-delusion.

Lane: If you're in a marriage typical of women in a suburban environment, they're comfortable, their husbands are making a decent living, they have a nice house, they have a social network, their kids are in good schools, they're reasonably happy, they go out, have nice clothes. Yet there is something lacking at the core of their existence.

They can't put their finger on it because they haven't embarked on the soul work some have done. Sometimes, it isn't until you find solitude, when you are on your own that you can truly start a new level of inner work.

Jane: I love that, but I don't necessarily think it's always true. I'm in a long-term relationship and yet I don't think I could have done any deeper work than I have done. I get what you're saying, though. It's the person who's cruising life. They may want to do it, but in reality, they'd rather go to the golf course or the book club. That's spiritual bypassing. It's no different to the shopaholic, the workaholic, the alcoholic. It doesn't matter what aholic, the person is numbing out from life.

There will be those reading this book who have people they care for and love deeply who fall into this category, and it's a case of letting them be. At some point for the majority, something will happen. There will be a crisis that will occur, a trauma perhaps. Not that I'm wishing this for anyone. It could be the loss of someone. It could be an illness. It could be a sudden bankruptcy in the family, something unexpected that shocks them. As they try to reconcile how that occurs, that's the entry point and their self-development will open up.

**The Tower Moment**

When I left my marriage, I did not realize I was leaving the family unit—and not just the man I married, but an entire ecosystem built around that life. I left behind a whole social circle, all my close friends, and everyone I was loosely or deeply acquainted with. At the time, I didn't fully understand what leaving meant. Everything felt free-flowing, as if I were just stepping out for a breath of air. I didn't have a plan. I didn't foresee the repercussions. I just knew I couldn't stay.

In the aftermath, it all hit. I went through multiple holidays alone —quiet, disorienting seasons where time seemed to stretch like cold, empty space. Christmas had always been full of warmth and tradition for me, a cherished ritual of light and togetherness. I lost that. I lost the joy in it, the meaning.

New Year's Eve was perhaps the sharpest cut. It had been important for me to kiss the man I loved at midnight. That moment meant something, especially for a girl raised in New York City, where the strike of twelve echoes with both glamour and gravity. Being alone at that hour—year after year—was a grief I hadn't anticipated.

Yet... while it was incredibly sad, it was also quietly, powerfully empowering.

Because what I was experiencing was nothing short of a Tower Moment.

In the Tarot, the Tower is the card that no one wants to pull—and yet, it is one of the most liberating forces in the entire deck. It represents the sudden collapse of a false structure. The shattering of an illusion. The lightning strike that topples the fortress you built on unstable ground.

When the Tower falls, you are thrown from it. The identity you clung to is gone. The social scripts, the traditions, the assumed roles—you watch them all crumble. In that moment, it feels like destruction. What it really is... is truth.

The Tower doesn't fall to punish you. It falls to free you.

You learn hard-won truths. You learn that the calendar is just a construct. That a date stamped with glitter and meaning doesn't define your value, your happiness, or your belonging. You begin to understand that holidays, while sacred in their own way, are not where love resides. Love is not bound by tradition. You learn to find joy in family whenever those rare, spontaneous moments of gathering occur. If it no longer has the holiday stamp on it—so be it. The moment is still holy.

Some people fill the void with work, and I did that at times. It's an understandable response: pour energy into the one container that still seems to hold structure. Eventually you realize that busy-ness is not healing. It's noise.

What most people fear—whether in divorce or death or spiritual awakening—is stepping into the "nothingness." That vast space where all the scaffolding disappears. Instead, here's the truth: when the structures beneath our feet crumble—every last one—what is not left is a void.

What is left is you.

Raw. Stripped down. Unmasked.

There, in that stark honesty, you find yourself. You begin again.

There is a reason for the removal of that most beloved structure of all: our emotional tether to family and social circles, especially during the holidays. When that is taken from us—whether through divorce, death, or distance—we are forced to reckon with what remains. It hurts. Yet it also clears the space for a deeper becoming.

The Tower card isn't just about collapse. It's about liberation. It's about watching the false fall away so the real can emerge.

As that illusion of safety is pulled away, we cannot let it bring us down. Not permanently. We may ache, we may rage, we may sleep through New Year's Eve. Yet eventually, we rise.

We rise by not rushing to fill the silence. I say—let the silence speak. Let the ache teach. Let the emptiness become a fertile space, not a fearful one.

Don't worry about filling it in the beginning. The growth will come. As long as you let it.

## Chapter 6
# Reality Pivots

I have a theory. I believe we are concentrating more deeply than ever before—diving beneath the surface, channeling from new levels of consciousness, and shifting how we process reality itself. What we're experiencing isn't just personal growth—it's a series of Reality Pivots. These are moments where everything you've known begins to tilt, dissolve, or reorder, and suddenly, you're standing in a different dimension of awareness.

The switch from one energetic terrain to another isn't always smooth. Sometimes it happens in the blink of an eye. Other times it's like molasses, slow and sticky, dragging up your deepest programming along the way. Either way, when a Reality Pivot hits, you may find yourself disconnected from linear function. Suddenly you can't do simple math, recall names, or finish a mundane task. What appears to be a glitch is actually a sign. Your consciousness is operating in a different bandwidth, one less tethered to left-brain logic and more attuned to symbolic, intuitive, right-brain knowing.

We're traveling in new energetic ecosystems, and our minds are recalibrating to process it. Instead of being hard on yourself for feeling disoriented or "offline," remember: you are accessing deeper truths, subtler frequencies, and multidimensional information flows.

This is not just a mental upgrade, but a metaphysical one. You are shifting from the laws of the material world to the Laws of the Universe. These include the Law of Vibration (everything is energy), the Law of Correspondence (as within, so without), the Law of Cause and Effect, the Law of Polarity, and of course, the Law of Attraction. These aren't just esoteric teachings—they're the scaffolding of reality.

Personally, I'm allowing things to stay fluid right now—trusting that what needs to land will land, in its own time and in the exact right form.

This book, like the energies moving through your life, is not organized by the old constructs of logic and control. It's a living, breathing map for the path you're actually walking. It's not a curriculum, but a compass.

We're not following an outline. We're following the flow.

That's why this chapter comes now—not at the beginning, and not in checklist form. Because you're no longer here to learn the laws the old way. You're here to embody the real ones. To feel them in your cells. To recognize them in the way life moves through you.

This book is a field. A resonant zone. It's not here to lecture but to mirror what you already know. Sometimes that knowledge is hidden beneath layers. Sometimes it arrives as déjà vu. Yet it's always there.

If you find yourself moving in and out of clarity, don't panic. This is what integration looks like. It doesn't always arrive in linear lines—it arrives in pulses, fragments, sensations, and sudden awakenings.

You are not scatterbrained. You're multidimensional.

Let it all land where it lands. Let the shift be magical, because it is.

Remember: you're not here to control the laws.

You're here to dance with them.

Jane: Another reason that you didn't want to go over the Laws of the Universe or anything like that is you didn't want to be influenced by outside thought.

Lane: A lot of what is out there is discordant with me. I want to keep this book strictly between me and Source, if that can be done. When I read other contemporary material, it's not so much to derive information as it is to feel into the field—just to see if a certain phrase unlocks something, triggers a download, or reveals a more resonant angle. One word, one strange metaphor, sometimes that's enough to crack open an entire transmission. These days I'm not looking for teachers anymore. I'm looking for echoes of truth.

When I read someone from another time, like the ancients, I have to jump an interpretive chasm. Their frequency was encoded for a different moment in history. Their words are veiled in an older energy that I have to interpret. When I get to the heart of what they're saying, the gold is there. The structure might not hold anymore, but the essence often does.

Let me be clear: I never take anyone's transmission as gospel. Not even the so-called masters. Why? Because this timeline—this chaotic, collapsing, and recalibrating world we're standing in—demands new forms. Even the most revered channeled wisdom has an expiration date when it comes to application. Cayce and Yogananda were lightning rods for the eons, but even they spoke through the filter of their era. Now, the signal has changed. The grid has shifted. The codes we need have to be reinterpreted—rewired for today's level of awakening.

## Reality Pivot 1: Your Inner Barometer

Take Cayce's comment on ego: "Ego is not the enemy of self-knowledge. It is the path to it."

That flips the entire New Age narrative on its head. We've been told to kill the ego, silence the ego, transcend the ego—but Cayce said no, walk through it. Integrate it. Let it point you inward.

Then he drops this gem: "It is in the application, not the knowledge, that the truth becomes part of thee."

There it is. That one sentence is a sacred wrecking ball to every book that tries to give you a checklist to God. Truth isn't a concept—it's embodied, or it's dead.

I've said this before and I'll say it again: I don't generally resonate with step-by-step plans. I don't respond to fill-in-the-blank workbooks. I want the essence to permeate my system, change my frequency, and become action. The way I navigate this life is through my inner barometer. This is ancient technology, built into our DNA.

Jane: Would I be right in saying that when you're reading books by other authors, you're using them as a scanning mechanism to determine what is in alignment?

Lane: Yes, and it's actually a validation either way. The resonance either rings like a tuning fork in my chest or it drops like a dead weight. Either way, it tells me something.

Jane: How can people learn to connect to their emotions and use this barometer, this scanning?

Lane: To know what is true for them versus what is a trigger for them versus what is relevant for them. That's the work. That's discernment. It's a muscle most people have never trained. The system we were raised in never wanted us to think that way—it wanted obedient consumers, not spiritually-connected scanners. When you start tuning your instrument, you realize that not everything that feels bad is false, and not everything that feels good is true.

You have to dissect the emotional signature: Is this resistance because the truth is uncomfortable? Or is it a signal that something's off, manipulative, out of sync with God-connection? That's where you develop what I call empirical truth. Not factual truth—facts can be manipulated, but truth that cannot be stolen or reframed by propaganda. You strip it down and what's left is what's real.

Jane: Some will say that includes fear.

Lane: Fear is imposed. It's injected, programmed, sold. It's not foundational. It's not a truth. It's an alarm bell, and when you hear it, the only real question is: What's beneath it? What's the wound it's covering? What's the lie it's protecting? It's just like ego. You follow it inward and you find the broken circuitry—and then you can rewire it.

When you finally strip it all away—the false histories, the fake science, the religions built on control, the government lies, the manmade diseases, the engineered division, the entire crumbling edifice of Western mind-control—you're left with just a few unbreakable truths. They don't require belief. They're self-evident.

For me, those truths are: The Creator. Personal integrity. Unconditional love.

You can't kill those. Not with fire. Not with censorship. Not even with mass psychosis. The mother whose child was murdered and still finds love? That's the God code. That's what survives the death of illusion.

Jane: I think this is a very important technique to talk about. If there is a potential grain of truth in it, if you get a bit of a nod of, hmm, that's a possibility, you hold it for further examination. I think that is a wonderful gift which we must highlight. If people were to add that one tool, their world would change immediately.

Lane: Exactly. That's the power of discernment—and it's a practice. Those of us who've been neck-deep in the awakening path, the truth movement, the disclosure timeline—we've had to get really damn good at it. We've had to scan whistleblowers and channelers and talking heads, Truthers, and spiritual influencers until our inner radar could ping a paid puppet from ten seconds of speech.

For the ones waking up now, the curve is faster. The tools are accessible. The grid is humming. What took me ten years might take a newcomer ten weeks. That's the acceleration we're in. That is, only if they practice. Only if they train their inner tech.

The first piece of that? Stop giving your power to someone else's "truth." Take it all in, run it through your system, and if it doesn't resonate—pause it. Don't reject it, don't adopt it. Just hold it in abeyance until truth confirms itself. Because it always does.

. . .

## Reality Pivot 2: Conscious Abeyance

Lane: Holding a possibility in abeyance is not the same as indecision. It's spiritual maturity. It's energetic discernment. It means you have a calibrated internal system—your soul barometer—and when something enters your field that doesn't fully resonate but might, you don't reject it, and you don't surrender to it either. You pause. You give it space. You say: "You may have truth in you, but I'm not giving you authority until it's earned."

This is the exact opposite of what we've been trained to do. We're conditioned to demand instant conclusions. Red pill or blue pill. Believe or reject. Friend or enemy. The thing is, life—and truth—doesn't work that way. A soul in evolution must sometimes sit with the unresolved, the incomplete, the not-yet-known. That's where the real upgrades happen.

I call this the practice of conscious abeyance. It's when you recognize that something may be partially true, or true at another dimensional level, or maybe just mistimed. You don't shut it out—but you don't let it run your programming either. You let it orbit until it settles into clarity.

It's not passivity, but precision.

Jane: That sounds incredibly freeing. Incredibly difficult for those who are used to black-and-white thinking.

Lane: That's why it's a reality pivot. Most people are so scared of being wrong that they'd rather pick a side than stay centered. It's important to understand that neutrality isn't weakness. When it's conscious, it's power. Think of a high-frequency tuning fork. It doesn't chase other notes—it just vibrates at its frequency, and anything out of harmony either rises to meet it or falls away.

That's how we're meant to operate in this new field.

We hold in abeyance what we don't yet understand. We don't need to shame it, and we definitely don't need to swallow it whole. We just say, "Not yet. I'm listening." And in that act, we reclaim our divine authority. We step outside the machine that demands instant allegiance and say: I choose to pause. I choose to feel. I choose to wait for truth to reveal itself on my timeline, not yours.

That's another reality pivot.

Jane: It leads to the first, doesn't it? Back to inner, or as I like to say, emotional barometer.

Lane: Exactly. You can't hold something consciously if you haven't trained your internal compass. If you're reactive or addicted to external validation, you'll collapse the moment a flashy teacher, partner, or politician demands your allegiance. On the other hand, if you've done the work—if you know what truth feels like in your body—you can hold anything. You can sit in the unknown without needing to solve it.

That's spiritual power.

## Reality Pivot 3: The Love Principle

Lane: There's not always a clean right or wrong. Just because someone is speaking a mistruth doesn't mean their heart is misaligned. This is where energy reading comes in—not the new-age fantasy version, but the raw, grounded, everyday human skill most people don't even realize they have. We're wired to feel the vibe of a room. We can tell when someone's radiating anxiety, joy, resentment. That's energy literacy.

The next layer of that—where it gets alchemical—is when you ask, where is this energy coming from? Not just what they're saying, but why they're saying it. What wound is speaking? What trauma is being protected? When you get curious instead of reactive, something inside you shifts. You unlock what I call the Love Principle.

Now let me be clear. This isn't virtue-signaling love. It's not handing out socks at Christmas or spooning out soup for a photo op—although kindness matters. This is soul-level love. Fierce love. Love that doesn't need to approve of someone's behavior to recognize their essence. You don't excuse harm—but you understand the human behind the mask.

Jane: What about those who harm others deliberately? Who weaponize their pain?

Lane: That's where the discernment piece comes in again. Here's the rebel line no one wants to say: Not everyone on this planet is operating from a human template. I'm not here to coddle evil. There are entities—yes, entities—whose actions are so dark, so devoid of conscience, that they do not belong here. Not everything masquerading in human skin is operating with a human soul. Some are deeply infiltrated. Some are synthetic. Some are here with a very different agenda. I say without apology: send them back.

However, for those who are human, no matter how lost or damaged, there is always a story. Always a why. That doesn't mean we let people roam free to destroy. It does mean we stop pretending that love is weakness. Love—real love—is the most terrifying force in the universe to those who operate in deception. Because it pierces illusion. It dissolves control systems. It sees straight through the costume and says, I see you... and I'm not afraid.

When you practice that kind of love? Judgment falls away naturally. Not because you worked on judgment, but because judgment can't survive where love has rooted itself.

Jane: What about triggers? We're still going to get triggered.

Lane: Of course we are. We're still peeling back layers of programming and distortion. Every time you choose love—especially when it's hard—you dismantle that programming. You accelerate your evolution. It's like spiritual rocket fuel. Forgiveness doesn't make you a doormat. It makes you a force field.

That's the third reality pivot. Lead with love, not fear. See the person, not the projection. When love becomes your lens, truth becomes a lot easier to spot.

## Reality Pivot 4: Past Life Memories

I think past life regressions are really interesting tools. You told me that you discovered you were not as a good person back in the Atlantean days.

Jane: It always makes me laugh when people play around with past lives and say, oh, I was a queen or a king at such and such a time.

Lane: There certainly are a lot of Cleopatras and King Arthurs running around.

Jane: What about the lifetime where you were the murderer or the rapist? I remember one where I was in charge of men that were placed in dungeons, where I abused them pretty badly.

Lane: We have all had what could be conceived as bad, as well as more—let's say more integrated—incarnations. We are collectively on the path of growing and learning, and not every step of that path is noble. Some lives, we play the oppressor. Other lives, the victim. It is through the full spectrum of experience that we gain the soul's deepest wisdom.

Jane: In one of the regressions, I remember looking into the eyes of a man that I despised because he never reacted to my abuse. He just took it on board. He was full of grace and inner peace. I remember the moment when I looked into his eyes and saw love because he knew I was just playing a role. I was experiencing a particular way of being for my own soul growth.

I'll never forget those eyes. It was very powerful. I remember thinking, I want to be like him. My role model came to me from the victim I was abusing.

Lane: Those lifetimes where you've not been the great person are very interesting to explore. There's a certain humility involved in uncovering times when you are not exhibiting the best of qualities. That humility is essential to healing and soul growth. The ego doesn't want to see it, but the soul demands it.

Jane: Atlantis was not one that I was very proud of.

Lane: You are unique to uncovering a past life where you were perpetrating evil. Usually, we're very protected against uncovering those lifetimes. There are safeguards. It may wound us deeply to learn that we hurt other people in previous incarnations. That's why the subconscious often blocks it—because most people aren't ready. On the other hand, when you are ready, when you're strong enough to see the shadow of your own soul, it becomes one of the most liberating revelations of your life. I've had at least one experience where I know I was doing things that were very bad. I did a particular regression years ago because I wanted to know what was going on between myself and a family member. I think selective past life memory is a self-protection device. At least for me it was.

Jane: I agree with that. There was a reason that I had to uncover this lifetime in Atlantis. I was one of three men who were leading the destruction of the Lemurians because in that lifetime I considered those people to be insipid, pathetic, and insignificant. Boring, delusional, uninteresting. I used terms that we would hear now from someone like Klaus Schwab.

Lane: Useless eaters.

Jane: Yes, that was exactly how I saw the Lemurians in that lifetime. I understand at a different level, therefore, where the World Economic Forum puppets are coming from. Now, do I agree with them in this lifetime? Not at all. I've signed up to fight the good fight against them.

Lane: That's amazing. I can remember two lifetimes during that period. One, I was a scientist and I did not know anything beyond my laboratory. I did not know how my work was being used to hurt others. I didn't care. No, it's more that I didn't want to care. I was tunnel-visioned, dissociated from the larger human experience. You've got your face in a microscope—or whatever the mechanics were back then—and you don't see anything beyond your task. It was selective myopia. Willful blindness.

The other lifetime I remember in Lemuria allows me to see how it all works—how light, consciousness, and compassion were the norm. It also allows me to feel where humanity is going. I can feel our new utopia. This isn't just a fantasy. It's a frequency that exists now, seeded within many of us.

This is part of the plan for humanity given to me by the Arcturians, which I'll be sharing with those who want it. Going back to your Atlantis lifetime. Basically, you destroyed my people (laughter).

Jane: Oh, yes. When I realized that, I also realized that my world in this lifetime is full of those beautiful people. I knew that my ego in this lifetime had the power to destroy every single relationship I had. Delving into this and the understanding I gained, I chose to use the emotional scanner technique. I did the scans to clear and then I would go through triggering content deliberately to test how I'm doing, healing this negative part of me, this power-hungry greed that I had. I don't have it now, but it took me a good 10 years to fully remove it.

Lane: The thing to remember is that you have control over the recall of past lives and also their residual effects. Just because you were once something doesn't mean you still are. The point isn't punishment or guilt—it's evolution. Feeling your way through all of it —the pain, the shame, the grace—will help you heal in this lifetime, as well as prevent possibly damaging actions on your part now.

If you can face the version of yourself who misused power, and love that version into transformation, you become a force of true redemption. That's the whole game.

**Reality Pivot 5: Inner Scanner Test**

Jane: I was raised in a family where I was to do my best to play in the elitist system and I loved it. I was drawn to celebrities. I was drawn to fame and fortune. Actually, fame and fortune were the byproduct. What I actually wanted was the power. I knew this was very dangerous and I did the work on this, a great deal of inner work with many amazing therapists and methods.

This went on until I got to a point where I completely trusted myself. Then along came COVID and the inner scanner tests were applied. I confirmed I wasn't for sale and I didn't go down the power path. I feel like I'm rock solid and stable now, but it did take a lot of work. Through all of that, I learned about the indoctrination.

# Lane Keller

I learned about discernment. I learned about judgment. I learned about love. I learned about finessing the scanning ability. It's a commitment to consistently scan. Like now, for example, I'm looking for what's still triggering me. I'll jump onto our newsfeed and I'll scan everything to see what I've not dealt with yet. What I get triggered by is what I've got to deal with now.

Lane: There is a fine line between being triggered and disgusted. It's a distinction that's rarely taught—especially in spiritual or healing spaces, where everything gets lumped into the category of "reaction" or "unresolved trauma." Truth is, not all emotional spikes are born of wounding. Some come from the soul's intelligence—its radar of resonance.

Jane: Oh yes, trigger will put me in fear.

Lane: That's exactly right. A trigger will generate a debilitating involuntary reaction. It hijacks you. A soul-level disgust, on the other hand, is your energetic firewall kicking in. It's your deeper knowing saying this is not right; this is not true; this is not mine. Instead of destabilizing, it clarifies.

For me, learning to distinguish the two was a game changer. When I first began tuning into what I now call my inner scanner, I couldn't tell the difference. I would feel the same physical charge in my system—tightness, heat, urgency—and assume it was all just trauma coming to the surface. Over time I began to notice that some reactions were actually a result of hyper-clarity. My disgust was an alarm—yes—but not because I was broken. Because something outside me was.

I had to learn to respect this signal. It wasn't ego or drama—it was discernment. It was my intuitive immune system.

Jane: It will disempower me versus disgust me. Disempowerment is very different. Fear is something I've got to deal with versus I can't believe those bastards think they're going to roll this out. I can't wait to watch the pushback.

Lane: Exactly. That second reaction? That's sacred rage. That's the soul saying, I remember who I am, and I will not comply. It doesn't shrink you—it sharpens you. That's a real revolution. Learning to scan the noise not with paranoia or panic, but with clarity. With sovereignty.

When I feel that fire now, I don't spiral—I scan. I don't shut down—I zoom out. I ask myself: Is this wounding, or is this wisdom? Am I being hijacked by fear, or is my soul telling me, this ain't it?

Jane: The scanning is interesting to me, and it's also a scan of knowledge, because they've created the matrix in such an intricate web. I think it will probably take the rest of this lifetime for me to fully understand just how brilliant a job they've done.

Lane: It is both terrifying and awe-inspiring—how well they've constructed the layers of illusion. Here's the paradox: the more intricate the matrix, the more finely tuned our scanner becomes. Every lie makes the truth stand out more starkly. Every manipulation sharpens our discernment. It's like spiritual sonar—we pulse out our presence, and everything false ricochets.

That's how we train. Not by escaping the matrix, but by learning to decode it from the inside out.

## Reality Pivot 6: Swap This for Blind Faith

I don't believe in faith for faith's sake. I live in Christ Consciousness, not as a doctrine, but as a frequency. I walk with belief in a Higher Power because I've tested it. I've lived it. My faith isn't blind—it's earned. It's not about following rules or parroting scriptures. It's about direct relationship.

I trust Source—and my guides—because over and over, they've shown me what alignment feels like. They flag the signal when something is off. They reroute me when danger is real. They don't promise immunity from hardship, but they do intervene when I'm still on my soul's path and the detour isn't necessary.

If I'm not meant to die that day, they'll yank me out of the ocean mid-riptide. That happened to me last summer—unexpected, swift, and unmistakably divine. Another time, in a foreign country, I fell down an embankment of steel and broken concrete. It should've been catastrophic. I had called for their help mid-fall, and they caught me. Not literally, but energetically. The damage stopped short of devastation. To me, that's evidence.

So, no—I don't just believe because someone told me to. I believe because I've lived through the miracle. Because I've learned what happens when you don't stay in resonance with God, or with Source. You get humbled. You reap what you sow. Karma isn't a threat—it's a law. You can't fake alignment. You either live it or you don't.

There has to be an understanding—deep and cellular—that unseen forces are at play. They are real. They are responsive. It only works if you are too. If you're acting from your heart and not harming others, if you're seeking truth and not control, if you're moving with reverence and not ego—they'll meet you. They'll walk beside you.

Yet if you're moving in deceit, or abusing your power, or breaking universal law, don't expect cosmic protection. You're on your own until you course correct.

That's what blind faith misses. Faith isn't a pass. It's a partnership. It asks you to show up with integrity—and then trust that the rest will be supported.

Jane: Would you like to talk more about faith?

Lane: I think this is a conclusion gathered from the evidence that you are protected, and a belief in a divinity. It's not an imposed belief because you went to a religious service and were told how it goes. It's from lived experience.

## Reality Pivot 7: Checking In

I have a secret superpower. Her name is Mom. For most of my life, she's been tuned in—claircognizant, energetically precise, and dead-on intuitive. For years, it made things simple. If I had a decision to make, I'd just say, Ma, can you check in for me? And she would.

During the pandemic, when the world was off its axis and travel felt like a gamble, I'd ask her: Can I fly at this time? She'd feel into it and say something like, you'll be fine. It would be better if it wasn't Mercury retrograde, but you'll be fine. She was always right. There was something incredibly reassuring about that—about knowing someone had the bandwidth to tune into higher guidance when I felt clouded.

Over time, I realized I needed to hone that compass for myself. I couldn't outsource my alignment. I had to learn to check in with Source directly. No middleman. No crutch. The process is simple—ask and listen. Sometimes you'll get a clear yes. Sometimes a definite no. Most often, you'll get a quiet neutrality. That's when you stay alert. Let the outer world confirm what your inner world is still processing.

If things start going sideways—flights switched, weird blocks, cancellations—you don't just shrug it off. You check in again. Ask, Is this redirect part of something higher? Am I not supposed to move right now? These aren't paranoid questions. They're reflections of discernment. Alignment is a living thing—it shifts. You've got to keep listening.

I remember missing a connecting flight to Rome once. I was furious at first—delays, a wasted hotel night, and not knowing a soul nearby. Then I dropped into acceptance. There's a reason for this. One I may never know. Still, I trust it. When you reach that place—not because someone told you to, but because you know—then you're no longer operating from fear or control. You're co-creating.

Checking in is not superstition. It's not asking the Universe to coddle you. It's real-time energetic calibration. The more you use it, the more precise it gets.

## Reality Pivot 8: Karmic Velocity

Karma is tricky. Karma is brilliant. Karma is relentless. If I'm being honest, I'd rather not experience it.

Jane: So, what do you do about that?

Lane: You learn your lessons quickly and effectively—and don't do it again. Karma isn't punishment, but pattern correction. Most people keep recycling the same loops because they don't get the message. They don't face the mirror. Karma can be lessened, even bypassed, when we shift from unconscious reaction to conscious integration. I've been refining this theory my whole life.

Jane: Can you eliminate harsh karmic lessons if you have learnt your lesson on the spot?

Lane: Yes. Part two of that is radical gratitude. You don't just mumble, thanks, Universe. You say it with your whole being. Thank you for that sharp, painful, revealing moment—because now I see clearly. Now I don't need to repeat it.

Feel it. Own it. Bless it. That's how you clear the field.

Nietzsche said it well—love your fate. Don't just survive your experiences—revere them. That shift alone dissolves karma before it ever calcifies.

Jane: When we find the gift in every experience, we don't need to repeat the experience. My question to someone would be, what is it that you now know about yourself that you didn't know about yourself prior to this experience?

As you identify what that is, whether it's positive or negative, you become conscious of it instead of it being a subconscious reaction.

Lane: We bring it to the conscious. We bring it to the light. Therefore, there is no need for that to be repeated.

Jane: That's what you've been saying, that the karma will dissipate.

Lane: Exactly. Yet it's more than a mindset. It's a covenant. I made one with God a long time ago—I was still a kid—and I said: God, I don't want karma. Not like that. Let me learn my lessons now. Teach me fast. Teach me clean. Just don't drag me through it all. That promise stuck. It's woven into me.

I still make little deals like that—with God, my guides, whatever benevolent intelligences are working with me. Not out of fear. Out of clarity. I don't want unnecessary pain. Instead, I'm willing to evolve.

On the spot. In real time. No delay. That's the key to karmic exit velocity.

## Reality Pivot 9: Memories, Covenants, and Contracts

Jane: Let's talk about covenants because I don't think people do what you do at all.

Lane: All right. I did my best to eradicate any soul contracts because I feel it is grossly wrong for us not to remember what we have contracted to before commencing our current lives.

I know this flies in the face of spiritual-type thinking. To me, this erasure—this selective amnesia about our soul's path—feels more like sabotage than protection. It reeks of manipulation. It feels like a false mechanism inserted by forces that want control, not growth. The veil isn't sacred—it's strategic. I don't trust it.

People say the veil of forgetfulness is a hallowed safeguard, but I only accept that in part. There's definitely truth in that. Still, the way it functions now? It's been weaponized. We should have clearer access to who we were, what we've agreed to, and why.

Jane: I do think that the veil has been hijacked and the dumbing down of the race has continued for a very long time as they've got more and more complex in their matrix and manipulation of the veil. I 100% agree that we should be remembering our past lives to have new experiences.

Lane: Exactly. The level of effort it took me just to access a handful of relevant past lives was insane. It took years. At one point, I went through two years of past life regressions just to understand a relationship that was emotionally challenging me. I loved him and he loved me, but it was elemental chaos—fire and water.

I couldn't make sense of the pattern until I tunneled back through time. What I learned didn't fix the relationship, but it helped me extract meaning from it. That's alchemy—when you grasp the energetic signature behind the madness. It opens a pathway—not just out of pain, but toward sovereignty. Toward higher perception.

The work was brutal. The insights were sacred. I do believe that it shouldn't have to be this hard.

Jane: So, at this point you renegotiated soul contracts and your covenants?

Lane: I did. That's the whole point of bringing up past lives—we need the full picture to make informed spiritual choices. If memory is the key to growth, then forced amnesia is a form of bondage.

I call BS on this idea that our contracts are unknowable, unreachable, or permanently binding. If I signed something in an astral dimension, I deserve to know what it says. I didn't come here to play blindfolded.

Jane: Me too.

Lane: I stand in my own authority, invoke my highest alignment, and say—out loud, with force—I refute and revoke any and all soul contracts I may have ever entered into without conscious remembrance or consent. They are null. They are void. They do not bind me.

I say this too, regularly, though: God, if there's something you want me to do—if there's a mission, a path, a purpose that's truly aligned—then show me. I'll walk it.

To do so I require conscious clarity.

That's my covenant now. It's not blind obedience. It's co-creation with Source—on clear terms.

## Reality Pivot 10: Isolating Your Purpose

What I mean by your purpose is the intuitive sense that you're on the right path—not because someone told you so, not because it's safe or strategic—but because you feel it in your bones. That is the subtle internal alignment, the magnetic resonance of yes. Of truth. Of home. Purpose isn't a title, a job, or a destiny handed down from above. It's an energy signature. A pull. A frequency that makes your heart expand and your soul sing.

## UNLEASHING THE REBEL WITHIN

It's helpful—even necessary—to remember why you came here. To ask yourself, beneath all the noise, what am I really here to do?

Jane: How do you do that?

Lane: Go back. Way back. Before the programming. Before the shame and conditioning and compromise. When you were still wild. When your inner world was intact and your dreams unfiltered. What did you long for as a child—not because someone praised you for it, but because it ignited your fire?

Then and now—what stirs your soul? What ignites your creative fire? If you didn't have to grind your way through a soul-killing job or pay the system to survive, what would you wake up excited to do? That's your compass. That's your resonance with Source. I promise you, it's not random. Your joy is a breadcrumb trail to your soul's purpose.

For me, it started with creativity. I never, not for a second, let go of any of my dreams. Not one of them.

Jane: What were your dreams when you were young?

Lane: This may sound egotistical, but it became my guiding principle: I knew I was here for something important. I felt it before I could name it. It is a vast, mysterious, hovering just outside of language—but unmistakable. I've carried that feeling like a pulse through my life. Sometimes it roars, other times it's whispered. But it never left.

Now, between you, me, and the readers of this book... my mom used to say, "Oh, you're such royalty. Load the dishwasher." I'd think, yes, I am royalty. I shouldn't have to do dishes. Needless to say, that didn't go over well.

But now? The Arcturians call me their queen. I don't say that to elevate myself—I say it because I've finally learned to receive who I am. Maybe it's symbolic. Maybe they have many queens. When I hear it, something ancient in me nods. Something remembers.

I've lived many lifetimes of drudgery and disillusionment. This one hasn't been all light either. Still, it's been lucid—rich with lessons and revealing moments. The core throughline, the one constant? Creativity.

I see new worlds. I write business plans that defy convention. I make beauty from scraps—whether it's a story, a piece of tree bark, a renovated home, or what's left in the fridge. I live by frequency now. Creativity is the channel.

I once wanted to be an actress. Then when I became a talent agent in New York and saw the underbelly of that world, I thought, nope. Not this. I pivoted into playwriting, then directing—where I could shape the narrative, collaborate in truth, and build from the bones of something real.

Subsequently, working with children deepened things. Their raw energy, their connection to spirit—it cracked open a new dimension of purpose. That's when I realized: I never left my dreams. I evolved with them. They weren't static. They braided into something larger. A mission.

This isn't unique to me. Creativity is a divine inheritance. It lives in every soul, waiting to be uncovered. When you activate it, when you stop suppressing it or outsourcing it, you remember why you came here.

The task is simple: find what's alive in you. What's raw and real. What still makes you tremble. That's your purpose. That's your rebellion. That's your revolution.

## Chapter 7
# States of Beingness

You've no doubt heard the term dimensions tossed around like spiritual seasoning—usually vague, fluffy, and divorced from anything you can sink your teeth into. The spiritual community loves to sprinkle it on everything: "I'm in 5D now." "He's stuck in 3D." "We're ascending to 12D by next Thursday." I get it. It's catchy. It sounds advanced. Yes, I suppose I'm technically a card-carrying member of the woo-woo set myself. That said, I have no patience for language that can't be explained without a decoder ring.

I'm interested in dimensional frameworks because they offer a way to describe the evolution of consciousness without resorting to religious dogma or New Age platitudes. More importantly, they help us track where we are on the spiral out of enslavement and into sovereignty.

Let's talk about 3D, 4D, and 5D.

These three dimensions aren't physical locations like houses you can move into—they're states of perception. Energetic bandwidths. While the scale goes higher—far higher—these three are the boots-on-the-ground battleground for most of us in this lifetime.

. . .

## Beyond the 3D Trap

When I say "3D," I'm not just talking about solid matter and time-space reality. I'm talking about a mindset—a manufactured consensus reality that's been deliberately programmed. Think of it as the operating system of the collective sleep state.

People in 3D reality trust the media. They trust Big Pharma. They trust their priest, their doctor, their elected officials. They trust the school system and the government, despite overwhelming evidence that these institutions are rigged to siphon our life force and keep us tame. They're what society calls "normal." They follow the rules. Sports events are their religion. They fill out their forms. They vaccinate on schedule. They go to church on Sunday and consume their daily dose of sanitized news without a hiccup.

Beneath it all is a refusal to question the structure they live inside. That's what keeps them stuck. It's not the sports or the religion or enabling relationships that chains them. It's the inability—or unwillingness—to see beyond the illusion. They're still asleep in the matrix, dreaming someone else's dream.

## 4D: Shadow Playground

Fourth dimension is trickier. This is where things start to bend and blur. The veil gets thinner. The psychic static gets louder. You begin to sense energies, entities, old wounds that live in your field. Welcome to the land of spiritual detox.

It's often glamorized as an "awakening," but make no mistake: this realm is booby-trapped. The fourth dimension is a psychological hall of mirrors. It's where the darkness dances in your peripheral vision. It's also where the worst of the astral parasites operate—the soul-sucking false light beings, the distorted serpentine frequencies, the "ascended" ones with hidden hooks. This is where you confront the trauma, the ego death, the seductive loops of shadow work that never quite resolve.

Now, some people insist this is a necessary passage. That we must "do our time" in 4D before we earn our way out. I call that cosmic gaslighting. That may be their path, but it doesn't have to be mine—or yours. I chose something different.

I didn't skip the healing, but I didn't sign up for endless purging rituals and inner exorcisms either. I chose to evolve through clarity, not chaos. Through discernment, not endless emotional flailing. You don't have to crawl through the underworld in order to wake up. Not unless you're still addicted to pain as proof of growth.

## 5D: Frequency of Freedom

Now we enter the territory of 5D—what I consider the first real taste of freedom. This is the state of being where you've unplugged from the matrix and stopped looking to false authorities for your truth. It's not about floating in a bliss bubble or performing spiritual perfection. It's about standing tall in your being. Clear perception. Unshakable resonance with the Laws of Source.

In 5D, you know who you are, even if you can't always explain it. You feel energy as clearly as sound or scent. You recognize distortion instantly. You walk into a room and sense what's off. You know when someone is lying, even if they're smiling sweetly. You can smell deception. Sometimes literally.

I've had moments—especially while house-hunting—where I'd be scrolling through listings and suddenly catch the stench of mold, rot, or desperation wafting through the screen. My body would recoil before my brain had even registered the data. That's 5D frequency discernment. It's subtle, but it's unmistakable.

In this dimension, you don't just believe in vibration—you live it. You become acutely aware of the frequency of words, of food, of environments, of people. You stop consuming garbage because you feel it degrades your field. You stop engaging in meaningless conversation. You stop compromising your essence just to "get along." You stop playing small.

The downside? It can get lonely. Your tolerance for mediocrity collapses. You can't pretend you care about the Super Bowl or celebrity gossip. You can't sit through sitcoms or political debates without feeling like you're being lobotomized. You feel deeply, but selectively. That's the point. You are no longer broadcasting your energy in all directions hoping to be loved. You are intentional. You are encoded with purpose.

This isn't a hierarchy—it's a frequency map. Anyone can climb it. Anyone can pivot. All the same, you cannot fake your way into 5D. You have to shed the layers, not wear them more convincingly. You have to burn the false self to ash and listen to the soul that's been whispering underneath all along.

When you do—when you finally let go of the comforting lies and face the raw, unsanitized truth—you realize that the 5D state was never "out there" waiting. It was always within you waiting for you to rebel.

**Navigating the Dimensions**

Jane: I think we're fully in the fourth-dimension demonic war, but I feel like I can just banish the interference and they don't get to Wi Fi me. I'm sure we've all got the hardware in us regardless of whether we've been vaxxed or not.

Lane: Yes, as far as I'm concerned, I left 3D a long time ago and went straight to 5D. It's not ego—it's alignment. Not everyone understands that kind of skip-step because they're still entangled in the drama of the fight. I don't battle demons. I don't play in their frequency field. If they want a war, they can have one—but not on my bandwidth.

That includes the fallout from the VAX, the 5G spiderweb, and the graphene trickery they've embedded into the human biome like sleeper code. It's real. Yet so is my choice to remain in integrity. I choose not to weaken myself by fighting shadows. I strengthen by vibrating above them.

We're in a planetary reboot—a full-spectrum clearing. Everything false is being exposed. This isn't just spiritual theory. This is boots-on-the-ground frequency warfare. The most dangerous thing they fear? A human who refuses to give away their inner authority.

Jane: So, what are we supposed to be doing? I think we know, but how do we navigate being in 5D, helping out, and yet not letting it affect us?

Lane: Honestly, I think we're doing it. We're navigating better than most. We're tracking the energies without being swallowed by them. Let's be clear—it's a bizarre position to hold. We're not in the 3D system anymore, yet we still walk through its remnants daily. We smell the rot, we hear the distortion, we see the hypnotized masses. Still, we don't fall for it. That's the work.

Every single so-called intel provider, guru type or spiritual whistleblower out there—I already know what they're going to say. I tune in, and within seconds, I sense the pattern. Some of them mean well. Some are on the payroll. Some are just recycling trauma porn because they haven't healed their own.

It's not nonsense—it's just no longer news. We've outgrown the noise.

What does interest me—what gives me hope—is the subtle uprising of unity. The quiet, steady dismantling of division. I see people, not ideologies, rising. I see a hunger for coherence that transcends identity and programmed loyalties.

This isn't about sides. It's not about tribes. It's not about who started what or who's suffered more. That's their trap. This is about all of us. The entire species. If we keep falling for binary thinking, we'll never break the loop.

So yes, when people step forward and say, "This is about liberation for all, not just justice for one," I know we're making headway. When the false narratives start to crack—when the media's spell begins to fail—I feel the grid loosen. That's what I'm watching for.

Jane: I agree. I said to somebody recently who was questioning the yes, no vote, which we had here in Australia with the Indigenous being recognized in the constitution. I said, we have to learn to get along. Until we can do that, the rest of it is just smoke and mirrors. I love that we're seeing people step up.

There was a cute little meme that popped up the other day that said, I'm not pro Russia, I'm not pro Ukraine, I'm not pro-Israel, I'm not pro Vaxx, I'm not pro Anti, and listed all of the different divisions ending with I'm Pro People. I think that articulates what you're saying in a different way.

## Moving Past 4D

Jane: I'm fascinated that you jumped 4D.

Lane: My mom and I have this perpetual back and forth on whether or not I skipped 4D, and I'm maintaining that I did.

She says, "But everyone has to go through it, it's part of the process." I push back: "Who says? Who laid down that rule? Some galactic guidance counselor handing out worksheets?" This is the very kind of conditioning we're here to disrupt. Just because something's been widely accepted or repeated ad nauseam in spiritual circles doesn't mean it's truth. A lot of so-called "process" is actually just programming.

Why does anyone have to crawl through hell to earn light? Why must pain be the tollbooth to evolution? I reject that premise. I've already endured the dark night of the soul. I've done my underworld tour. I have no interest in a lifetime pass to purgatory. The cult of suffering runs deep on this planet, and I call it out every time I see it.

What truly sealed the deal for me—what made me draw the line —my significant other at the time, the twin flame, was battling in 4D realms while he slept. Real warfare. Not metaphoric. Full-on astral combat. He'd wake up with literal bruises, scratches, wounds on his body from whatever he'd been doing in the dreamspace. Some of the things he shared were horrifying—dark entities, dismemberments, energy traps. Still, he insisted this was part of the process.

To me, that was the final straw. The death knell for my tolerance of that entire dimension's mythology. I decided, in no uncertain terms: I will not participate in that paradigm. I will not train in the dark dojo. I will not fight in the shadows to prove I deserve the light. I am light.

As a result, I did what I do best: I chose. I chose to anchor myself in 5D—or whatever you want to call it—and move forward from there. My 5D self isn't perfect. It's human, yes, but it's committed. It strives to remain in forward motion, rooted in unconditional love and spiritually-connected authority. I'm not saying I never slip. We all get triggered. When I do, I see it as a spotlight flashing on a wound. Oh, look—there's the bullseye. Better clear that.

Jane: I remember when I was on a zoom with these allegedly beautiful humanitarians. One of the men said, when we talk to XYZ person, we need to be speaking in 3D language. I thought to myself, you patronizing sod. That statement is contradictory to what I believe 5D is, and you've just outed yourself. That kind of talk is a sure tip off that you've got a lot of healing to still do.

Lane: That's so true. Spiritual elitism is alive and thriving—especially among those who think they've graduated into 5D, when they've really just enrolled in a new hierarchy with better branding.

There's a smugness there. A condescension that sneaks in when someone thinks they've ascended, but are really just spiritualizing their unhealed ego. You can hear it in their tone. You can feel it in their vibration. The irony is, the very belief that you're better than someone else because you're "more awakened" is the surest sign you haven't actually made it out of 3D.

True resonance doesn't broadcast superiority. It radiates clarity. It recognizes divinity in everyone—not just those who speak the same coded language. That's why I use "5D" as shorthand—because it's efficient. Let me be clear, though: I don't like labels. I never have. This trend of turning dimensional language into social rank makes my blood curdle.

We were meant to transcend the game, not glamorize it.

. . .

## Egoic Mind Roadblock

I've been in those "elite" circles—the ones with penthouses and private jets—and I've also spent time with those who've scraped by in broken systems, caught in survival mode. I can tell you this: I see them all as equals. Status doesn't mean a thing if you're not operating from soul-level integrity. The exception I make is when people are actively harming others. That's where the line is drawn.

Harm doesn't always look like violence. It can look like hoarding all the access, gatekeeping the land, the water, the food. It can look like owning the coastline and putting up fences so that the rest of us—the so-called riffraff—can't reach the ocean. Take a look at what Bill Gates has done with farmland. Or the Bush family with water rights. What they've done is scoop up the earth's vital resources and sealed them off under the banner of ownership. If you've ever driven the coasts of America, you'll see how this elitism plays out in real time: massive estates blocking public beach access, gates and private security keeping the people out. These aren't homes—they're monuments to disconnection.

This is why I love the town I'm in now. You can still get to the beach on every block. No gatekeepers. No high towers guarding the sunrise. Just sea, sky, and soul. Believe me, that's rare. Most towns—especially in Florida—are carved up by golf courses, strip malls, and gilded, grotesque displays of status. The irony? None of it is actually beautiful. It's not in harmony with the land. It's soulless. Just money flexing its power.

True beauty blends with nature. Sustainable, intuitive, sacred design is what we should be building—something alive, not these mausoleums of ego and excess. The ego's vision of paradise is always sterile, hierarchical, and disconnected from the organic flow of the Earth.

This gets to the root of the matter: elitism is antithetical to ascension. You cannot elevate into higher realms of consciousness while clutching desperately to the trappings of separation and control. The more tightly you grip earthly illusions of status, the more dense your energy becomes.

Let's talk more about density. That word is used a lot in spiritual circles, but I have sat with it for a long time to understand what it really means. For me, density is the gravitational pull of the 3D construct. It's the heaviness of material obsession, of being trapped in the physical without conscious awareness of why.

In this dense 3D world, we see patterns like:
- Using sex as currency or escape
- Taking from others to gain power
- Building wealth through manipulation
- Overindulgence, gluttony, addiction
- Numbing out with substances
- Victimhood used as identity
- Anger and reactivity worn as armor

All of this is ego territory. All of it is service to self.

The plot thickens. Service to self doesn't just mean being selfish in the obvious sense. It means that every single thought, word, or action is filtered through thoughts like: what does this give me? How do I win? How do I stay in control?

It's subtle, but insidious. The way to break it is discipline of awareness.

Let's get concrete:

3D consciousness is the egoic mind.

That's another term that's been tossed around like confetti—service to self—but it still holds weight. Every action has to be examined through that lens:

Am I feeding my ego, or am I acting from alignment?

Am I trying to gain something externally, or am I offering something from a deeper source?

Every single thing you do and say, every thought that comes into your head, must be examined to isolate where it's coming from and why. This is how you dissolve the egoic structure. Not with incense or mantras or pretending to be "above it all." With sober, unrelenting self-inquiry. Where did that thought come from? Was that action really for the good of all—or just for the good of me?

You want a real practice? Try this:

Get into a conversation with someone and say nothing. Don't interrupt. Don't fix. Don't wait for your turn to speak. Just listen. Give them the one thing almost no one gets in this world—your full, nonjudgmental presence.

Don't share your version. Don't one-up their story with your own. Don't say, "Yeah? I did that 20 years ago." That's service to ego. That's a reflexive need to center yourself in the experience.

Instead, sit there. Hold space. Let them be seen. That's service to other. That's breaking the 3D trance.

Jane: That's a great exercise.

Lane: It is. It's deceptively simple. When you stop trying to prove or impress, when you let go of being the one who knows, the whole game shifts. This isn't about being "good." This is about getting free.

## A Dimensional Test

How can you not feel for both sides in a war? Why would you pick a side? We're not talking about those orchestrating the killings, here, but about the people. Both sides are suffering. Both peoples have been caught in cycles of manipulation, trauma, displacement, and lies. Why not practice love for all of them and send that energy out to the universe instead of letting propaganda infect your heart with rage and tribalism? Send out love like a force field—wide, unwavering, and uncaptured. War is a test. Not just of politics or alliances, but of dimensional awareness.

War is not merely about religion, borders, or historical claims. It is about frequency. About where we choose to sit in the spectrum of human evolution. Are we going to let this light-versus-dark war keep us tethered in reaction, or are we going to break the cycle and rise into unity consciousness? Yes, unity consciousness is a buzzword. Truth often gets mocked into cliché so people forget its power. That said, unity consciousness is real—and it's strong enough to undo the programming.

It starts with the ego. That sneaky parasite of 3D consciousness. We've got to realize that most of our ego stuff comes from one central wound: the illusion that we're not enough. The feeling of being unworthy, unloved, unseen. The compulsion to prove our value, to be praised, to be chosen, to be validated. However, when you really look at it—when you dismantle the wiring—you see that the need for outside recognition is a hollow exchange. It's not love. It's not truth. It's survival-level psychology built on programming and false rewards.

We've all done it. We've chased applause, approval, validation from partners or peers or parents. Ultimately, the only recognition that matters is the one that comes from within. Because outside recognition is transactional. It's given to you in a moment when it serves someone else. When it no longer does, it's withdrawn.

Why would you let your soul be controlled by a currency that unstable?

Instead, feel good about your own self. Feel rooted in your integrity, your choices, your personal authenticity. That kind of frequency changes everything. Others will begin to love and appreciate you—not because of what you perform—but because of how you make them feel. Because of the way your energy helps them remember their own light.

Love your own self. Fiercely. Gently. Unapologetically. Love others just as much, if that's possible. At least try to. This is the surest path to 5D—not by preaching, but by embodying.

Jane: I don't know how easy that is. It's difficult for some.

Lane: If you had no food except one loaf of bread, would you give it to somebody on the street? Or would you instead keep it for yourself and your dog and maybe your neighbor?

Jane: That's a toughie. I know people do it and I admire those who can really put others before themselves. I think in that situation,

I'm going to put my hand out and say, no, I'm feeding my children and animals first.

Lane: I don't disagree. I'm certainly not at the point of saying, "I've got a loaf of bread left and I'll give it to somebody on the street and that's all I've got and I don't know where the next one's coming from." It's a really good test though. I also have another test of generosity. If you commit an act of kindness, whether it's leaving a bag of groceries on your neighbor's doorstep or some other random act, can you do it and not tell anyone?

Jane: If the majority of the world chose to do random acts of kindness tomorrow, and then told everybody about it, it's actually going to create a really good movement in a really good energetic way. I'd be happy for it, but I do understand the ability to be able to gift without telling anyone is a great spiritual growth.

Lane: Yes, so we are talking about 3D to 5D. Maybe it's a bad test. The 3D person can do that random act and spread love, and that's beautiful motivation and encouragement for others. The 5D person would do it and not tell anyone because it's not about receiving anything back or others saying, "Oh my gosh, you're such a good person." Instead, they would hand the person on the street the bread, give them some money and then tell the world they observed someone else doing it. Maybe that's how you accomplish both at one time.

## Chapter 8
# Frequency Jumping

Let's be honest—this whole ascension business can sound a little "out there." That said, jumping dimensions isn't about floating off the planet in some glitter-dusted trance. It's about mastering your energy so precisely, so purposefully, that you refuse to be dragged down by low-density nonsense.

Here are some unapologetic tools to navigate the dimensional landscape and rise into your highest state of clarity, creativity, and conscious rebellion.

**Frequency Jump 1: Stay in Sync**

Passion. Joy. Creation. These are not abstract concepts—they're sacred states of alignment. When you're in sync with them, you're in sync with Source. That's Godliness. That's sovereignty.

Every time you create something from nothing, you are echoing the blueprint of the universe itself. Whether you're designing toenail art, polishing rocks into gems, writing a novel, cooking from instinct, or dreaming up ways to serve others—you are in the infinite current. You have surpassed being a consumer and are instead a Creator.

The problem? Too many people have been shamed out of their creative birthright. Maybe a second-grade teacher sneered at your wobbly tree sketch. Maybe someone told you dancing was frivolous. Maybe the system convinced you to chase productivity over passion. That ends now.

You are creative. Your true self is wired for it. If you've forgotten, it's only because you've been buried under the rubble of conformity, obligation, and judgment. It's time to dig yourself out.

Start with what lights you up. Follow the trail of your own curiosity. What fascinates you? What makes your heart beat louder? What could you lose hours doing, without watching the clock? That's the frequency of your soul trying to pull you out of the 3D muck.

Yes—passion, vibration, and creativity are intimately linked. Raise one, and the others follow. Raise all three, and you are rewriting your reality.

## Frequency Jump 2: Swap This for Apathy

Who gave anyone the right to sit on the sidelines while the world is on fire?

We are in a battle—energetically, spiritually, and psychologically—for the soul of humanity. Yet, millions are still hiding out in their comfortable bubbles, sipping their lattes, pretending nothing's wrong. Hoping someone else will fix it. That someone else will take the risk, speak the truth, question the system, expose the fraud, carry the burden, bleed on the front lines.

How about a simple, cold truth? It's not okay to let 2% of the people do 98% of the heavy lifting. That karmic debt doesn't just disappear. If you're coasting while others are rising, it will catch up with you. Inaction is not neutrality—it is a choice. In this dimensional split we're in, that choice speaks volumes about your frequency.

No, I'm not talking about feel-good performances of charity. Buying Girl Scout cookies doesn't count. Booking a table at some ritzy philanthropic gala, where 80% of the proceeds go to the marketing agency? Still not it. Even feeding the poor, while noble and necessary, is not what I'm pointing to here.

What's required now is razor-sharp perception—and the courage to speak the truth as you see it. That is authenticity. Not performance. Not politeness. Not parroting what's acceptable. Authenticity is the raw, unfiltered alignment of your inner knowing with your outer voice.

Most people are secretly terrified of authenticity. They fear being disliked, rejected, or targeted. Yet the cost of staying silent is far higher. The weight of suppressing your truth—of playing nice while your insides are being hollowed out—drags you into density. It chokes your light and chains your spirit. It brings on dissatisfaction and illness.

That's what keeps you stuck in 3D.

Claiming authenticity lifts you, even if it's clumsy at first. Even if it costs you friendships, jobs, or family approval. The more you live in integrity with your core—the more you speak your own language, stand in your own shoes, and walk the walk with courage, kindness, and conviction—the stronger you become. The more *you* you become. That is the fast lane to 5D.

Because 5D isn't a place, it's a frequency. It's not an escape pod—it's a conscious choice to burn brighter, rise higher, and stop playing small. It's a knowing. A fierce, untouchable clarity. It's the refusal to betray your own soul, even when everyone around you is still asleep.

In 5D, you don't weigh every action against fear. You don't agonize over whether to say what needs to be said. You are the action. You are the light. You are the frequency others feel, even if they can't name it. You're no longer bogged down by petty dramas, social theater, or manufactured fear.

You become a force that doesn't apologize for existing.

If you feel apathetic or disconnected—swap it. For authenticity. For discernment. For action. For unapologetic truth. That's the rebel work. That's how you jump dimensions.

. . .

## Lane Keller

### Frequency Jump 3: Eradicate Ego

I have an excellent tool for ego that I haven't yet discussed. It works beautifully. Like magic. What is it?

Take the word "I" out of your vocabulary.

Yes, that's right. Try it for just one day. Every time you are about to say "I" substitute "we." Not in a fake way. Not in a way that erases personal identity. Instead, do it in a way that expands consciousness. Believe me, it works. The shift happens faster than you'd expect. Things start to feel lighter—less charged, less personal, less sticky. You stop looping in your own story and start recognizing the collective symphony we're all part of.

As you drop "I" from your speech, you will literally feel yourself rising. It's subtle but unmistakable—like a helium lift in your chest, a release of some invisible burden you didn't know you were dragging. You start to float into upper dimensional awareness—not because you're dissociating, but because you're expanding.

You're stepping out of the cage of personal identity and into the field of interconnectedness. That shift is a dimensional jump.

You can actually break out of the egoic mind in just 24 hours. You don't need a 10-day Vipassana retreat. You don't need to chant mantras in a cave. Just stop saying "I."

It's like giving up sugar. The first couple days are rough. You feel the absence like a ghost limb—you don't even realize how often "I" dominates your vocabulary until you try to eliminate it. Yet once you do? The cravings vanish. The hold dissolves. The system rewires. Until, of course, you "taste" it again. Then the pull starts to sneak back in. The good news? It's a quick turnaround. You now know how to shift it. You've glimpsed another way of being, and once you've had that taste, you can return anytime.

Don't use the word "I." At least not unconsciously. See what happens.

For those of you flipping pages and thinking, hey, wait a minute. You're using "I" right now. You're absolutely right. Sometimes "I" serves a purpose—especially when relaying personal experience in service of something larger. That's what this book is doing. It's not to spotlight the self, but to connect through it. To show you what's possible by reflecting lived authenticity.

Here is a golden tip. In conversations, in everyday moments, in group exchanges use "we." *We* is the portal. We shifts the tone. We dissolves the hierarchy. We reminds us that we're not solo satellites trying to outrun each other in orbit. We are nodes in the same intelligence. When we speak from that place, we access something far bigger than any one voice.

Try it. Not because it's trendy or spiritual. Do it because it's practical dimensional alchemy.

Drop the ego, and watch your frequency lift.

## Frequency Jump 4: Identify Your Real Goal

When people see you doing good work, they often say, "That's creating really good karma for you." I'll smile, maybe nod, and respond, "That's great—how nice." Yet, I'm not doing it for karma.

I'm not stacking spiritual brownie points. I'm not angling for some cosmic reward or insurance policy for the next life. I do it because someone needs attention in that moment. Because the world needs truth—raw, unfiltered, unpopular truth—spoken aloud. I act because something needs doing, and no one else is stepping up.

That's the real goal: to respond to what is needed, not what will make you look good, feel spiritual, or be praised. The ego loves to masquerade as goodness when it's really after validation. But the soul? The soul acts because it must. No fanfare, no waiting for credit. Just motion toward coherence.

Jane: I wonder if that's just something ingrained.

Lane: I don't know where that comes from exactly. Maybe it's a soul memory. Maybe it's bloodline. Or maybe it's just the result of being raised by people who lived according to the Golden Rule and expected you to be a kind and decent being. Wherever it originates, the action doesn't come from calculation or moral math. It comes from inner alignment. It needs to be done, so you do it. Period. You're not performing for karma, or to be seen, or to impress some heavenly ledger keeper. You're acting in rhythm with your own knowing.

Jane: The vast majority of people, in my opinion, don't do that. They've got to learn these things. They've got to learn because the childhood trauma happens so young that they move into a defensive, subconscious, fear-based behavior—where they're always watching their backs, shielding their hearts, and making moves for safety instead of truth. Whereas you skipped that through your very different upbringing.

Lane: My mom had the plaque in the bathroom growing up. It was the Golden Rule from Jesus: "Do unto others as you would have others do unto you." It wasn't just a nice saying. It was the answer to virtually everything. That was our moral compass. That was the default.

When I respond to something, it's not complicated. I just ask: What would I want someone to do if I were on the other side of this? Then I do that. No grand deliberation, no performative virtue. It's instinctual now. A rhythm. A way of walking through the world with integrity that doesn't require overthinking.

That's the real dimensional upgrade. The rebel upgrade. Not thinking about how to be good—but being it, because it is how I would want myself, or one of my loved ones, to be treated.

## Frequency Jump 5: Release Trauma Consciousness

We have to rise out of trauma consciousness if we want to jump dimensions. There's no way around it.

This doesn't mean denying the existence of trauma. It means refusing to build your identity around it. Trauma is real—but so is your capacity to transcend it. What keeps so many stuck in 3D isn't just the trauma itself, but the attachment to it. The looping stories. The habitual excuses. The refusal to release the identity that was forged in suffering.

That's what 3D is. It's not just a place, or a state of consciousness. It's a trapdoor of justification. It's the voice that says: I was abandoned, I was betrayed, I was silenced, so now I get to numb out, lash out, shut down, or stay small.

I want to be clear—we're not talking here about deep, acute trauma that legitimately requires years of conscious support and processing. That kind of pain deserves tenderness and careful attention. What I am calling out is the culture of perpetual trauma as an identity badge. Trauma porn, as I mentioned earlier in the book. The "oh well, I was wounded as a child" mentality that becomes a lifelong permission slip to eat junk, treat others poorly, avoid truth, and never take full responsibility for your impact.

That's the kind of trauma consciousness that anchors you in the density. That's what binds you to 3D.

Let's be honest—everyone has been traumatized. Everyone. Maybe not to the same extent. Maybe not in the same exact way. None of us got out of childhood—or adulthood—without emotional bruises. If you're here on this planet, in this time, in this body, it's because your soul signed up for the school of experience. You were put into this life on purpose. Not to crumble. Instead, to rise.

The real question is:

Are you going to let the trauma define you? Or are you going to turn it into firewood?

Are you going to use it as a reason to spiral downward, or as the very material you use to build your wings?

Yes, purging it may be difficult. It may feel like a death. It may take every ounce of strength you've got left. However, if you want to jump dimensions, you've got to stop dragging the dead body of your old story around with you. You've got to make the conscious choice:

I will not build my temple on a foundation of pain.

I don't believe the Creator gives us any challenge we're not capable of transmuting. That doesn't mean it'll be easy. It does mean it's possible. With that possibility comes power.

You are not your trauma. You are not your history. You are not the scars, or the labels, or the diagnoses.

You are what rises from all of that.

Let that be your reality.

## **Frequency Jump 6: Don't Buy Into Separatist Thought**

Separatist thinking is one of the biggest traps of the 3D matrix. It's seductive. It masquerades as intelligence, as morality, as certainty. At its core, it is still separation—and separation is the opposite of Source.

The moment you think, I know better, you're in danger. The moment you feel, I've read more, studied more, awakened more, and therefore I'm superior, you've slipped right back into ego. Ego is density. Ego is division. Ego is the veil between you and truth.

Let me tell you something: the more you truly know, the less certain you become. That's true wisdom. As you rise in consciousness, you begin to see how infinite, layered, and mysterious this whole reality actually is. Certainty softens into humility. Knowledge sharpens into discernment. The mouth finally learns when to stay closed.

I say, the more I know, the less I know—because with awareness comes the realization of how much remains hidden.

This is why separatist thinking is so dangerous. It doesn't just breed ego and elitism. It opens the door to mass control. We're being served carefully curated division across every axis of life—political, spiritual, social, sexual—and told it's part of progress.

It's not progress. It's programming.

Let's call it what it is: indoctrination. It's clever. It doesn't scream tyranny. It whispers virtue. It wraps control in the language of compassion, science, or justice. It tells you you're fighting for the greater good—when in reality, you're being used as a pawn in someone else's game.

Take the LGBTQ+ discourse. This has been a massive dimensional test—not because of the individuals involved, but because of the manipulation riding on top of it. We haven't been asked to love one another unconditionally. We've been ordered to conform, to comply, to recite the correct slogans or risk being exiled. Children have been fast-tracked into irreversible hormonal and surgical interventions before they've had time to explore who they are. This isn't liberation but exploitation disguised as identity. Real confusion and pain are being hijacked and monetized, and anyone trying to slow down or question the process is labeled a bigot. Some see it as compassion, but in reality it's coercion.

The same goes for ANTIFA, for the vax wars, for every faction you're being pushed to either idolize or hate. Every time you pick a side without investigating the machinery behind it, you lose a little piece of your inner authority. The issue is never what you see on the surface. The issue is always the agenda behind it.

Let's go deeper. Look at abortion. You're told it's about bodily autonomy. A woman's right to choose. Of course, dominion over one's own body is sacred. But when that truth is used to hide late-term fetal harvesting, organ trafficking, and rituals that cross into spiritual inversion, it stops being about women's rights. It becomes something far more sinister. The surface narrative has been curated so perfectly that anyone who questions it is automatically dismissed as anti-woman. Ask yourself—who benefits from that taboo? Who profits from keeping the real story off-limits?

Then there's climate change. It has become a secular religion—complete with moral superiority, forbidden questions, and public shame rituals for anyone who doubts the orthodoxy. What if, under the guise of "saving the planet," entire populations are being nudged into deeper levels of surveillance, restricted movement, and loss of personal freedom? What if the real issue isn't about the Earth at all—but about using the Earth as leverage for total control?

These narratives are not black and white. They are layered, distorted, weaponized. The real war is not between red and blue, or pro and anti anything. The real war is between manipulation and discernment. Between programming and perception. Between fear and higher alignment.

Many so called liberal or progressive individuals sincerely believe they are working for humanity's good—and in many cases, their hearts are genuinely aligned with healing. The same can be said of many on the other "side." The real divide is not between people. It's between those who question and those who obey. Between those who seek real truth and those who recite assigned beliefs.

The systems we've been taught to trust—education, media, medicine, science, religion—have all been compromised in some form. That doesn't mean truth doesn't exist within them. It means we can no longer afford blind allegiance. Radical self-inquiry is the only compass we can trust now.

The radical truth, the thing that some forget when triggered by rhetoric, is that when it comes down to it people want the same thing: peace, to act in freedom, safety for children, financial freedom, and a healed planet. We've been manipulated into believing that our neighbor is the enemy. That someone who disagrees is dangerous. That those with opposing views are somehow less human.

As a result, we separate. We divide. We vilify. We believe we are more moral, more informed, more awakened—without ever pausing to ask why we believe what we believe.

That's the trap.

Separatism of any kind—whether it's spiritual, political, racial, gender-based, or ideological—keeps us locked in 3D. It feeds the ego. It binds us to density. The moment you feel the need to correct someone, to shame someone, to prove you're more evolved, more enlightened, more aware—that's the signal. That's your ego showing up in spiritual drag.

Because what gives anyone the right to control another?

The higher dimensions aren't about sameness. They're about harmony. Harmony doesn't require agreement. It requires presence. Respect. A fierce refusal to play into the divide-and-conquer scripts of the false matrix.

Ascension isn't about being right. It's about being real.

It's not about obedience. It's about awareness.

Unity consciousness isn't some ethereal ideal. It's a battlefield. Every time you choose not to fall for the trap of separation—every time you question instead of comply—you are rebelling against the oldest lie in history:

That we are meant to fight each other.

We are not. We are meant to rise—together.

We are not enemies. We are a species under siege by ideas that weren't ours to begin with.

We don't need to agree on every issue. We do need to reclaim our right to think critically, speak truthfully, and love without being told who to fear.

That's what 5D looks like. That's the frequency of liberation.

## Frequency Jump 7: Allow Free Will

Free will is not a courtesy. It's not a gift you extend to others because you're feeling generous or spiritually evolved. It is a universal law. It's a Source-endowed contract written into the very nature of this reality. Every one of us has free will—granted not by governments, not by religious systems, but by Creation itself. Violating someone else's free will is a surefire way to sabotage your own growth, no matter how noble or righteous your intentions seem.

The hard truth is: trying to control another person's choices is spiritual trespass.

You can speak your truth. You can offer insights, warnings, even compelling arguments. That's your right. That's your voice. Once your truth is shared, it is important to step back. Because if the person you're speaking with is an adult, they get to choose. Period. Whether it's aligned with your worldview or not. Whether it "makes sense" or not. Whether it infuriates you or not. Their path is theirs to walk. Their karma is theirs to carry.

If you force their hand—emotionally, spiritually, intellectually, or physically—you don't just interfere with their soul's evolution. You sign up to inherit the energetic consequences of that coercion. You want to take on someone else's karma? I don't think so.

That is the opposite of personal authority and sovereignty. That is spiritual codependence masquerading as conviction.

This is one of the greatest challenges of moving into 5D consciousness: letting go of the compulsive need to change, fix, or educate others. That drive often comes from a distorted place—fear, frustration, or unprocessed trauma dressed up as guidance. True elevation means detaching from that need and understanding that your job is to embody your truth, not to enforce it.

Because let's be real: when you're still trying to make people behave a certain way, you're operating from control, fear, or hierarchy. That's 3D territory—plain and simple.

In 5D, we leave behind not just the controlling people in our lives, but the controlling tendencies within ourselves. We stop playing God in other people's journeys. We stop inserting ourselves into timelines that aren't ours to edit. We learn to trust the architecture of divine timing—even when it's messy, even when it hurts, even when it looks like someone we love is making the "wrong" choice.

Because maybe it isn't the wrong choice. Maybe that's exactly the choice their soul needs to make in order to grow. Maybe they need the fire. Maybe they need the fallout. That's not up to you. That's between them and their higher self.

Now, here's the paradox: you must also protect your free will just as fiercely.

Freedom means you are in command of your own frequency, your own choices, your own narrative. That kind of freedom is magnetic—but it's also threatening to those still living in chains. People will try to steal your freedom, often without realizing it. They'll try to make you feel guilty, selfish, or "unloving" for not doing what they want you to do. They'll push emotional buttons. They'll accuse you of being too harsh or too detached.

Don't fall for it.

Don't let yourself be manipulated by the enslaved. Instead, model what liberation looks like.

Yes, there will always be things happening in the world designed to strip you of your choices—social systems, media narratives, medical mandates, institutional gaslighting. That's the test. Are you secure enough in your own authenticity to stand tall, even when the external world tries to shake you?

Because sovereignty is not just a word. It's a vibration. It's a lifestyle. It must be defended.

Guard your 5Dness with everything you've got. Because once you taste true freedom—mental, emotional, spiritual—you'll realize just how many people are still trapped in cages they've been taught to worship.

You'll see clearly: real freedom means honoring yours—and everyone else's. Even when it hurts. Even when it defies logic. Even when it breaks your heart.

You are not here to save the world by controlling it.

You are here to show what it looks like to be free within it.


## Frequency Jump 8: Avoid Energy Vampires

We all have these energetic drains in our lives. Some are obvious—others are masters of disguise. They don't always know they're doing it, but that doesn't make the effect any less real. They cling to you like static, always needing something, always seeking validation, always looking for a place to dump their negativity. These people leave you drained after every interaction, feeling like you've been emotionally mugged, sometimes not even realizing why you're so tired until much later.

This isn't about abandoning those who are genuinely in pain or need. This is about identifying those who perpetually siphon energy and refuse to evolve—who stay stuck in the same story, crisis, or loop, and want to keep you stuck with them. That's 3D consciousness in its purest form. Now for the twist: if you allow it, you become complicit in the dysfunction.

That's where the radical part comes in.

Part of jumping dimensions is learning to create an inviolable forcefield. That means setting boundaries like your life depends on it—because energetically, it does. Do not allow yourself to be anyone's dumping ground. Do not carry other people's emotional weight when they refuse to do their own inner work.

If someone consistently leaves you feeling heavy, hopeless, guilty, pessimistic—or like your joy just got hijacked—you need space. You need distance. You need spiritual discernment.

Can you be a friend from afar? Absolutely. Don't let guilt or false loyalty tether you to someone who is committed to draining you. Compassion does not mean codependence. Love does not mean proximity.

The rebellious act here is choosing your own frequency. Refusing to be pulled down by those who aren't willing to rise. Walking away without apology, because your clarity, peace, and purpose are too sacred to be squandered.

This doesn't make you cold. It makes you conscious.

Protect your field. Guard your joy. Remember: no one gets to ride shotgun in your energetic vehicle unless they're willing to help fuel the journey.

## Frequency Jump 9: Bye-Bye Addictions

Addictions are not just bad habits—they're spiritual anchors. They drag you down into the densest frequencies, disconnect you from Source, and keep you locked in a cycle of false satisfaction and subtle self-sabotage.

Let's name them plainly: alcohol, hard drugs, baseless sex, adoration, pharmaceuticals, sugar, processed food, social media, porn, plastic surgery, even an obsession with productivity. These aren't just vices—they are systems. Systems placed before us, often deliberately, to short-circuit our awareness and clog our spiritual pathways.

## UNLEASHING THE REBEL WITHIN

Addictions keep us in a state of perpetual yearning—never quite full, never quite clear, always reaching for the next fix. In that haze of craving, our authentic self gets muffled. Our Creator connection weakens. We drift further from our essence and closer to the constructs designed to enslave us.

Now, this isn't about perfectionism. I'm not saying you can't enjoy a glass of wine. I do. I'm often too much in my head, and I appreciate the gentle loosening that a little wine offers in a social setting. The test is: Can you stop? Can you go without it? Can you sit in stillness with no props, no numbing, no noise?

If the answer is no—if the absence of your chosen substance brings panic, anger, or emptiness—it's not helping you rise. It's holding you hostage.

Originally, plant medicines were sacred tools. They were used to bridge worlds, to travel across dimensions, to open the third eye in reverence and ritual. The Vedic sages of India wrote the Rig Veda under the influence of soma—an entheogenic compound derived from plants like cannabis and ayahuasca. These were not party drugs. These were portals.

Let's be real, however: the drugs of today are not the sacred sacraments of old. Most of them are chemical perversions, stripped of spirit and pulsing with distortion. Even "natural" substances like ayahuasca or psilocybin come with risks—especially when used carelessly or without proper spiritual hygiene.

Opening dimensional doors without discernment is no small thing. I've seen people unravel. I've seen them fracture. Yes, some return wiser. Others don't return at all, or worse, they return altered, with fractures in their field that invite parasitic energies. What starts as exploration can end in possession.

It's the same with Ouija boards, séance games, witchcraft, and the trend of demon courting disguised as shadow work. If you're inviting in entities or using substances to bypass your inner process, you're not ascending—you're outsourcing your power.

The darkest trap of all? The seductive rebranding of Satanism and occultism as "empowerment." This is exploding among younger generations—often disguised as "sex magick," "left-hand path," liberation, or cool, aesthetic rebellion. Let's not mince words. Anything that overrides another's free will, invokes entities, or feeds on manipulation is not freedom. It's enslavement. It's inversion. It doesn't end well.

Witchcraft may claim to be white or benevolent, but the line is razor-thin. Once you're meddling with energy that wasn't born of Divine Source—or using force rather than frequency—you're in dangerous territory. People who cast spells or call in demons because it seems edgy or powerful don't always know they're gambling with their soul. Too many never come back. Their essence leaves, and what remains is a vessel controlled by something else.

Bypassing addiction is not just about quitting negative habits. It's about reclaiming your intrinsic self from the parasitic systems that feed on your disempowerment.

Real spiritual rebellion means choosing presence over numbing, clarity over fog, and Source over shortcut. You don't need substances or false light to experience other dimensions. You are the portal. You were built for this. You just forgot.

No drug, no demon, no dopamine hit is worth sacrificing your alignment with divine Source.

If you truly want to rise, start here: Let go of anything that clouds your field or weakens your will. Don't just detox your body. Detox your choices and your cravings. Detox your soul.

This is what it means to jump dimensions.


## Frequency Jump 10: Rebel into the Real You

I'll share a final tool. It's fire.

Choosing 5D is an act of rebellion. Not a casual shift. Not an ethereal wish. It is a conscious, relentless refusal to be enslaved by the systems that have governed this Earth for millennia.

To rise into 5D is to burn the mask of compliance.

## UNLEASHING THE REBEL WITHIN

It is to say, with every breath:
- I will not be ruled by fear.
- I will not fight battles designed to keep me distracted.
- I will not conform to narratives that pit me against others.
- I will not perform obedience and call it goodness.
- I will not let my mind be colonized by fake morality.

This is about clarity with teeth. Presence with purpose. Personal authority with spine.

5D is not about floating away. It is about seeing clearly and acting accordingly.

You are here to rebel—against shame, against programming, against the sedated half-life of 3D density. You are here to become fully, ferociously, undeniably you.

This is not rebellion for rebellion's sake, but the sacred uprising that cracks illusion, frees perception, and makes space for your soul to lead.

Your true self is not tame. It is revolutionary.

The next phase of this journey will demand that you stand in that truth.

Because we're about to walk into deeper territory. We're going to talk about cognitive dissonance. The lies you've been told—and the ones you've told yourself. The distortions you've accepted as reality. The systems you've fed with your energy without realizing it.

We're going to dissolve illusion and meet truth face-to-face.

You will need your clearest sight, your strongest heart, and your most rebellious spirit.

The jump is over. You've crossed the dimensional threshold.

Now it's time to tear down the veil.

# Phase II: Cracks in the Illusion

"We are supposed to become a race of leaders—not a race of sheep. We are supposed to be chiefs. That is what they teach their people, nobody falls behind. We all evolve together."
—Alex Collier, Andromedan Contactee

# A Note Before You Begin

This next phase may feel different. Heavier. Sharper. Confronting.
That's because it is.
Phase II dives into the core distortions of our modern world—media manipulation, manufactured fear, medical coercion, engineered conflict, and the systematic suppression of human sovereignty. While the section contains solutions, the tone here shifts for a reason: the illusions must break before clarity can rise.
You may feel resistance, grief, anger, or disbelief.
That's natural. You are not alone.
You are always in charge of your pace.
If the material feels off-putting, or too intense at this time, skip ahead to Phase III, where the focus turns toward healing, rebuilding, and grounded empowerment. These later phases are filled with explanations, resonance, and hope. You can return to this phase when —and if—you feel ready.
There is no wrong way to walk this path.
Only your way, in your time.

## Chapter 9
# Awakening in the Physical World

We've explored how to transform your internal landscape—how to change your thinking, raise your frequency, and become the most aligned, authentic version of yourself. That work is sacred. Inner transformation is not only the seed of all outward change—it's the fuel of personal sovereignty.

The rebel's truth? Inner healing alone is not enough.

If you perfect your inner world but close your eyes to the world around you—especially the harm being done to others—you are spiritually bypassing. This is the opposite of ascension. Spiritual bypassing may be the final frontier of sabotage. It wears a peaceful mask but hides consequences. It masquerades as awakening while secretly reinforcing denial. Because ignoring the physical world we inhabit—its structures, its suffering, its active manipulation—and pretending everything is fine in the name of "love and light" is not spiritual. It's avoidance.

The physical world you inhabit is not a neutral place. It is not as it appears. Beneath the gloss of progress and comfort lies a veil thick with illusion, distraction, and calculated deception. Behind that veil operates a multi-layered, coordinated cabal of entities, institutions, and ideologies that do not honor love or cherish creativity. They do not care about truth, children, innocence, or your right to evolve.

This hidden force does not value your essence. It fears it. Because when humans awaken to who they truly are, the entire false matrix collapses. That awakening doesn't happen in isolation. It doesn't happen in mountaintop monasteries detached from the world's pain. It happens here on Earth when we dare to bring consciousness into the chaos.

You cannot rise while choosing to remain in darkness. Real ascension is not separate from awareness—it requires it. If you want to help birth a higher world, you must be willing to see the one we're in with clear eyes.

That means pulling back the curtain. It means allowing the veil to drop, even if what you see shakes you. It means recognizing that silence in the face of evil is a form of complicity. Inaction isn't only "doing nothing," it is also refusing to look. It's choosing the comfort of ignorance over the discomfort of truth. That is a decision with energetic consequences.

As you begin to taste Oneness, you'll feel the weight of injustice. Not just out there—but in you. Because as consciousness expands, the illusion of separation collapses. You begin to realize that every act of harm against another is an act against yourself. Every child trafficked, every truth suppressed, every soul silenced reverberates in the collective field that includes you and those close to you.

Ascension isn't about escaping the world. It's about embodying truth within it. It's about having the courage to look at what's been hidden. To pull back the veil and speak what others are afraid to say.

We are in a full-blown spiritual war. It is playing out in schools, in hospitals, in trafficking rings, in media pipelines, in policy decisions, and in your child's classroom.

Let's be blunt: there's no more mountaintop sitting allowed. The fate of humanity is what's at stake.

You don't get to meditate your way out of this. You don't get to chant peace while others are being systematically destroyed. That's sedation, not ascension. It's exactly what they want.

Does this mean you have to become a full-time activist? Not at all. It does mean you must become aware. You must become vocal. You must be willing to disturb the peace if the peace is built on lies. Sometimes that means challenging school boards. Sometimes that means exposing child trafficking. Sometimes that means having one courageous conversation that shakes someone awake.

How is it possible to transcend the world while others suffer? The wounded are not "others." They are fragments of the collective Self. As long as they are trapped in cages—literal or spiritual—you are not truly free.

Unity consciousness doesn't mean retreat. It means responsibility. It means understanding, in your bones, that what happens to another is happening to you. Ascension is radical presence. It is rebellion, rooted in love.

Your personal evolution and the planet's evolution are not separate. They are mirrors. Until we stop pretending that one can flourish while the other is poisoned, true healing will elude us. Truth cannot thrive in a consciousness riddled with denial.

This next phase requires vision. Vision requires courage.

Are you ready to see what's there?

## The Unfortunate Truth

There is a dark intelligence that has worked quietly, and sometimes loudly, against humanity for millennia. This force has infected nearly every institution we once believed sacred—governments, healthcare, education, religion, banking, food systems. Its power is not in bombs. Its power is in programming.

Under its grip, we've become numb. Docile. Confused. Distracted. Disconnected from our bodies, our birthrights, and our brilliance.

Left alone, without interference, humans are capable of

extraordinary genius and Source-connection. Instead, under the weight of this shadow force, we've become spiritual orphans inside a system that feeds off our disconnection.

To name every player and tactic would require volumes. All the same, you should know this much: disclosure is here. It has begun by the time these words reach your eyes. Watch closely. Because as the curtain is pulled back, you'll need discernment and not fear.

Let the truths empower you. Let them remind you of what you already know. Because you do know. You always have. Ignoring things never made them go away.

## A Word of Warning

Some of what you're about to hear may sound like conspiracy theory—a term that was invented to discredit truth-seekers. I am not asking you to believe blindly. I am asking you to research, investigate, and discern.

This information comes not from fantasy, but from decades of intense, verifiable inquiry. The truth is not fragile. Still, your programming might be. That's okay. Let it crack.

## Shadow World Players

Let's start with this: The Khazarian Mafia. It is the world's oldest, most organized occult crime syndicate. It has cloaked itself in false identities, infiltrated systems at the highest levels, and weaponized ancient tools of control—including Babylonian money magick—to enslave humanity through debt and dependency.

The Vatican is also not what it seems. I understand this will trigger devout Catholics. Still, truth is not about comfort. Look closely at the Jesuit Oath. The corruption reaches far beyond what most can fathom and is Luciferian in nature.

You won't find names of the players in your history books. You won't hear about their deeds on the nightly news. These factions rely on secrecy. Their greatest trick has been convincing you they don't exist.

They hide behind identities. The Khazarian Mafia, for instance, is not Jewish—though it cloaks itself in that identity. Like others in this dark alliance, it practices Ba'al worship, Luciferian magic, and sacrificial inversion. These are not metaphors. These are rituals, and they are very real.

## Multiple Rings, One Agenda

The web of control stretches globally. It has been coordinated through puppets like George Soros, Henry Kissinger, Bill Gates, Klaus Schwab—figures who appear humanitarian on the surface while orchestrating devastation beneath. Now a new generation has risen to carry the torch.

Their faces may be younger, but their allegiance is the same. Olivier Schwab, son of Klaus Schwab, quietly helps steer the World Economic Forum's technocratic future. Yuval Noah Harari, a WEF darling, openly questions free will and champions a post-human world. Larry Page and Sergey Brin, the architects behind Google, now preside over the largest surveillance empire in human history, cloaked in algorithmic benevolence. Their AI protégé, Demis Hassabis of DeepMind, builds machines that learn faster than children, with little oversight and limitless funding.

This next wave doesn't need guns or gulags. They wield data, biotech, narrative, and predictive code. They don't shout. They whisper in boardrooms, program in basements, and smile from TED stages—convincing you it's all for your benefit.

No, it's not. It's for control. If you're not awake to that, you're not truly free.

The rings of influence spread through every major corridor of global control: the WEF, WHO, UN, FDA, CDC, CPS, IRS, NSA, TSA, and beyond. Nearly every three-letter agency is compromised —acting not as protectors of the people, but as enforcers of a hidden agenda. The Federal Reserve isn't federal. Homeland Security, FEMA, and the CIA have staged countless false flags and psychological operations, all designed to destabilize, distract, and divide.

These aren't random incidents, but coordinated chess moves.

The endgame is to dismantle free will and fracture the human spirit. To make obedience feel virtuous and rebellion feel dangerous.

However, they can't do this in the light. Their power depends on shadows, on deception, on your complicity.

They only win if you stay quiet.

## Eyes Open, Gloves Off

Whether these truths are new to you or already burned into your bones, this is your reminder: your clarity is essential.

The fog is lifting. The matrix is glitching. The gloves are off.

If you've made it this far, you're no stranger to the undercurrents. You may have already questioned the media, the money, the medicine, the so-called experts, the endless wars, the poisoned skies, the scripted narratives, and the digital leash tightening around your neck.

You may have sensed that something was off. That things don't add up. That there's more to this life, and to this world, than what we've been spoon-fed.

Good. That knowing is your edge.

In the chapters ahead, we'll strip away the false storylines, confront cognitive dissonance, and bring to light what has been hidden in plain sight. You'll need your discernment and your inner rebel, wide awake.

These chapters reveal what you weren't supposed to see.

## Chapter 10
# Unmasking the Machine

Let's not mince words. Behind the global structures we've been taught to trust—governments, health authorities, banks, schools, organized religion—lurks a shadow force. A parasitic presence that has burrowed into every layer of our world, sowing disconnection, control, and spiritual paralysis. I call them the Dark—not the elite, not the globalists, not the shadow government. Parasites. That's what they are.

This force is not a recent invention. It has been operating for a millennia, camouflaged behind the machinery of civilization. Their goal? To keep humanity disempowered, disconnected, distracted, and dependent. They mean for us to be the perpetual work horse and financial battery.

They've corrupted our food supply with toxins and GMOs. They've turned medicine into a profit-driven weapon while burying the truth about indigenous cures and our natural healing abilities. They've taught our children lies through education systems designed to break spirit, not build it. They've created false religions to shame the body and distort the Divine. They've built a financial system designed to trap you in eternal debt servitude.

Once you see it, you can't unsee it. The world you've been taught to love is not the world that exists. Pretending otherwise empowers your captors.

Truth doesn't require permission. If you're going to ascend in any real way—if you're going to be part of the healing of this planet—you're going to need to stop running from the uncomfortable and face what's been hiding in plain sight.

The truth may not always be pretty. Yet it is always freeing.

## Bloodlines & Bankrolls

The Khazarian Mafia, the Vatican Jesuit Order, and the old-world bloodline families are not relics of a conspiratorial past—they are active architects of the world we inhabit. Their fingerprints are on everything from interest rates to international treaties, biotech rollouts to billion-dollar bailouts. These aren't disconnected power players. They are factions of an ancient, interwoven machine—ritualistic, hierarchical, and obsessive in their quest to dominate through deception.

The Khazarian lineage itself didn't vanish. It evolved, cloaking itself behind rebranded surnames, front organizations, and philanthropic façades. They masquerade as political leaders, religious authorities, or global innovators, but their allegiance is not to the people. It is to a shadow priesthood of control—an esoteric network that thrives on hierarchy, secrecy, and the extraction of power through spiritual inversion.

They are masters of inversion. The Vatican shields its true influence behind stained glass and sacred texts—but beneath the robes lies a dark marriage of empire and sorcery. The Jesuit Order, far from being a neutral religious society, functions as the intellectual and geopolitical espionage arm of this spiritual cartel. Their role? To infiltrate, indoctrinate, and manipulate—shaping educational systems, seeding ideological wars, and obscuring metaphysical truths.

Meanwhile, the so-called "noble" bloodlines—Rothschilds, Rockefellers, Windsors, Orsinis, Payseurs, and their generations of intermarried kin—continue to hoard planetary wealth and steer geopolitical outcomes. Their DNA is not just a matter of genetics, but a matter of preservation. Through selective breeding and ancestral ritual, they maintain a multi-generational spiritual hierarchy designed to keep themselves in alignment with what they perceive as divine rule backed not by Source, but by a corrupt inversion of what is moral, loving and just.

The global chessboard is their theater. Wars are their currency. Epidemics, their leverage. Disasters—both natural and engineered—are not "unfortunate events," but large-scale energy-harvesting mechanisms. Behind the scenes of every humanitarian response or economic summit is a contract. A spell. A trade in human autonomy for subjugation.

Understand that this is about seeing the machine so that you can avoid it. The moment you stop following systems designed to dominate, you reclaim the authority to dismantle them. These systems were built to harm you with intention.

The deeper truth—the one they've tried for centuries to bury—is that they are few. You are many. Their survival depends on illusion. Your awakening ends it.

### **Dark Fuel: Trauma as Currency**

Let's talk about the engine that fuels their entire control matrix: trauma. Not just any trauma—but engineered, ritualized, weaponized trauma. The kind that fractures the psyche, splinters the soul, and severs the human connection to Source. The kind that is programmed, triggered, and replicated across generations.

Satanic Ritual Abuse (SRA) is not fringe theory. It's the hidden scaffolding beneath global institutions. Its methods have been systematized and widely dispensed through government programs like MK-Ultra and Project Monarch, black-budget operations seeded by bloodline elites and institutionalized under the guise of national security and psychiatric experimentation.

Through repeated trauma—rape, electroshock, isolation, deprivation, forced drugging, and ritualized torture— subjects, very often children, are broken open. Dissociation becomes survival. In those cracks, the programmers go to work: creating alters, installing scripts, embedding handlers, layering trauma loops into the subconscious. The subjects aren't just victims. They are assets. Built to obey, perform, seduce, spy, kill, or self-destruct on command.

Every scream, every tear, every betrayal is harvested as loosh—this is life force energy for nonphysical entities who feed on pain. This is the metaphysical component most people miss: it's not only about domination. It's about sustenance. The rituals open portals. The blood seals contracts. The terror fuels the dark grid.

Mind control programming doesn't stop at underground chambers or elite estates like seen in the film, *Eyes Wide Shut*. The very culture we consume—music videos, awards shows, fashion runways, magazine covers—is coded with symbols and triggers. Public trauma rituals are cloaked as entertainment. Mass shootings, school tragedies, and high-profile deaths often follow uncanny patterns, with dates, numerology, and media scripting echoing with dark ceremonial rites.

The same families show up again and again. The same motifs. The same foundations. Royals and billionaires acquire children by the thousands, yet we never see them again. Hollywood and music stars emerge overnight with handlers, eventual breakdowns, and "reinvention" after rehab.

Ask yourself why trauma survivors with no connection to one other describe the same symbols, same language, same rituals.

This isn't random. It's a system.

The elites who run it were often victims themselves—broken, programmed, and spiritually inverted from birth. That doesn't excuse them. It does explain the loyalty and the silence, as well as the generational lockstep.

You want to dismantle the cabal? Start with its power source.

Until we stop feeding the global trauma engine, we'll be rearranging shadows. Real freedom means exposing the root system: the occult rituals, the stolen children, the dark contracts. Only then can we collapse the grid they feed from.

## Brotherhood or Blood Oath

Freemasonry is a name you've likely heard—often mentioned in the same breath as fraternity, charity, or tradition. At the lower levels, that's not entirely wrong. Many Masons are good men. Their lodges raise funds for local causes, sponsor scholarships, and support widows and orphans. The tenets of moral development, personal integrity, and fraternal support are genuine—at the base.

That's not where the story ends.

What most members don't realize is that Freemasonry is a compartmentalized system. Like an iceberg, the public-facing structure is only the tip. As one rises through the degrees—particularly beyond the publicly acknowledged 33rd—everything changes. The teachings become more esoteric, the oaths more binding, and the symbols more charged. The Light they speak of is not metaphorical—it's Luciferian.

By the time initiates reach the highest degrees, they are no longer part of a fraternity. They are part of a priesthood—sworn to secrecy above all else. These oaths supersede family, conscience, and law. Secrecy becomes sacrament. Violation of that sacrament comes with consequences: ritual expulsion, spiritual targeting, and in some cases —literal death or character assassination.

At the hidden levels—sometimes referred to as "The Inner Order"—members are hand-selected, not promoted. These levels are not visible on charts. They are not found in handbooks. They exist in a closed circuit of bloodline ties, hidden rites, and occult allegiances. Here, Lucifer is not denied—he is revered as the bearer of illumination, the liberator of man from the 'tyranny' of God. Rituals become darker. The manipulation of energy, intent, and sacrifice becomes explicit. The line between brotherhood and blackmail blurs.

Freemasonry, like many ancient institutions, was infiltrated, not invented for evil. Its roots trace back to stone guilds, sacred geometry, and the architecture of holy creation. Over time, it was hijacked—first by opportunists, then by occultists, then by those who sought to weaponize its structure for global influence. The Masonic system became a perfect vessel for covert power: hierarchical, self-policing, oath-bound, and masked by benevolence.

The infiltration didn't stop at lodges. Masonic influence can be traced through the founding of the United States, the Vatican's inner chambers, intelligence agencies, the music industry, and Hollywood. Look closely at national monuments, corporate logos, and world capitals—you'll find the same symbols echoed again and again. The square and compass. The all-seeing eye. The capstone of the pyramid. These are not coincidences. They are signatures.

To those reading this who are part of Masonic lodges—and who joined in good faith to better themselves or serve their community—this is a call to discernment. You may be walking a noble path. Still, I urge you: Do not ascend further. Do not chase the hidden knowledge they dangle as a prize. What lies beyond the veil is not enlightenment. It is ensnarement.

The true light does not require blood oaths or secrecy to shine.

## The Machine Has a Name

You've heard the term. Maybe you dismissed it. However, the Deep State is no myth. It is the operational arm of the parasite class—the shadow mechanism behind the veil of democracy and diplomacy.

It goes by many names: the Cabal. The Elite. The Shadow Government. Illuminati. Jesuit Order. Council of 300. CFR and Trilateral Commission members. SES. Bilderbergs. Khazarian Mafia. The Rothschild Central Bank Network. Globalists. The UN-WEF

Consortium. Call it what you like. The label is distraction. The function is what matters.

This machine isn't a theory. It's an interlocking web of financial dynasties, intelligence networks, and spiritual perversion—embedded in every institution you were raised to trust. Government. Healthcare. Media. Tech. Education. Defense. Religion. It operates like a parasite inside a host, manipulating from within.

The structure is hierarchical and cellular. Most people inside it have no idea of what they're truly serving. Compartmentalization keeps the foot soldiers blind. Orders come from above, cloaked in layers of bureaucracy, humanitarian language, or with labels like, "science."

There are two kinds of players: puppets and puppet masters.

The puppets are carefully selected, groomed, and elevated—entertainers, politicians, CEOs, doctors, influencers. If they don't comply, they're blackmailed or removed. If they do, they're rewarded with power, prestige, and protection. Nonetheless, they are not in charge. They're the face of the machine, not its brain.

The puppet masters operate decades in advance. They write the scripts for your crises, your revolutions, your "breakthroughs." They manufacture chaos then offer their prepackaged solutions. Every crisis becomes a conduit for control. Every event serves a ritual purpose.

They tell you the science is settled—when science is never settled. They tell you that silencing dissent is necessary for public safety. They tell you that masks save lives, that lockdowns are compassion, that untested injections are "safe and effective." They tell you men can be women and children can consent. They tell you that objecting to these things is dangerous.

The more absurd the narrative they put forth, the more obedient the populace must become. Once truth and fiction are blurred, once logic is replaced by fear, the machine wins.

These are not separate movements. They are coordinated psychological operations designed to fracture reason, disrupt family structure, and erode personal freedom. The battlefield is your mind. The goal is your submission.

Once you see it, the sleight of hand becomes obvious. The buzzwords lose their power. The actors lose their masks. The machine becomes visible—not just as a theory, but as an enemy.

When that happens, the spell breaks.

## You Are the Disruption

As the old structures fall, they will not go quietly. They will not admit defeat. They will not hand over the reins and say "you win." Instead, they will double down on fear. They will do their utmost to manufacture more division, distraction and dread.

They'll stir up race wars, gender wars, class wars, religious wars—anything to keep you from noticing that they are the ones behind the curtain. They will deploy "new crises" to distract from the truth. Expect it. Recognize it. Refuse to be baited.

You are not here to be a passive observer. You are not here to wait for a savior, a politician, or a disclosure date.

You are the disclosure.

Your frequency, your clarity, your voice, your integrity—these are the weapons that dissolve the dark. Every time you choose coherence over chaos, you fracture their control. Every time you choose truth over comfort, you collapse another program. Every time you refuse to play their game, you rewrite the rules.

## No More Bypass

This next phase of growth—this unmasking of the physical world—demands something deeper than spiritual platitudes. It demands the rebellious clarity of a warrior-seer. It demands the heart of a mystic and the spine of a soldier.

Because what you're about to face is not just global in scale. It is personal. You will see how you, too, were programmed. How you participated in your own hypnosis. How you defended illusions that felt safe. How parts of you may be clinging to the very system that harms you.

That's okay. There is no shame in it. We've all been duped by mass hypnosis. The danger is in not awakening at all.

The physical world must be looked at head-on. Not in avoidance. Not in blind rage. But faced in lucid defiance.

## Chapter 11
# Puncturing the Cabal Veil

When you begin to truly pierce the veil of illusion cast by the parasite class, you'll start noticing that their strongest weapons aren't always bullets, mandates, or weapons of mass destruction. Often, it's rhetoric. Language. Subtle manipulations of logic and perception designed to keep you confused, ashamed, and divided. The mind, after all, is the first battleground.

Some of the topics in the following list were identified on the now lost boards of 8chan—one of the gathering places of digital dissent, where whistleblowers and researchers dropped breadcrumbs too dangerous to be seen by the masses. These boards, like the similarly dismantled VOAT—demonized in the mainstream—were where truths were decoded. On those boards, no one used their real names. Not because of cowardice, but because telling the truth in a world ruled by deception is a dangerous act.

Here are some the most common manipulation tactics used by the parasite class and their media foot soldiers.

. . .

## Generalizations

This is one of the laziest yet corrosive tactics—blanket statements that require no thought, nuance, or critical evaluation. It's how division is sewn into the fabric of everyday conversation.

"All democrats are pedophiles."

"All Trump supporters are racist."

"All men are toxic."

"All women are crazy."

"All conspiracy theorists are mentally ill."

It's stupid. More dangerously, it's effective. Because generalizations tap into fear, tribalism, and identity—fostering hostility where dialogue should live. They divide by race, gender, belief system, and background. They are used to fracture the human collective into small, angry groups. This is 3D consciousness tethered to illusion, and it's intentional.


## Gaslighting

Borrowed from the Hitchcock film *Gaslight*, this tactic has become a signature move of both narcissists and governments alike. The essence of gaslighting is this: make the other person question their reality.

"You're overreacting."

"You're being dramatic."

"You're not well."

"Why are you always so negative?"

"You really believe that stuff?"

Or, better:

"That's anti-Semitic."

"You're a homophobe."

"You're transphobic."

"You're an Islamophobe."

Accusations have become the new silencers. Using labels that carry emotional and social taboo, cause targets to retreat or suffer the backlash. That's the point.

Gaslighting works by creating a double bind: you are forced to defend yourself against a fabricated accusation—one designed to entrap. The suggestion of the alleged offense lingers regardless of evidence. It shifts the burden of proof and puts the accused on trial for daring to state things too clearly.

It's what your emotionally manipulative ex said before turning your friends against you. What the media says when you question their narrative.

The parasite class uses this technique consistently: accuse a political opponent of the crimes he cannot defend. Imply mental instability in the truth-teller. Call the whistleblower unhinged. Call the mom speaking out at a school board meeting a terrorist. Call the citizen asking questions a conspiracy theorist.

Once the public hears the claim, the stain sticks.

Gaslighting is not just personal abuse—it is a state-sponsored strategy. The only antidote is clarity and the courage to trust what you know, even when no one else does.

## Projection

This is one of the oldest tricks in the psychological warfare playbook: accuse others of what you, yourself are doing. It's another way of disarming opposition and deflecting scrutiny. On the personal level, it can be subconscious—a knee-jerk defense. In politics, it's a deliberate decoy.

If I accuse you of lying first, I redirect attention from my own deception. If I call you a threat to democracy, I don't have to explain the surveillance I authorized or the censorship I helped enforce. If I label you dangerous or unhinged, I protect myself from accountability.

In current times, projection is everywhere.

The same agencies that call for the blacklisting of independent journalists for spreading "misinformation" coordinate narrative control behind the scenes. The media voices demanding transparency are the same ones laundering state-approved talking points. The political figures calling for "unity" are simultaneously fueling division through race, identity, and fear.

Look at the recent disclosures: leaked internal memos reveal how health officials, big tech, and intelligence bodies worked together to suppress dissent while accusing critics of being anti-science. Education boards decry "disinformation" while quietly approving curriculums that rewrite history. Banks and financial platforms deplatform users in the name of safety, while laundering billions for criminal networks.

Projection is a weaponized inversion of truth. Say it first, say it loud, and brand the opposition before they have a chance to speak.

The smear is the strategy. Once the label sticks—"denier," "phobe," "conspiracy theorist"—the real conversation dies.

When you see a sudden media blitz, a viral accusation, or a chorus of outrage on repeat, ask: what truth is this trying to bury? What crime is being hidden in plain sight by pointing the finger elsewhere?

Because in today's upside-down world, the louder the accusation, the deeper the confession.

**Misdirection**

This is the magician's classic sleight of hand. While you're focused on one hand waving in the air, the other is planting the trick. Politicians and media use it constantly to deceive.

Case in point: the evidence that the Russia collusion hoax—used to justify surveillance, censorship, and years of political sabotage—was orchestrated not just by intelligence insiders, but knowingly greenlit by a former president. The goal? Undermine the increasingly popular upstart before he took office. Rig the perception. Control the narrative. Ensure the "outsider" doesn't disrupt the system.

Meanwhile, the unsecured server and tens of thousands of deleted emails—many pointing to deeply troubling connections—are once again buried and met with the same strategy: deny, distract, and deflect.

Ask a real question, and watch what happens. Instead of answers, you get accusations.

When questioned about election interference or intelligence corruption, you're called an extremist. When footage emerges of child trafficking or war crimes, you're told it's Russian disinformation. When the truth gets too close, they pivot—not to logic, but to emotion.

Misdirection isn't just about changing the subject. It's about hijacking the listener's attention, replacing investigation with indignation, and diverting truth with trauma. A dead son is invoked to shield a live scandal. A buzzword is deployed to shut down dissent. A war is started in time to bury a leak.

This isn't governance. It's theater. You are the intended audience—kept in the dark by the blinding flash of stagecraft.

Once you stop watching the hand in the air, you'll start seeing the one behind the curtain. You'll realize the real magic trick is how long they've kept us hypnotized.

**False Equivalence**

This tactic thrives on lazy logic. It draws a false parallel between two unrelated events or actions, flattening the moral terrain so that atrocities and offenses blur into one gray, forgettable smear. It's how war crimes become footnotes, and how whistleblowers get treated like felons.

"You're upset that intelligence agencies violated constitutional rights? Well, every government makes mistakes."

"Sure, they authorized gain-of-function research, but that's no worse than any other global health misstep."

"Okay, so the surveillance state expanded again—but didn't your side want better security too?"

False equivalence dilutes outrage. It numbs discernment. It treats systemic abuse and casual rudeness as moral equals, so that neither can be held accountable. When nothing is uniquely evil, nothing requires urgent change.

This tactic is everywhere, from televised debates to social media pile-ons. It's used to dismiss the release of damning documents by saying, "That's just politics." It's how the exposure of child exploitation rings gets buried beneath scandals about misgendering. It's how calls for transparency are compared to "witch hunts," while actual cover-ups are shrugged off as routine.

It is hypocrisy weaponized to look like balance. It is spiritual poison.

Because when the mind is trained to see all things as equal, it becomes blind to both beauty and evil. That's the aim: to strip you of discernment. To make you question your gut. To make you stop noticing what matters.

This is a favorite move in the parasite playbook: reduce everything to noise, and you'll never hear the signal.

Once you recognize it—once you stop arguing in their sandbox of illusions—the spell begins to break. Clarity returns. With clarity comes sovereignty.

That's how the magician loses their grip. Not when you play their game better, but when the rebel in you refuses to play at all.

**False Flags**

If you've heard the term false flag before and assumed it was some wild theory, it's time to erase that conditioning. False flags are not speculative. They are a well-documented tool of control used throughout history—particularly by regimes that want to consolidate power without resistance. They are staged or manipulated events designed to provoke a specific public response. They work almost every time.

Take 9/11, one of the most impactful false flag operations in modern history. On that day, fear became a weapon. The narrative was pre-crafted—foreign terrorists, religious extremism, collapsing towers. What followed was an instant surrender of our freedoms: the Patriot Act, the rise of the surveillance state, biometric tracking, warrantless wiretaps, airport strip searches. All in the name of "safety." Most Americans, in their trauma, nodded along. The bogeyman was terrifying, so we handed over our rights in exchange for feeling protected. That was no accident. That was programming.

Fear is the most potent tool of the parasite class. It's the master key that unlocks obedience. This is why I repeatedly emphasize eradicating fear from your system—not just as an emotion, but as a frequency. Because fear will be used against you, again and again, to make you submit.

False flags are almost always followed by the "solution" the architects planned in advance. School shootings are designed to eliminate the Second Amendment—one of the final blocks against total tyranny. The right to bear arms is not just about self-defense. It's about defense against corrupt government. That's why, to them, it must be destroyed.

Ex-CIA agent Milton William "Bill" Cooper saw it coming. He predicted school shooting false flags before they began, warning that they would be rolled out across the country in a coordinated effort to soften public resistance to gun control. Then—Columbine. Sandy Hook. Parkland. Uvalde. Each time, one or two unstable shooters. Each time, a wave of grief and terror. Each time, a renewed call to disarm the public. Cooper was duly murdered on his own front lawn after blowing the whistle. They don't forgive truth-tellers.

Let me be clear: this does not mean innocent people weren't harmed or killed. Real lives were lost. Children died. However, context matters. The suffering was engineered. There were signs and clues: the shooter had been hearing voices, was on psychotropic meds, had a mysteriously absent family. Details are scrubbed from the internet before the story breaks. Social media warriors now spot these patterns within hours of the events. Still, the mainstream narrative rolls forward.

The Boston Marathon bombing was a clear false flag. Ads were posted beforehand calling for "crisis actors." Eyewitnesses saw drill operations in progress the day before. The footage, the inconsistencies, the scripted elements—all point to orchestration. Again, people were hurt. Nonetheless, the event served a greater purpose: trauma, surveillance justification, the tightening of federal control.

More recently, mass shooter events at high-profile shopping centers and LGBTQ+ gatherings have been suspiciously timed to distract from politically damaging revelations—like classified document leaks, high-level corruption trials, or the resurfacing of intelligence reports exposing long-buried criminal activity among global elites. When something damning is about to surface, a bloody headline appears to hijack the public's attention. It's not a fluke. It's the formula.

This is how it works. A high-profile, emotionally charged event occurs. Innocents die. The public is shocked, grieving, afraid. In that emotional vacuum, the parasite class introduces "solutions"—usually in the form of increased control, surveillance, censorship, or disarmament. The problem was engineered to justify the solution.

Understanding this doesn't make you heartless. It makes you clear-eyed. Waking up doesn't mean to deny suffering. It means recognizing who is profiting from it—and refusing to give them your permission.

Once you see through the mechanics of the false flag, you become immune to its power. You no longer react in fear. You stop handing over your personal freedom for a false sense of safety. That, above all, is what they fear most: a populace that sees the game and walks away from the table.

. . .

# UNLEASHING THE REBEL WITHIN

## Virtue Signaling

Virtue signaling remains one of the sneakiest tools of moral manipulation in modern society. On the surface, it appears as public goodness—people declaring their righteous values or virtuous choices. Yet scratch the surface, and it's a hollow performance—designed not to help others, but to elevate the self.

At its core, virtue signaling says: Look at me. I am good. Not because of what I do, but because of what I say. That's where the deception begins. It's usually divorced from real-world action and deeply rooted in ego. It demands applause while offering little substance.

You see this in celebrities parroting scripted causes while vacationing on private jets. In influencers posting waving flags without understanding the geopolitical mechanics. In CEOs parroting DEI mantras to appease institutional overlords like BlackRock and Vanguard—who use your retirement funds to force ideological compliance in alignment with a one world government.

Hollywood has perfected the game. Award shows are stages for moral theater—actors draped in designer gowns and hundred-thousand-dollar jewels using their three-minute speeches to echo whatever cause is trending. From "Time's Up" pins to "#StandWith" movements to climate guilt admonishments, these declarations are rarely matched by meaningful effort. Behind closed doors, these same individuals remain blindly complicit in the very systems they claim to oppose—child exploitation rings, corporate profiteering, and globalist power structures.

Brands and institutions are no strangers to the charade. Pharma giants preach compassion while lobbying for lack of controls that harm millions. Technology gurus champion free speech in public, while deplatforming dissenting voices. Governments slap rainbow flags on their social feeds while selling weapons to regimes that criminalize the identities they claim to protect.

Let's be honest: the true heroes of the world aren't broadcasting their goodness. They don't need applause or hashtags. They're quietly rebuilding communities, holding trauma for others, planting food, protecting children, exposing corruption—often at great personal risk. You rarely hear them speak about it, because they're too busy doing.

The paradox of virtue signaling is that it becomes a mask for moral emptiness. The louder someone screams about their righteousness, the more you should wonder what they're trying to hide, or compensate for.

This performative morality is now embedded in school curriculums, healthcare policies, ESG investment schemes, and corporate HR trainings. It's a smokescreen. A tool for controlling the narrative while distracting from the decay beneath.

When you stop falling for it—when you demand authentic integrity instead of posturing—you pierce the veil of one of the parasite class's favorite manipulations. Because it's never been about goodness. It's about control cloaked in moral camouflage.

## The Tyranny of the Label

Closely related to virtue signaling is the weaponization of identity. Once rooted in movements for justice, identity politics has morphed into a psyop of division—splintering humanity into increasingly fragile tribes, each convinced their pain is most sacred, their voice most urgent, their rage most righteous.

Let's be clear: many groups have endured harm, oppression, and real generational trauma. That is not in question. However, the moment pain is politicized, gamified, or used as a bludgeon against others, it stops being about healing and becomes being about control.

Today, identity is a weapon, not a window. Social algorithms feed outrage loops that reward victim signaling. Universities teach oppression olympics. DEI departments masquerading under rebranded names like, "Belonging," "Community Engagement," or "Student Development," enforce ideology over dialogue. Children are taught to view themselves as oppressed or oppressor based on unwarranted traits that have been applied to them, and which say nothing about the content of their character.

Instead of uniting around common humanity, people are trained to reduce themselves to race, gender orientation, trauma category, political alignment, and neurotype labels. Once designated, they're taught to weaponize that identity against others. It becomes a shield, a sword, and a currency—in one.

Meanwhile, the puppetmasters funding these divisions via NGOs, think tanks, hedge funds, and tax-exempt billionaire foundations, have no interest in justice. They are not fighting for rights. They are orchestrating chaos. The more divided the people, the easier they are to steer. While communities turn on one another in manufactured moral outrage, the real parasites loot the treasury, rig the elections, buy up farmland, censor dissent, create pandemics and rewrite history in real time.

It gets worse.

While the media fixates on things like pronouns and identity grievances, veterans sleep on sidewalks. Children overdose in bathrooms. Farmers go bankrupt. Water rights are hoarded and bought up. Girls are sterilized in gender clinics. The architects of this broken machine remain cloaked in untouchability.

Ironically, those who have suffered most—the exploited, the working poor, the trafficked, the veterans, the forgotten—are the quietest. They're too busy surviving. Too proud to beg. Too awake to perform. They don't need influencer activism. They need freedom.

The tragedy of identity politics is that it replaces actual empowerment with curated outrage. It offers a hollow sense of belonging built on resentment and not healing. It keeps people enslaved—psychologically, emotionally, spiritually—within a system that never intended to set them free.

Rejecting identity politics does not mean rejecting compassion or a rightful redress of harm. It means refusing to be manipulated. It means refusing to live in a cage of labels. True liberation begins when you remember who you are beyond the narrative—beyond the script—beyond the tribe.

Not a victim. Not a symbol. Instead, a sovereign being, ungovernable and whole.

## Social Engineering

Social engineering didn't begin with social media. It began with war.

After World War II, Project Paperclip quietly brought hundreds of Nazi scientists, psychologists, propagandists, and mind control experts into U.S. institutions under the guise of national defense. What they seeded was insidious: a new world model of psychological warfare. Many say we never stopped fighting that war—it just changed tactics. Look into the Bush family and their Nazi-linked financial roots. That's just one thread. Follow it further and you'll find names like Dulles, Harriman, Morgan Chase, and Rockefeller—all pillars of "respectable" society, and all deeply complicit.

The postwar rise of social engineering was not an accident. It was a plan—backed by banks, think tanks, and intelligence agencies—to remake public consciousness. The Tavistock Institute in London became a global epicenter of this effort. Tavistock is behind the weaponization of psychology, the mass normalization of propaganda (renamed "public relations"), and the systematic erosion of critical thought. Edward Bernays, dubbed the father of PR and a nephew of Sigmund Freud, taught corporations and governments how to manipulate public opinion through emotion, fear, and repetition.

If you want to know how entire populations are steered—look no further.

Imposed narratives—climate panic, DEI culture, synthetic feminism, transhumanism, "anti-racism" as rebranded collectivism—are not grassroots movements. They are engineered paradigms designed to divide and distract. Climate change, for instance, has never been a left/right issue. It has been a globally coordinated psychological operation, used to justify land grabs, resource control, and carbon-based social credit systems. Yes, Mother Earth is being harmed. Just not in the way they insist.

The scientists who dissented? Silenced. The data? Heavily redacted. The media? Controlled. They are not engaging in debate, but reading from scripts.

Feminism is a perfect case study. While true equality is a righteous goal, the Women's Liberation movement—funded by groups like the Rockefeller Foundation—was never just about rights. It was about disrupting the family unit, doubling the tax base, and sending children into government care at increasingly younger ages. The nuclear family posed a threat to centralized control. As a result, it had to be weakened—under the banner of empowerment. In a process that stretches even further back, women were pitted against men to create more separation. Divide and conquer.

The same tactic has played out in low-income communities. Ghettos were deliberately constructed. Drugs deliberately flooded in. Food deserts deliberately created. Fathers were removed via corporatized incarceration. Mothers became dependent on government programs. Generational trauma was cemented—then blamed on culture instead of policy.

This is how the parasite class operates: they hijack legitimate grievances and repackage them into programs that deepen dependency, division, and despair.

None of this means that progress hasn't been made. It has. Consciousness has expanded. Human dignity matters more than it once did. Still, engineered narratives always come with a trap. If you can't spot who's funding the outrage, you're likely still in the spell.

To truly liberate ourselves, we must separate natural justice from manufactured movements. We must reclaim our right to unite—not under artificial ideologies, but in clarity, autonomy, and shared sovereignty.

## Chapter 12
# Body Wars

What compromises the immune system? What are the true stressors?

You may not like the answer unless you've already broken through the mainstream illusion. Let's start with one of the biggest offenders:

Medicines.

Yes, medicines—pharmaceuticals of all kinds. These include over-the-counter pills, prescription drugs, injections, antibiotics, psychiatric meds, and hormonal therapies. All of them, without exception, come with side effects. Side effects are not arbitrary. They burden the body. They mask symptoms. And the medicine? It never actually cures anything.

Let me repeat that: no pharmaceutical has ever cured a disease. It only masks the symptoms. Not that that doesn't have some value.

Some of you may say, "Wait, what about life-saving treatments? What about emergencies?"

Sure—if you get into a car accident, by all means, go to the hospital. Emergency medicine is often miraculous and life-saving. But chronic illness? Cancer? Autoimmune conditions? These are not cured—they are managed, often at an excruciating cost.

Some believe radiation or chemotherapy "saved" them. Let's be honest: what actually happened? The body was flooded with life-threatening toxicity, killing not just cancer cells but healthy ones too. If you're lucky, you enter a window of remission. Still, you're not free —you're on the scan treadmill now. Every six months, you return for tests. You wait. You hope. You fear. It's not healing—they've replaced the disease with a pattern: a lifelong ritual of anxiety, checkups, and dependency.

I'm not here to make your decisions for you. If you find a certain treatment necessary, that's your choice. Just know this: for nearly every condition you face, there is a natural solution. It may take more work, more patience, and more personal responsibility—but the outcome may be far more lasting and far less harmful.

## The Great Medical Hijack

The fact remains: medicine does not cure disease. It has never cured disease. Its business model depends on managing symptoms—creating dependency, not liberation. The trillion-dollar pharmaceutical and health care complex is not about healing. It is about revenue. The system will never allow for permanent cures. Why would it? Cures cut off cash flow.

If you're skeptical, ask yourself: why do alternative cancer cures get silenced or outlawed? Why are holistic doctors mysteriously found dead? Why is nutritional therapy not taught in medical school?

The answer lies in history. In the early 1900s, the Rockefeller family—oil tycoons with a vested interest in chemical-based pharmaceuticals—began infiltrating medical education. They offered lavish endowments to medical schools on one condition: abandon all natural healing modalities. Homeopathy, herbalism, energy medicine, and nutritional therapy were systematically discredited and purged from the curriculum. What replaced them? Patented drugs. Petroleum-based pills. A new religion of pharmaceuticals backed by white coats and government grants.

The public? They were told it was science. However, it was always business.

Look closely and you'll see that cures for cancer and countless other diseases exist. Many of them have been known for decades. Some involve raw food, detoxification, fasting, mineral therapy, frequency medicine, herbal regimens, and emotional healing. Many come from indigenous traditions that are being wiped out systematically—because their knowledge threatens the corporate model.

The cures are out there. You have to dig. Discern. Charlatans exist in every field, including natural health. That doesn't mean truth isn't available. It just means you need to sharpen your inner radar.

**The Biohack Blind Spot**

How do we protect our children—especially if we choose not to vaccinate? Or even if we did vaccinate, but now want to support and restore them?

We start by removing immune system stressors.

Pharmaceuticals are one. The next is adulterated food. By that, I mean any food that has been processed, irradiated, sprayed, laced with preservatives, or genetically tampered with. Real food is whole. Real food is clean and doesn't need a label.

Here's the catch: even so-called "organic" food has been compromised.

Thanks to the FDA (led at the time by a former pharmaceutical CEO, naturally), the definition of "organic" was quietly loosened after heavy lobbying by Walmart and other corporate giants. Market research had shown their customers wanted organic goods but wouldn't pay more for them—so they changed the game. Not by offering better food, but by diluting the organic standards.

Now, a box of glyphosate-laced cereal can be sold as "organic." Why? Because it contains some organic ingredients, or it met a degraded standard of the original version. It's all marketing theater.

It works—because it allows parents to feel better while feeding their children sugar bombs sprayed with pesticides and laced with seed oils. This is by design.

What we need—what our bodies crave—is food like our forefathers grew. Food raised in living soil, watered with clean, filtered water, grown without chemical interference. That's getting harder and harder to find. It's been systematically eliminated.

If you've seen documentaries like *Food, Inc.*, you have glimpsed the machine we're up against.

The question remains: how do we get real food into our diets now?

If you don't grow it yourself...

If you don't have access to a local farmer's market that isn't owned by Big Ag...

If you can't trust the labels...

What do you do?

We'll get into solutions next—but before we do, let's zoom out for a moment.

Yes, I know some people will hear all this and say, "You're just beating the same tired drum." In a way, I am. Fortunately, the song is changing. There is a massive surge of socially active parents who are putting the pieces together. From sharing birth plans and detox protocols to reading ingredient labels on camera, they're waking up. Thank God they are.

We've seen the election of RFK Jr. to lead the Department of Health and Human Services—a man who, for decades, was smeared, shadow-banned, and publicly dismantled for daring to question vaccine toxins, water pollution, and the incestuous marriage between Big Pharma and Big Government. His appointment alone has signaled a tectonic shift. A ripple in the matrix. A breach in the illusion of consensus. It means doors are finally cracking open. Still, let's not kid ourselves—the opposition is a behemoth. Decades of regulatory capture. Entire government agencies run by the very industries they're meant to police. A medical establishment trained to mock, dismiss, and destroy anything outside the pharmaceutical paradigm. Billions in lobby money. Coordinated media takedowns. Generational programming. Every step someone like RFK Jr. takes, is scrutinized, ridiculed, and obstructed

The machine doesn't implode in a day. The house of cards falls slowly, one card at a time. The awakening isn't a lightning bolt—but a slow burn. A mother reading an ingredient label for the first time. A father saying no to one more booster. A teenager ditching seed oils and lighting up from the inside out. This is what revolution actually looks like. Not just lawsuits and elections—but millions of micro-decisions to reclaim personal authority.

Yes, the tide is turning. Yet there is still a massive blind spot when it comes to seeing the whole picture.

You cannot eat GMO products and call yourself holistic.

You cannot drown your meals in seed oils, or hand your toddler a McNugget, and then post about your daily mushroom stack and buttered coffee and claim you're biohacking your way to health.

You cannot pop magnesium at night after a day of glyphosate, Red dye #40, and synthetic fragrance and claim you're "addressing your body chemistry."

How can this be wellness? It's physical bypassing through supplements.

True health starts at the root.

It's not about hacking the brain. It's about liberating the entire being. That means clean soil, clean air, clean water, and clean thought. It means listening to your body as an ecosystem, not a tech interface. It means unlearning the illusion that you can out-supplement poison.

Your body is sacred technology. Yet it only works when all

systems—physical, emotional, spiritual, nutritional—are in actual alignment.

**From Poison to Power**

There is something else that still isn't being talked about enough.

If you're still drinking tap water, you're absorbing a neurochemical cocktail: fluoride (a known pineal gland calcifier), chlorine, pharmaceutical residue, heavy metals, and microplastics. If you're drinking it out of plastic? Add estrogenic disruptors to the list. Bottled water is not the solution—it's the illusion of one.

Beyond that? The air you breathe.

Smart meters, microwaves, 5G towers, WiFi routers, and satellites aren't just conveniences. They're constant frequency fields—pulsing through your home, interrupting your mitochondrial communication, disrupting melatonin production, and impairing cellular repair. EMF exposure is a silent saboteur. When you combine it with heavy metals already in your tissues, the effects multiply.

We're not just dealing with poison in the food and water. We're being attacked at the vibrational level.

Still—there's more.

You can eat cleanly, detox regularly, and still miss the root cause of illness if you're holding onto unprocessed grief, rage, guilt, or spiritual dissonance. This part matters. Your frequency is your immune field. Disease doesn't just come from what enters your mouth—it comes from what festers unspoken. From the truths you don't admit. From the life you're afraid to live.

No pill—natural or pharmaceutical—can fix that.

Then what do we do?

We localize. We connect. We unplug.

Victory isn't global—it's local. It's you, your neighbor, your land. It's a shared cow. A co-op order. A garden revival. It's bringing medicine back to the kitchen. It's breaking bread with allies instead of waiting for saviors.

If you're ready to stop managing symptoms and start reclaiming your inner authority—cell by cell, soul by soul—let's move on.

Because the deepest roots of personal power aren't found in supplements or supply chains. They're found in the home.

If we're truly serious about reclaiming the future, we have to start with those inheriting it.

The next frontier is not just your nervous system—it's your child's, and the rebellion begins in the classroom.

# Chapter 13
# Raising Lions

A quiet travesty has unfolded across Western nations—not just in the medicine cabinet, but in the classroom.

Our school systems, once envisioned as pathways to empowerment, have become machinery for control. From kindergarten through college, the structure of education runs counter to how children naturally learn. We prize conformity and compliance over creativity and critical thinking. Standardized testing rules the day. Schools that don't meet artificial benchmarks risk losing not only minds along the way, but their funding.

Teachers have little flexibility. Parents even less. Children—especially the sensitive, the independent, or the neurodivergent—are forced to sit still, suppress themselves, and absorb pre-approved content designed not to awaken minds, but to condition them.

What's wrong with our school systems?

In short, nearly everything. The structure of education runs counter to how children naturally learn.

If a child doesn't "fit the mold"—if they're creative, spirited, or can't sit still in a fluorescent-lit box for hours—they are flagged.

Often, these are the children who are awake, aware, and attuned to a deeper truth—and yet labeled as a problem.

Why are they disruptive? Are they unruly, or are they reacting to a toxic home, processed food, sugar overload, chemical-laced water, heavy metals in their environment, or vaccine injury? These children often cannot focus not because something is wrong with them—but because everything they have absorbed is wrong.

Let's name two culprits: sugar and dairy. Both are inflammatory and deeply disruptive to the nervous system. Sugar—especially in the form of juice, cereals, processed snacks, and hidden sweeteners—is not a treat but a neurological assault. Dairy, despite its revered place in the food pyramid, is not a health food. It's an allergen, a mucus-producing, immune-suppressing substance.

**The Child Industrial Complex**

Enter Ritalin, Adderall, and an entirely new suite of amphetamines and psychotropics that are routinely prescribed to children as young as five. In some states, it's become routine to recommend these drugs before trying dietary changes, emotional support, or lifestyle modifications.

Let's be honest: this is not about healing and never has been.

If your child resists conformity, expresses divergent thinking, or questions authority, the system will try to suppress it. When the behavior seems unruly or doesn't fit the narrow definition of "normal," drugs become the enforcement tool.

Even worse, psychotropic medications—originally developed for adults with severe psychiatric disorders—are being prescribed to school-age children under the guise of "support." What we are doing is medicating gifted, empathic, nonconforming children into submission.

**Nourish to Flourish**

Get back to basics. Start with food. Change their diet fully and immediately. No sugar. No dairy. No white flour. No additives. No GMOs. It may take time. It may take a battle of wills. Your child's future health and mental clarity depend on it.

If your child has been vaccinated—or you suspect injury or immune disruption—seek naturopathic support or the care of a classical homeopath. This last distinction is critical. Classical homeopathy uses one remedy at a time, tailored precisely to the individual. Combination remedies, though popular, treat surface symptoms and dilute the deeper healing process.

Chiropractic care is also essential—especially in early development. It aligns the body, calms the nervous system, and allows the child to grow into their body without unnecessary interference. Other helpful therapies include craniosacral adjustments, acupuncture, and naturopathic medicine.

Try to eliminate gluten and genetically modified grains, which are inflammatory and hard to digest. Be cautious with dairy alternatives: soy is often genetically modified, rice milk can be high in arsenic, almond milk can carry chemical additives, and generally all of the "alternatives" contain an enormous amount of seed oils. One of the best options is organic coconut milk—it's nutrient-dense, clean, and has a natural sweetness that kids tend to love. For infants or toddlers, organic goat milk—if tolerated—can be a viable option, structurally closer to human breast milk than cow's.

I used to rotate milks in our household. Once, I poured an alternative milk into a regular carton in order to get my toddler son to drink it. When he caught me, he was furious—and refused to touch it again. Very much with children is psychological. You have to stay sharp. You have to be ahead of them, not in trickery, but in understanding.

Of course, emotional stress must be minimized. Don't argue or complain about lack of money or relationship problems in front of your kids. Don't pretend children don't notice. They do. They sense everything. Many so-called behavior problems are cries for harmony.

. . .

**Education as Liberation**

The public school system is designed to make outliers feel like failures. If your child shows promise in ways that don't align with standardized benchmarks, they are deemed deficient.

If possible, co-educate. This doesn't mean expensive tutoring to help them pass school metrics. It means offering alternative worldviews and knowledge sources that empower their spirit. If you can homeschool, consider it seriously. Not every family can, but those who do often discover a renewed relationship with learning—on both sides.

Whether you homeschool or simply supplement, the goal is to awaken the thinker, the explorer, the creative soul. Help them question. Help them know themselves.

Because in the end, personal freedom begins with the right to think freely. Everything else follows from there.

**Beyond the Treadmill**

Back to the school system and the trap it sets: the tests, the benchmarks, the race to the top. You know the drill—ace the standardized tests, get into the right school, earn a spot in a name-brand college, and then... what? Get spit out into a life that looks just like everyone else's. That entire mindset is rooted in the fear of not achieving a goal that is illusory.

If you want a regimented life, if you want your children to do what everyone else does, then stay on the treadmill. On the other hand, if you're here reading this, chances are you're already questioning the system.

Now for the truth: your child is going to walk their own path—whether you allow it or resist it. You cannot mold their spirit into your fantasy of success. You shouldn't.

Take Harvard, for instance. I've had relatives and friends who've worked inside the Ivy League machine. One is a counselor who deals directly with students, and he's been blunt: depression, disconnection, and suicidal ideation are rampant among those who feel like they don't fit the mold. Many are overwhelmed not by academic pressure, but by the crushing pressure of expectation and conformity.

Don't be seduced by glossy brochures or prestigious names. These institutions often churn out system-loyal individuals who continue to prop up the very world we are trying to transform. They are not necessarily bastions of truth. They are factories of obedience dressed in tweed and tradition.

Rethink the framework of what success looks like. Question what you've been told. Question where the path is leading, and whether it's really yours or your child's. There are countless beautiful, intelligent, vibrant children who are labeled "underachievers" simply because they fail to mimic a broken curriculum. What looks like malfunction is early resistance. Honor it, hone it, and nurture it. Do not let it die or be drugged into submission, but help shape it into something meaningful and lasting. These are our future entrepreneurs, artists, writers, and out of the box thinkers.

It's common to succumb to pressure from teachers, administrators, or doctors who recommend putting your child on drugs for the sake of performance. You might see a temporary improvement in grades. But what price are you willing to pay for that bump in GPA?

Drugs create dependency and alter brain chemistry. They interfere with emotional development. They carry lasting side effects that may not show up until years later. Depression, anxiety and mood disorders are often signs of deep toxicity and unresolved imbalances. They can be addressed, but not through suppression. Never through sedation.

Also consider the psychological and EMF stress of digital exposure—smartphones, video games, and the constant dopamine hit of social media. These rewire the brain, feed toxicity and increase instability. This is all part of the picture. You cannot separate mental wellness from physical, emotional, and digital environments.

Protect your child. Be brave enough to say no to what everyone else is doing and address the root causes.

## The Rebel's Remedy

Before we leave this topic, we must speak plainly about our disappearing health freedoms.

Whether or not you believe in them, if you're forced to vaccinate your child with no legal recourse, with the vaccine manufacturers not even held liable for any damage they may cause, you're not free. When you're compelled to put your child on pharmaceuticals so they can remain in school, you're not free. When hospitals overrule parental rights and perform medical procedures against your will—even kidnapping children under the guise of "protective services"—you're not free.

When food is chemically altered, genetically modified, sprayed with biotechnological agents like Apeel (Bill Gates' unlabeled "invisible coating" found on produce nationwide), and you are not even told, you are not free.

When labeling GMO food is discouraged because it might trigger consumer hesitation, you are not free. When organic farms are criminalized, raw milk producers raided, and backyard gardens bulldozed under zoning codes manipulated by agro-giants—you are not free.

Don't think for a moment these things are rare. Violations are occurring all over the world—and especially in the so-called lands of the free.

It goes deeper. When you're forced to participate in centralized insurance systems, when your medical data is mined and sold, when you are denied access to natural remedies because they haven't been "approved" by entities funded by pharmaceutical companies—what part of that sounds like choice?

If you think these measures are here for your protection, look closer. Look at who profits. Follow the money.

Ask yourself: who's making the rules? Who's behind the

mandates, the regulations, the suppression of natural medicine, the denial of food integrity, the targeting of healers and farmers?

More often than not, it's people sitting on the boards of biotech companies, pharmaceutical giants, and chemical conglomerates. These are not unbiased actors. These are not truth-seekers. They are profit-makers. The regulatory agencies meant to protect us are in bed with them.

What is the answer?

Do not follow the company line.

Question everything. Examine who is saying what—and why. Cross-reference, dig deeper, use discernment. Make solid choices for you and your child. The illusion of freedom is paper-thin.

We are nearing a critical threshold—not just in health rights, but in human rights.

You address this by not asking for permission. Reclaim your body. Reclaim your children. Reclaim the rebel's right to natural wellbeing.

That is called freedom.

## Chapter 14
# Breaking the Code

Now that you've gotten a sense of what has been going on without your knowledge—how deeply the threads of manipulation run, how subtly your perceptions have been shaped—it's time to ask: what can you do about it?

We are not helpless. We are not pawns. We are not mere bystanders in a rigged game of societal control. Becoming aware is not just a first step—it is an act of rebellion. From that awareness, powerful actions become possible. You can begin, today, to pull yourself out of the matrix of deceit.

The first step? Turn off the programming—literally.

**Code Breaker 1: Turn It All Off**

Yes, you love your favorite TV show. You've grown up with certain characters, you have your guilty pleasures, your cinematic comfort food. Time for more truth: you are not watching TV; TV is watching you. Not in the Orwellian, literal surveillance sense (although let's be honest, that too)—but in the sense that every frame, every commercial, every scripted laugh track, every word— is designed to train you. This may seem to be "entertainment," but it's entrainment. A carefully coded hypnotic device meant to keep you passive, compliant, and numb.

Here's the rebellion: take your TV back—or better yet, remove it altogether.

You don't need to go cold turkey. Start by shifting the way you consume content. Get off the cable leash. Figure out how to access your favorite shows without the mind-numbing barrage of commercials. You can watch virtually any show or film you want without being bombarded by pharmaceutical ads or political propaganda once you learn to navigate online archives. A little digital literacy goes a long way.

Once you do this, something shifts. You begin to reclaim your time. Your consciousness. Your mental real estate.

Then something even more interesting happens: you lose interest.

Without the nonstop flow of triggers and targeted manipulation, you start to realize that most of what you thought you "had to watch" was filler. Noise. Programming for the sake of filling time. Your list of "must-see shows" begins to shrink. First down to a few. Then one. Then, maybe none.

You're not losing something. You're gaining something.

You're gaining your free will back. Your mind back. Your imagination back. With it, you're claiming the right to choose your input and to stop being passively fed by a system that profits off your attention.

This is how the rebel's path further unfolds—not with fire and protest, but with awareness and a quiet refusal to be hypnotized.

Ready for the next code?

## Code Breaker 2: Conscientious Consumerism

You've begun stepping off the mental conveyor belt by disconnecting from TV programming. Now, it's time to examine another layer of the matrix: your habits as a consumer.

Every purchase you make is a vote. A signal. A thread in the web of energy, intention, and influence that ties you to the larger system. The question is—do you know what you're voting for?

Consumerism is one of the most deeply embedded programs in our lives. It's not just about having things—it's about needing to have them. Wanting the next. Grasping for the new. It's engineered greed and dissatisfaction, crafted by corporations who have spent billions figuring out how to make you feel incomplete until you buy their solution.

Here's the rebel's move: double-check every purchase. Before you click "buy," before you swipe your card, ask yourself—Do I really need this? Is this truly aligned with the life I'm choosing to live?

Let me be the first to admit : I love beautiful clothes. I love gorgeous shoes. I have too many shoes, and I don't hide it. The difference is—I see it. I see the program. I feel the pull. I consciously choose what I will and will not allow to hook me.

This is about reclaiming agency.

The cult of consumerism is everywhere: Black Friday, Grey Thursday, Cyber Monday—a trifecta of engineered madness. These are not holidays. These are rituals of zombie consumerism, ceremonies of mindless acquisition.

You do not have to participate.

You can begin, right now, to disrupt the system by living differently. Buy only what you need. When you buy, buy from those who reflect your values. Boycott the companies who fund censorship, push pharmaceuticals, exploit workers, or promote division. Research their ties. Look deeper than the label.

Every time you choose not to buy something you don't need, you create a crack in the control grid. Every time you support a local artisan or an ethical small business, you strengthen the parallel economy of freedom.

Consumerism is not just about spending money—it's about spending energy. Life force. As rebels, we guard that life force like gold.

Remember, your worth was never meant to be measured in handbags or square footage. Your identity cannot be bought—only reclaimed.

Next time you feel the urge to consume, stop. Breathe. Ask: Who am I without this purchase?

Chances are, you'll like the answer.

Ready for the next code?

## Code Breaker 3: Desexualize Your Kids

If you're still looking for the smoking gun that proves society has been hijacked—look no further than the hypersexualization of children.

Some will call this religious zeal. But this is not about shaming sexuality or promoting puritan ideals. This is about waking up to the disturbing and deliberate manipulations that are unfolding in front of us. We are being desensitized to the sexualization of minors—and that desensitization is a key tactic in the collapse of moral, emotional, and spiritual clarity.

We are immersed in a culture that feeds children adult imagery, language, and behavior long before their nervous systems, emotional maturity, or spiritual discernment is ready to integrate it. You don't need a degree in psychology to see what this does to a developing psyche. When children become oversexed at increasingly younger ages, it's not progress—it's a sign of the decay of society.

This may seem like fringe opinion, but it's observable. Track it over the last 20 years: as pop stars shed more clothes, as social media influencers twerk into algorithmic stardom, as apps replace human intimacy and porn replaces physical connection, children mimic what they see. They become both objects of the system and consumers of it. Their identities form around distorted models of self-worth and interpersonal relationships.

The end result? We are erasing the joy of discovery. We are gutting the sacredness of connection. We are turning divine union into a punchline.

The idea of age-appropriate, conscious monogamous sex with a loving partner has become an afterthought, even a source of mockery. There is something sacred in preserving the integrity of sexual energy until it can be held with reverence. When that reverence is removed, the body becomes transactional. The soul goes unrecognized. A generation grows up confusing hyperstimulation with love.

What do we do?

We reclaim the home as a sacred space—not just physically, but emotionally and vibrationally. We question what our kids are exposed to and how. We watch what's sneaking through their screens, their schools, their TikTok feeds, and their "sex ed" curriculums disguised as empowerment. We remember that true empowerment begins with boundaries, not indulgence.

There is nothing old-fashioned about protecting innocence. There is nothing regressive about safeguarding childhood. In fact, it's one of the most revolutionary acts a parent can make right now.

Some people will say, "If I homeschool, won't my child miss out on socialization?" Ask yourself—what kind of socialization are we talking about? The kind that pressures 8-year-olds into gender confusion and sixth graders into watching porn as part of sex ed? Or the kind that fosters values, creativity, curiosity, and genuine relationships?

You may feel unequipped to homeschool, or believe your job makes it impossible. This is where the next wave of rebellion comes in: community. You find others who see what you see. You band together. You organize learning pods, demonstrations, school board speeches, hire ethical tutors, share responsibilities, create microschools, or set up supervised homeschooling support while you work remotely.

There are solutions. They won't come from the top down. They will come from the ground up—from you, the awake parent, the alert soul, the rebel with clarity.

It's time to reject the myth that protecting your child's sacredness is prudish or outdated. It is neither. It is wise. It is brave. It may be one of the most crucial things you ever do.

Your children are not vessels for ideology. They are beautiful beings full of possibility—here to love, to create, and to blossom into who they truly are.

Let them unfold on their own timeline, not the one forced on them by a collapsing culture.

## Code Breaker 4: Support Local Government

Let's circle back to the question of government—because this one's big.

If you've begun to awaken to the manufactured matrix of control, you've probably noticed the same pattern everywhere: decisions are made from the top down, and the people at the top? They don't know you. They don't represent you. They probably don't respect you, and they sure as hell aren't working for your freedom.

That's why the rebellion begins close to home.

Government should be kept as local as possible—physically, energetically, and structurally. It's a principle that's been lost in the fog of bureaucracy and globalism. It's an essential one if we are going to reclaim real power as individuals and communities.

The more removed the government is from you personally, the more automated, impersonal, and unaccountable it becomes. You get filtered out. Your voice becomes static. Your actual needs—your clean food, your clean water, your right to parent, your bodily autonomy—are lost in a sea of manufactured talking points and corporate lobbying.

This may seem like a partisan issue, but it's about proximity.

The closer your leaders are to your street, your school, your water supply, your land, your kids—the more power you have to influence them. If you can show up to a town hall and look your representative in the eye—if you can rally five neighbors to do the same—you are already doing more to shape the future than any social media argument or federal petition drive ever could.

There is a growing movement—often ignored or demonized by mainstream outlets—that supports the idea of states reclaiming autonomy, decentralizing authority, and stepping out of the chokehold of federal mandates that no longer serve the people. At its root, this movement is not about fragmentation. It's about restoring self-governance at the level where it actually matters.

Even if that idea feels too radical right now, one thing is undeniable: local government is where your rebellion can gain traction.

You don't have to agree with everything happening in your state or town, but you do have the ability to vet candidates, attend meetings, ask hard questions, and support those who actually represent your values. If you're not sure who those people are—start finding out. Look into their funding sources. Watch how they vote. Follow their trail. If they're bought, call it out. If they're clean, support them. Don't wait for some mythical savior. The fight for freedom is fought block by block.

Local government is the last firewall between your autonomy and total centralization.

Show up. Speak up. Get your boots on the ground. Because the rebels of the future won't be hiding in bunkers—they'll be running for school board, managing farmers' markets, building parallel communities, and taking back one town at a time.

Let the revolution be relational. Let it be close. Let it start with you.

## Code Breaker 5: Dump the Brainwashing

Let's face another hard truth: if you've lived in modern society for more than five minutes, you've been brainwashed. Maybe not in the dramatic, dystopian sense—but certainly in the slow-drip, culture-soaked, algorithm-curated, education-conditioned way that numbs your instincts and installs someone else's beliefs as your own.

Where does it come from? Everywhere.

It pours in from the internet, floods you through TV, seeps in through films. It's woven into the school curriculum, blasted through headlines, echoed by politicians, and reinforced by well-meaning friends who've swallowed the script. You don't even realize it's happening. That's the point. That's how good it is.

School is perhaps the biggest and earliest conduit. We are taught not how to think but what to think. We're graded on obedience, not originality. Conditioned to seek approval instead of truth. Designed to memorize, regurgitate, and fall in line.

Yet your mind is not theirs to program.

How then, do you break the spell?

First, you unplug from the usual input. Take a break from headlines. Question your daily sources of information. Ask: Who benefits if I believe this? Who profits from my fear, my conformity, my distraction?

Then, return to your source.

Get quiet. Let your intuition come online again—not the knee-jerk reaction shaped by trauma or media, but your real inner knowing. The one that whispers instead of shouts. The one that sees through the noise and says, wait. This doesn't feel right.

Once that voice gets louder, let your mind work with it. True intelligence isn't just logic or facts. It's the unbreakable fusion of your intellect, your gut, and your heart. That's your built-in inner barometer. That's how you know what's real.

This isn't just about breaking free—it's about reclaiming the rebellious brilliance that was always yours.

Reprogram yourself... or someone else will do it for you.

Ready for the next code?

. . .

## Code Breaker 6: Vibrational Harmony

Discernment is your superpower. It's the compass you use when there's no map. The inner sonar that cuts through the noise and propaganda to say: This feels true. That does not.

What is discernment, really?

Some say it's a mix of heart and head—intuition married with intellect. Others frame it as left-brain logic paired with right-brain creativity. In real life, it's messier than that. It's not a formula—it's a feeling. A layered, personal calibration that arises when you stop outsourcing your judgment and start listening to something deeper.

For me, discernment begins with rigorous investigation. I don't take things at face value, and I don't blindly accept claims—especially not from those in power or with something to gain. I research, I compare, I challenge assumptions. This is about peeling back every layer of a narrative until what remains is raw and real.

Then comes the intuitive resonance. That "click" inside when you come across something that aligns—not just mentally, but energetically. It's not just satisfying your logic. It's vibrating in a way that matches your internal knowing.

This is what I call vibrational harmony.

It's when all the things you've uncovered on your truth-seeking path begin to echo a similar tone. Your gut says yes. Your spirit settles. You can feel it in your cells.

We are energetic beings in an ecosphere of frequency. Words carry frequency. Beliefs carry frequency. Truth carries frequency. Once you attune to that, you can detect the lies not just through data —but through dissonance.

The world is rigged with falsehoods presented as common sense. When you slow down, drop into your own being, and refuse to be coerced by fear or pressure, you'll feel when something is off. You'll know. That knowing will lead you to the next piece.

This is the final step in reclaiming your unprogrammed life: using your own frequency to filter the flood of noise. Reconnecting to that inner tuning fork that rings only when something is aligned.

## UNLEASHING THE REBEL WITHIN

Not because someone told you, but because your whole being says: Yes. This is true for me.

That, my rebellious friend, is how you unplug from the machine.

# Phase III: The Rebel Path

"Don't you know yet?
It is your Light that lights the world."
—Rumi

## Chapter 15
# Signal vs. Static

You've made it this far for a reason.

You've cut through the noise. You've questioned the scripts. You've felt the burn of truth as it stripped away illusion after illusion. In the midst of all this dismantling, a new challenge emerges—one quieter, subtler, but just as crucial:

How do you know what to trust?

Because once you step outside the matrix, the terrain doesn't instantly become clear. If anything, it gets foggier at first. Your mind starts racing to fill in the gaps. Your heart starts pulling in directions that scare you. The static is everywhere—inside you, around you, online, in your relationships. Everyone's got an opinion. Everyone's got a download. Everyone's selling a path to truth.

Which one is real?

This is where the rebel must go inward—not to escape, but to calibrate. The next level of growth isn't just about breaking chains. It's about becoming the tuning fork for what's real.

To do that, you need to discern between signal and static.

You need to distinguish the sacred whisper of your inner knowing from the frantic chatter of fear, ego, and programming. To do that, you must learn how to balance the head and the heart—not as enemies, but as twin engines of truth.

Let's get into it.

Let's talk about intuition. Logic. Emotion. Discernment. Let's decode the noise. Most of all—let's find the frequency that's yours to follow.

Because that frequency? That's where the real rebellion lives.

## When Your Gut Beats Google

Knowing that you need discernment and actually feeling it are two different things.

How do you tell the difference?

Is it with the mind? The heart? A gut feeling you can't explain?

For some, the journey starts with research. For others, it begins with a strange discomfort—something that doesn't sit right, even when you can't explain why. A subtle dissonance. A tightening in the chest. A flicker of unease when a voice or message just... doesn't land.

Here's the thing: that feeling isn't just moodiness or being judgmental. Rather, it's teaching you to detect truth.

Is the intellect the starting point? For some, yes. For others, it's the heart. Sometimes it's not a conscious process at all—it's just a subtle inner sense that something's off. A discomfort. A vibration that grates. A tension you can't quite name but feel in your gut.

I used to think this feeling was me being impatient or judgmental. Certain people on social media would cause me to prickle emotionally. Their tone, their face, their vibe—didn't land right. I couldn't listen. Their voices were too grating, too smug, too fast, too fake. I'd scroll past, irritated, assuming it was me.

Then the pattern emerged.

Time and again, the very people I couldn't stomach turned out to be something other than they appeared—for instance, posing as truth-tellers while subtly undermining the truth. Eventually, I realized: my body knew before my brain did. My inner barometer had been quietly pinging.

That "annoyance" wasn't intolerance. It was truth detection.

It wasn't personal. It was vibrational. Their frequency didn't resonate, and my intuition screamed before I had words to back it up. Once I learned to trust that feeling—once I started listening instead of brushing it off—it became one of my most valuable tools.

Their truth, if it even was truth, wasn't my truth. That distinction matters. Because discernment isn't just about information—it's about internal alignment. It's about resonance. The more I follow that inner compass, the more precise it becomes. It has evolved into a kind of internal radar.

Now? My inner barometer is on at all times.

Do I still research? Absolutely. Yet, the landscape has changed. The digital battlefield has shifted. I don't rely solely on external data —I rely on calibration. Many others are now doing the same. Intuition is spiking across the collective, accelerated in no small part by the phenomenon known as Q.

Say what you will—Q awakened millions to the realization that we were being played. That narratives were being carefully constructed. That clues were being seeded. That we were being trained to stop trusting ourselves.

The drops—short, cryptic, often coded—weren't there to give answers. They were designed to prompt questions. To wake up the researchers. It wasn't about following blindly. It was about learning to dig. Millions did.

Whether you were part of that movement or not, the Q phenomenon cracked open a level of discernment that changed the culture. Researchers became decentralized. Codebreakers emerged. Suddenly, "trust your gut" became more than a New Age cliché and transformed into a survival skill.

No matter where you stand on any polarizing figure, the message remains: you must learn to discern.

Discernment is the rebel's compass. It's what keeps you from falling for the next shiny savior, the next PSYOP, the next seductive half-truth wrapped in comforting language. It's what separates your voice from the static.

## That Inner Alarm

Some people are born with a highly attuned intuitive compass. They just know. They walk into a room and sense the energetic currents. They hear a voice and instantly feel whether to lean in—or run. They don't need proof; their nervous system tells them everything.

Others—many of us—have to rebuild this compass over time. We've been trained out of it. Schooled out of it. Gaslit into doubting ourselves. We were taught that "proof" comes from external authority. That only experts can know what's real. That feeling something in your bones isn't good enough.

Fortunately, your internal alarm system is real. Like any skill, it sharpens with practice.

When you're first rebuilding your discernment, it can feel messy. One day you trust your gut, the next you second-guess it. You might wonder: Am I being paranoid, or perceptive? Is this judgment or intuition?

That's where the "both/and" approach comes in. You need both your head and your heart. Your logic and your instincts. Think of it like triangulation. When multiple senses are telling you the same thing—when your mind, body, and spirit all say yes (or no)—that's when you know you're on to something.

This doesn't mean your discernment will be perfect. You'll misread signals. You'll be fooled. You'll get swept up in false hope or righteous rage or clever distractions.

Each time you come back to your center, you get stronger.

This is why it's so dangerous to cling to beliefs as if they're sacred relics. Once your mind becomes rigid—once you've decided you already know—you stop learning. You stop sensing. You filter out reality in order to preserve your worldview.

Unquestioned beliefs are mental prisons for they keep your inner barometer stuck on low.

Here's the rub: the more you cling to dogma, the easier it is to manipulate you. That's how cults work. That's how political parties work. That's how mainstream media works. They depend on your willingness to believe something without questioning the source.

Truth doesn't need your loyalty. It doesn't demand obedience. It just asks to be felt.

If you want to raise your inner barometer capacity, start with this radical act: hold nothing sacred. Not your teachers. Not your parents. Not your traditions. Not authors like me.

That doesn't mean becoming cynical or cold-hearted. It means becoming precise, curious and fiercely honest. It means staying in motion—always calibrating, always testing, always listening deeper.

When your alarm goes off, don't silence it. Ask why. When something triggers you, don't dismiss it. Look underneath. When someone's words feel just a little "off," pay attention. Energy doesn't lie.

## Your Freedom Depends on Doubt

Some people have a very developed sense of intuition and instantly come up with answers that prove correct. For those who are still sharpening this inner compass, this is something that bears repeating: you must keep your mind open to all interpretations and analyses. Even the ones you've previously dismissed or the ones that make you uncomfortable.

You're now probably thinking, how on earth do I do that? It starts by holding no belief sacred. Yes, I mean none.

This is where most people freeze up. We're taught that some beliefs must never be questioned. That to even examine certain ideas is dangerous or offensive. This is the very mechanism that keeps the matrix of illusion intact. Unquestioned belief systems don't just limit you—they imprison you.

It's not about having no values. It's about having the courage to test every value you hold.

Yes, I believe in certain things. I believe there is a Universal Creator. I call this force—neither male nor female, but possibly both—God or Source. My concept is probably not everyone else's concept of God. Some call Him Creator, some say the Universe, some say Spirit or Light or All That Is. That's the point.

You don't have to adopt anyone else's name, structure, or belief about the Divine. You do have to stay open, however. Open to interpretations. Open to paradox. Open to multiple lenses of understanding.

Because here's the truth: unless you do this, your inner barometer will be stuck on a low setting. You'll fall for old scripts dressed in new clothing. You'll miss the programming coded into "helpful" advice. You'll confuse dogma with wisdom and be blind to the sleight-of-hand that happens in both religion and science.

Every single thing we've been taught is not necessarily correct. In fact, it most probably is incorrect. Let that settle in. That includes history, medicine, nutrition, education, politics, relationships, and even basic assumptions about your body, your mind, and your purpose on this planet.

The answer is simple, but it's radical: question everything.

I know I've said this before. Other people have said it as well. Yes, it's in danger of becoming another cliché with people printing it on T-shirts and bumper stickers. I mean it—deeply, sincerely. Question everything—but also, do not dismiss new or uncomfortable information out of hand. Not because it's trendy, but because it's the only way out of the web of lies we've been living in.

This is called reclaiming your right to think for yourself.

## No More Grazing on Lies

In the writing field, editors have a saying: "don't hold any sacred cows." That means the brilliant passage you stayed up all night crafting, the one that flowed through you like celestial poetry? It might need to go. The sentence you thought was your magnum opus might be the very one that dulls the edge of your message.

Letting go can feel brutal. The rebel truth? What doesn't serve the whole must burn.

If you want your work—or your worldview—to evolve into something sharper, truer, and more powerful, you must be willing to cut loose the pieces you're overly attached to. This takes courage. It also takes humility.

The same principle applies not just to writing, but to your beliefs.

Yes, I'm talking about your assumptions. Your rules. Your "truths" that no one's allowed to touch. The things you've inherited without ever examining. The things you defend out of loyalty, tradition, or fear.

These are your sacred cows. They're in the way.

The path to clear thinking authenticity requires a kind of spiritual editing. You must be willing to slash and burn what no longer serves. This includes the beliefs you thought defined you, and the identities you've clung to for safety, inclusion, or validation.

This does not leave you empty or unmoored, but instead, clutter-free and clear so that the real you can emerge.

How do you begin?

You do this by subjecting every one of your cows to examination. That means you inspect everything you've arbitrarily accepted as fact. Everything your parents, teachers, religious leaders, scientists, or news anchors ever told you. Everything the culture praises or demonizes. Everything.

Because here's the twist that unravels the whole damn knot:

The fact is, there are no facts.

Let that detonate gently in your mind.

What we've been sold as "fact" is often opinion wrapped in authority. It's data cooked to serve a narrative. It's propaganda dressed up in peer-reviewed clothing. It's history written by the victors. It's tradition masquerading as truth.

Talk about your mind twisters.

If you want out of the maze, if you want your discernment to be razor-sharp and your lie detector fully activated, you must start by slaying your own sacred cows.

Because until you do, you're not really free.

## **Limiting Beliefs**

Limiting beliefs include things like: My religion is the only way to heaven. My government cares about the people. Or, we need banks because they have to hold our money.

These are the kind of unconscious beliefs that sneak in early, dress up as truth, and burrow deep. They rarely feel like beliefs at all. They feel like common sense. Like gravity. Like the sky is blue. That's how thoroughly programmed we've been.

Time for the flip: belief is not truth. "Limiting beliefs" is not just a buzzword—it's a trap door in your consciousness that you've probably never opened.

Let's try opening it now.

How about reversing your thinking that money is necessary to: we don't need money?

It sounds wild at first—until you understand that fiat currency is a fiction. An agreement. A construct. That there are other ways of commerce. Barter. Community exchange. Decentralized systems. Sound currencies. Possibilities that don't depend on being chained to debt.

Here's another belief reversal: religions were created as systems of control. Instead of offering spiritual liberation, many became tools for obedience, guilt, and tribalism. Perhaps not all, but enough to warrant deep reflection.

Still more: trillions of dollars in debt is not a real thing. Fiat is fake. It is based on nothing. They print money up.

Yet we accept that debt—national, personal, generational—as a binding force. As if it were moral and essential. What if it's neither?

How about the limiting belief that we are anything less than Source-connected sovereign beings?

That one sits at the root of nearly all disempowerment. That we can't determine our own fates. That we need permission to thrive. That our value comes from outside approval or institutional validation.

Now flip it: we *can* determine what's right for us and our families. Our rights aren't granted by governments or enshrined in legalese. They are intrinsic to us. They are inalienable. They exist because we exist. They are part of human law. Or, God's law.

Let's go deeper. What about the belief—especially in the States—that we are a democracy?

We are not. America is a constitutional republic. There's a big difference. A democracy cedes control to others through the vocal strength of the majority. A republic holds that voting power in the hands of the people—each person, not just the loudest bloc.

Or at least, it did—until the United States was unlawfully reformed as a corporate entity in 1871 by the banking cabal. That restructuring reclassified the republic into a business, and you—yes, you—into a commodity. A debt instrument. A vessel for labor and tax extraction.

Let's look at some more limiting beliefs. Jesus, or Yeshua, was born on December 25th. False. That was a convenient overlap with the Roman festival of Saturnalia. How about this one: Killing infidels will send you to heaven. That your appendix is unnecessary. That your uterus is expendable once you're done giving birth. That dementia is part of the life cycle. That sex and passion fade with age.

None of it is inherently true.

Illness is not a natural phase of aging. Sex doesn't die unless we let it. December 25th is a marker of religious assimilation, not a cosmic timestamp. Our organs are not random extras. Sacred union doesn't wither—it deepens.

If any of this causes discomfort, good. That's the point. You're pressing against the edges of your programming. On the other side of those edges is something rare: clarity.

## Unaware Friends

Many people around us are just steps away from becoming full-blown bots—if they're not there already. You can recognize them easily: the glazed-over look when you veer off-script in conversation, the discomfort that creeps in when the topic drifts away from makeup trends, football stats, or celebrity gossip. The moment you bring up something deep or real, they short-circuit. You can almost hear the internal error message flashing: This does not compute.

Common sense says: don't engage directly. Not because you're superior, but because their belief systems act like automated defense grids. They will reflexively regurgitate whatever the media machine has fed them—word-for-word, without a single moment of critical thought. No pause. No filter. No self-check. Just echo. Just loop. Try challenging them ever-so gently, and you may find yourself on the receiving end of a merciless verbal lashing. You've threatened the illusion that protects them. You've chipped away at the glossy armor of their curated reality. Fear will fight back.

Because behind every limiting belief—every robotic regurgitation of "that's just how it is"—is fear.

The fear that you can't do something. Or that something new shouldn't be done. Or that if something changes, it will bring ruin. That's what limiting beliefs do. They plant the idea that there are no alternatives. No off-ramps. No way out. Just fate, decay, inevitability.

I'll offer another one: I'm going to die from ____ disease. Fill in the blank with whatever illness the system is using to keep people terrified and obedient.

Or this: If we get rid of the IRS, how will taxes be collected? How will the government run?

Let's get something straight. Your taxes aren't running the government. They're in part paying interest on fake debt to the Federal Reserve—a privately owned entity that has nothing to do with your government and everything to do with your enslavement. The other parts have been funneled into slush funds that return to cabal coffers, with very little going to the efforts they purport to support. You've been sold a story, and that story keeps you compliant.

Let's look at another belief worth smashing: Everyone gets old and sick. False. I know plenty of people aging gracefully—people who are in better shape, sharper minds, and stronger bodies than folks half their age. No, dementia isn't inevitable. That's a scam. Dementia is driven by environmental poisons, flu shot toxicity, food-induced inflammation, and glucose mismanagement. You've been programmed to expect decline. That decline is engineered.

Then there's the social belief: If I break from my friends, my church, my family, or my social circle and start questioning the narrative, they'll reject me.

This is perhaps the most widespread straightjacket of all. People want to stay in "the club." That club might be a place of worship. It might be a school parent group, a workplace clique, a family dynamic, or an entire neighborhood of performative belonging. It's the club of consensus reality—the one you'll be expelled from the moment you start thinking for yourself.

What's really behind this fear of exile? Fear of being challenged. Fear of no longer being liked. Fear of being alone. What if you flip it? What if instead of fearing disapproval, you embraced your role as an outlier? What if you walked away and started your own club—one built on truth, integrity, and independent thought?

That's how revolutions begin.

## Starve the Parasites

Now let's go deeper. The real currency of control isn't just money—it's energy. Emotional energy. The dark side has cultivated humanity like a harvest crop of fear, sadness, despair, and trauma.

Why? Because those lower vibrational states feed them. This is what many call loosh—the term describing the energetic sustenance extracted from suffering.

Wars, famines, terrorist events, media panic—all of it generates loosh. It keeps humanity weak, reactive, divided, and vulnerable. It keeps the dark parasites strong. Fear is their food. Despair is their drug. We are their supply line.

Now for what they fear most: Joy. Unity. Laughter. Love. Authenticity. These higher frequencies make them wither. They can't feed on harmony. That's why they attack it. That's why they ridicule it. That's why peace is never the true goal.

Once you understand this, everything changes. You stop giving them what they want. You stop feeding the beast.

You start choosing joy—radically, defiantly. You start moving toward unity—not artificial "unity" under a regime, but genuine soul resonance with your fellow humans. You begin vibrating higher. You start remembering who you are: an infinite and divine being. Not a serf. Not a statistic. Not a lab rat.

This is another step in the real rebellion: to reclaim the frequency of life.

Separation, fear, and loosh are not your nature. They are the weapon used against your nature. Your true self is whole, loving, expansive, and clear. No matter how many times they try to shut that down—you can rise again.

You've broken the code. Now keep going.

## Chapter 16
# Staying Ignited

We've all been there—the only one at the dinner table talking about the FDA, the AMA, or the puppeteers behind the scenes, while everyone shifts uncomfortably in their seats. You see it in their eyes: the polite panic, the blank stares, the rush to change the subject. You're not being rude. You're refusing to swallow the script.

Welcome to life outside the grid.

You didn't come here to win popularity contests. You came here to wake up—and maybe, just maybe, to rattle a few cages along the way. Here's the twist: waking others up isn't about ranting louder. It's about embodying the frequency of truth so clearly, so unapologetically, that it becomes impossible to ignore.

Let's lay down a few rebel-ground rules for navigating the unawakened terrain without torching your relationships.

**Shine—Don't Shout**

It's important to get something straight: you're not here to convert anyone. Evangelism arises from ego. Preaching "your truth" is the same, and both fall flat. What changes people is presence—your unshakeable clarity, your refusal to live a lie, your quiet confidence in the face of mass illusion.

Yes, it's maddening to watch people sleepwalk through life. Yes, it hurts when the people you love parrot propaganda like it's gospel. Now for the rebellious truth: it is not your job to rescue anyone.

Your job is to stay ignited.

Be the proof. Be the pulse. Be the walking contradiction to their programmed expectations. Live with so much coherence, so much radical authenticity, that your being speaks louder than any lecture could.

Still, what about those rare moments—those cracks in the armor—when someone shows a flicker of curiosity? Maybe you're on a call, or sitting next to someone on a plane, and suddenly they ask. They lean in. The glaze in their eyes clears.

That's your cue, but —listen up —don't dump the whole download. You are not here to override another's path. Sharing information, even when it's your lived truth, isn't about force—it's about offering perspective, so that when curiosity arises, something real might be found and give way to dialogue. The point isn't to convert, but to offer another lens, so that if someone wants to look deeper, the door is open.

In other words, this isn't the time to go full Q drop or down the abortion rabbit hole. Drip the truth like nectar. Just enough to spark something. Let them want more. Don't rob them of the dignity of discovering things for themselves.

Yes, I've been burned. Called crazy. Mocked. Dismissed. The funny thing is, though, most of what I said back then is coming true now. Those same people? Quiet. Watching. Recalculating. This is how it works.

If you've been scorched, good. Welcome to the front lines.

## Staying Ignited 1: Keep Emotions Out of It

Now for another hard-earned truth: the second you get emotional, you lose your power.

This isn't about you being right. This is about truth breaking chains. The second you take things personally, you shrink into their game. The rebel doesn't play by those rules.

Stay cool. Stay sharp. Stay sovereign.

You don't need everyone to agree. You just need to be the frequency. One grounded conversation can ripple across timelines. One spark. One heart. That's all it takes.

## Staying Ignited 2: Back Off from Groupthink

You'll know it when you hear it: the lifeless repetition of media mantras, the smug recantation of "listen to the science," the automated shutdown when things get uncomfortable.

It's important to remember that this is their programming talking.

Don't waste your breath arguing with a closed loop. If someone is running scripts, let them. It's not your job to override the code. Your job is to protect your energy and know when to disengage.

Discernment is your greatest weapon.

## Staying Ignited 3: Listen

This part's underrated. Actually listen.

Not to agree, necessarily, but to understand. Why? Because their resistance teaches you where the programming lives. Their arguments reveal the exact pressure points the system installed. When you listen without reacting, you learn how to address it.

Also? Listening shows strength. It builds trust. It sets you apart.

When they talk, take mental notes. Not to win the debate—but to understand the war.

## Staying Ignited 4: Sidestep Tricks

They will come at you. Not out of malice, but because they don't know any better. The system trained them to do this. Emotional baiting, faulty logic, hearsay dressed up as fact, gaslighting, ridicule, and every psychological defense in the book may come out to play.

Let them. You? You don't flinch.

Don't stoop. Don't retaliate. Don't explain yourself to death. Just stand there—rooted, calm, wide awake. Make your presence the disrupter.

You don't need to prove a damn thing. You're not auditioning. You're not defending. You're here to remind them—without saying a word—that there is another way.

If you choose to speak, let it be simple, steady, and strong:

"I've done my own thinking. This isn't blind belief—it's the result of a lot of digging, a lot of sifting, and a lot of unlearning. I'm not here to convince you. However, if you ever want to talk about it, I'm open."

Then step back. Let the seed root. Let it be.

Most of all—keep being who you are. Loudly. Quietly. Unapologetically. Authentically.

Because sometimes the most radical thing you can do is simply not back down.


**Staying Ignited 5: Purge Your Limiting Beliefs**

Let's get brutally honest. How can you call out other people's programming—their blind spots, their refusal to see the truth—if you're still quietly shackled by your own?

That's the unseen layer of rebellion. It's not just about expunging the lies outside you. It's about hunting down the ones that still live inside.

Limiting beliefs don't always scream. Sometimes they whisper. "I can't do this." "If I speak up, I'll lose everything." "If I don't get my kid into the right school, their life will collapse." It's the domino delusion—the kind of fear programming that makes you plan your entire life around imagined disasters.

What looks like intelligence is indoctrination.

We weren't meant to live in boxes. Those boxes? They're held shut by fear.

One of the early truth-tellers in this modern disclosure wave, David Icke, said it best: "the opposite of fear is unconditional love." At first, that might sound vague. However, it's vibrational law. Fear is a low, dense frequency. Love—real, unconditional, frequency-splitting love—is the highest in the cosmos.

The only thing that might rival it? Authenticity. When those two meet you become unstoppable.

Those who've made contact with off-planet intelligences—yes, we're going there—report that these beings are fascinated by the human capacity to feel love. It's wild to them. We carry a frequency they don't fully understand.

Now for the catch: high and low frequencies cannot coexist in the same body for long. One will dominate. One will dissolve the other.

The question becomes: Which are you choosing to run on?

## Staying Ignited 6: Love Yourself

Start here. Not with loving the world. Not with healing humanity. With loving yourself. Fiercely. Unconditionally. Without apologies.

Because fear, at its core, is a side effect of disconnection from self.

It's rooted in the most insidious belief of all—that you are not capable, not worthy, not enough, not divinely aligned and protected. That something out there has authority over you.

Lies. All of it.

You are a multidimensional being with the capacity to heal, lead, shift timelines, and reroute entire narratives. Until you remember that, you're easy prey.

Now think about the rest of the low-vibe emotional soup: hatred, rage, jealousy, resentment. These don't just poison the collective—they eat you from the inside. They break down your soul's immune system. They feed the parasitic matrix that survives off your pain.

Want to stop feeding the dark? Start choosing love.

Next time someone triggers you, picture them inside a giant, absurdly pink fuzzy heart. Add unicorns. Fluffy clouds. Whatever works. Don't do it for them. Do it to reclaim your power.

People are wounded. Most are walking around in pain they can't articulate. Maybe what they need most is someone who refuses to play the same old game. Maybe what they need is you—fully awake, radically clear, and not backing down from love.

## Staying Ignited 7: Be Aware of Indoctrination

It's everywhere. In every ad, every school board meeting, every influencer post pretending to be "authentic." Indoctrination is the air we've been breathing since birth.

Now you know. You don't get to pretend you don't.

You don't get to say, "Well, everyone else is doing it," and call that discernment. You don't get to shrug off your role in protecting your kids from toxic culture and then wonder why they're anxious, confused, or desperate for approval.

Awareness is your weapon. Use it.

Say no to the casual poison. Monitor what your kids consume—not from fear, but from leadership. Explain what's wrong, why it's wrong, and how to see through it. That builds trust. That builds discernment. That builds real connection.

Let's try a real-world example: a father found out his eleven-year-old daughter was reading a best-selling YA series that ended with a teen pregnancy. She was on the final chapter when he stepped in and removed the book. She was furious—until he explained why. He wasn't trying to control her. He was trying to protect her mind.

He let her finish that last chapter. As for the next book? She'd wait. A few years. She agreed.

That's good parenting. Kids—especially these old-soul kids being born now—want that kind of clarity. They're relieved when someone draws a line and says, "This isn't for you yet."

At ten, eleven, twelve years old—why should they be wrestling with adult-level themes like sex, trauma, and betrayal?

Answer: they shouldn't. Full stop.

They don't need a faster track to adulthood. They need protection. They need truth. Most of all—they need you to wake up to the culture they're being steeped in before it steals the best parts of them.

Instead, rebel. Say no. Set the boundaries. Be the adult they remember wasn't afraid to lead.

## Staying Ignited 8: Embrace Direct Connection

This one's going to rattle a few cages, but we're not here to stay safe.

If you've made it this far in the book, you've already unhooked from the comfort of the mainstream. Let's cut straight to it: Religion was designed to divide and disempower. Period.

We are not meant to be sinners groveling for forgiveness. We are meant to be directly connected to Source—not through intermediaries, not through guilt, and certainly not through fear.

Look at history with clear eyes. Many of the greatest atrocities perpetrated on this planet were done in the name of religion: the Inquisition, the Crusades, St. Bartholomew's Day massacre, the Holocaust, the Armenian genocide, the Ottoman-Byzantine wars, the Serbo-Croatian exterminations. The list is long, and many chapters have been scrubbed from public knowledge.

The truth echoes through the eons: the hands that preached peace often wielded the sword.

This is not an attack on one religion. Christianity, Islam, Judaism—all have blood on their hands. The Ottoman Empire rivaled ancient

Rome in its brutality. No doctrine is innocent when it becomes a weapon of control. The moment a faith appoints itself as gatekeeper to the highest planes, it becomes a cage.

Let's face the truth: you don't need anyone to tell you how to find God. You don't need doctrines. You don't need rituals. You don't need a priest, a pastor, a rabbi, or a sheikh. You don't need to kneel in public shame or confess your soul to a human dressed in sacred robes.

Your soul is your business. Your redemption, your healing, your truth—it's between you and Source. No middleman required.

Would you hand your child over to strangers and let them raise them as they see fit? We've already done this in schools. Would you do the same with your spiritual essence?

Religions, for all their community and ceremony, were engineered to suppress your power and insert a hierarchy between you and the Creator. You were never meant to be small. You were never meant to be arbitrarily obedient, caged, and ashamed.

You were meant to remember that the kingdom of heaven is within you.

Yes—churches, shrines, mosques and synagogues offer warmth, ritual, and a sense of belonging. There's beauty in shared prayer and communal reverence. On the other hand, when you surrender your discernment to another, when you outsource your God-connection, you become complicit in the crimes committed under that banner.

The only true path to your divinity is through authenticity and unconditional love. Follow the Golden Rule, and do no harm. That's it. No dogma required.

## Staying Ignited 9: Love Right Side Up

From the time you're old enough to date, the programming kicks in: find someone with money. Looks. Social clout. A good provider. A respectable partner. Someone you can "build a life with."

It's not just upside down. It's sabotage.

Because what if the real purpose of love wasn't to look good on paper—but to ignite your soul?

What if love wasn't about finding the safest option—but about risking everything for something real?

We've been conditioned to chase the checklist: the career, the status, the stable future. What we need—what our souls need—is a partner who meets us in truth. Someone who's brave enough to walk the path of awakening with us. Someone whose heart pulses in sync with ours, even when the world makes no sense.

Not someone who plays the role of "provider" while their spirit is numb. Not someone who ticks the boxes but leaves you starving for intimacy. Not someone whose love depends on whether you're performing acceptably in the matrix.

No. What we need is divine union—the merging of two souls willing to evolve, stretch, grieve, burn, and rise together. A partner who's not afraid of the shadows. Who sees your fire and says: Let's go higher.

If your goals are still defined by external validation—wealth, beauty, social alignment—you may miss the one who was meant for you. You may overlook the soul who would walk beside you in purpose, in passion, in wild, untamed love.

Ask yourself: What are you really looking for?

Are you trying to secure status, or ignite a frequency?

Because when two souls come together in true resonance—unpolished, unfiltered, and unafraid—everything becomes possible.

Love can rewrite timelines. It can dissolve lifetimes of fear. It can bring heaven down to earth.

It can do this only if you have the courage to seek the real thing.

## Staying Ignited 10: Know that you are Divine

At the root of every limiting belief—whether it's societal, religious, or personal—is fear. At the root of fear is disconnection.

Disconnection from self. From Source. From truth. From love.

## UNLEASHING THE REBEL WITHIN

We've been programmed to chase false authority, surrender our infinite birthright, and seek approval from institutions and figures who do not know us, do not care for us, and do not speak for the Creator.

You are not broken. You are not separate from God. You are not a sinner in need of saving. You are a spark of infinite love, here to reclaim your wholeness.

When you strip away the rituals, the dogma, the indoctrination—what remains?

Love.

Not the conditional love we've been sold. Not the performance-based love that demands you shrink to fit in. The kind of love that remembers who you are, and asks nothing in return except that you show up in truth.

This kind of love is revolutionary. It dissolves programming. It dissolves fear. It dismantles the illusion of unworthiness and separation. It doesn't require a priest or a temple or a rulebook. It lives in your breath, your body, and your being.

When you begin to see yourself clearly—truly see—you stop asking for permission to be whole. You stop fearing judgment. You stop needing validation. Because you know.

You know you are eternal and sovereign. You know you are love. You know your freedom is not something that can be given or taken—it is your birthright.

When you walk through this world with that kind of knowing, everything begins to change. The people who once ignored you start to listen. The ones who tried to gaslight you begin to question themselves. The ones who felt lost may find light through you—not because you preached to them, but because you stood in your truth.

So, love yourself—not as a strategy, or as a slogan, but as a sacred act of rebellion.

Love yourself because they told you not to.

Love yourself because the system profits from your doubt.

## Lane Keller

Love yourself because you are the only one who can remember who you were before the programming began.

Then love others. Not blindly. Not passively. Instead, do it from that same deep place of knowing.

Because the world doesn't need more tolerance. It needs more truth. It needs more rebels rooted in love.

That's how we dismantle the matrix. That's how we change the game.

That's how we come home.

## Chapter 17
# Electromagnetic Reality

An undercurrent of dark worship has infiltrated our planet and is vying for control of our lives—and most people are still too lulled by distraction to see it. I personally don't know if the pitchfork-wielding guy in red exists, or if that image was just another cartoon designed to keep us from noticing the real danger. What does exist—provably, traceably, and pervasively—is a contingent of individuals who pursue an antihuman agenda in the dark one's name. Whether these individuals are fully human or something else entirely—reptoid, hybrid, bloodline, or possessed—is almost beside the point. What matters is this: a portion of the population is actively perpetuating a form of evil so sickening, so twisted, and so grotesque that most people can't even fathom it. That disbelief is the dark side's greatest shield.

These individuals will do anything—anything—for power. For youth. For greed. For access. For control. For energy. For status. For things they think they value. These things come at a staggering cost: the cost of humanity itself. The sacrifice of innocence is the highest currency in their world. They are feeding off what's pure in order to gain more of what's perverse. This isn't metaphor or theory. It's not some ancient myth you can brush off. It's happening right now—and it's structured, protected, and sustained through systems of blackmail, coercion, and global complicity.

Whether the red guy, or his son, or the goat-headed Baph guy exists as an entity is secondary. The fact that there are people—celebrities, elites, financiers, politicians, and even educators and influencers—who practice sex magick, ritual abuse, and sacrificial rites involving children is what we must confront. Because it does exist. It will continue unless enough of us stop looking away and start naming it.

If you want to go deeper on this, I point to a docuseries I produced with LifeSource called *Alice in Pedoland*. It's available on Rumble, and you'll find the links at LifeSource.global and in the back of this book. I warn you—it doesn't tiptoe or sugarcoat. However, it does guide you gently through the darkness so you can face it head-on. Because that's the only way we'll ever break it.

The depths to which the dark ones go can be beyond human comprehension. Yet, this is the force that must be met. If we're serious about reclaiming this world, then we must become the kind of beings who aren't afraid to look the darkness straight in the eye and command: "Not on my watch."


### What Are You in Service To?

Jane: It's been suggested that we're looking at 10 to 35% of individuals who worship the dark. A football team took a photo with us in Australia. It was the Aussie Rules grand finals, and three guys at the front of the photo were doing some sort of Illuminati symbolism with their hands. It was obvious. I have worked in elite sports for 24 years. Some of my family's best friends are retired elite athletes. My daughter is an elite pro athlete. So, I've been around that environment a lot. It's clear to me that there are athletes who are part of the satanic worshipping sect. How did those three in the photo get selected, recruited, brainwashed, manipulated or blackmailed into participating? Why those three and why not the three next to them? This is where I ask, how low down does this go? Because it's in my everyday circle.

Lane: Does this concern you, it being so close?

Jane: It doesn't scare me because we are powerful. It's not an issue. But it interests me. There's a lot of blackmail, obviously. There's a lot of coercion to go into the cults that do evil stuff.

Lane: Satanism is, in my opinion, directly connected to hedonism. As we get into a more hedonistic society, the practice of Satanism becomes the quest for the unbridled power they think they can acquire from practicing the occult. This goes back to the black wizard, Alistair Crowley and his teachings. His famous saying is "do as thou wilt," which means do as you will without repercussions or any morality other than to do what makes you feel good. There's no moral high ground except to serve yourself and whomever you are worshipping in evil's name.

As long as you're doing what you want to do without concern of the harm you are doing to others, or even yourself, you are in service to the dark. To me, those things are grossly connected. Look at all the kids who are being sucked into this because yes, God has left the building, so to speak, with prayer and unconditional love drummed out of daily life. Our motto in America used to be In God We Trust. Now we trust no one.

Jane: Australia was actually founded as an atheistic country. We were a prison cult, an uncivilized outpost that seemed free but which has actually been under the control of tyrants administering fear. We're seeing the repercussions of that now. One of the reasons we had the most people compliant during Covid was because of fear—fear of death, fear of not following the rules, fear of what the authorities could do to you. There is no spirituality here.

## Addressing Evil

Jane: How as a human being do you begin to address this evil?

When reacting to this how about saying to yourself, are you coming from fear or are you coming from love?

Lane: That saying doesn't necessarily resonate with me because I don't understand it on an emotional level. I don't comprehend it because I'm always coming from love. I've left fear so far behind I can no longer grasp the feeling. For me personally, I say, when you feel fear, you're creating emotional food for them. This is what they want. This is what they feed on. They love when you're distressed or behaving in a hateful way because you are feeding them. You're adding energy to their power grid.

Why would anyone feel hatred? Even in the darkest moments of your life, when people have done you wrong, you shouldn't hate. You might slip and say, I hate this or that, but you shouldn't feel it. The dark side loves that. They want us to hate each other. Good, they think. They fight each other and not us. They don't have to lift a finger if they've got us warring with our neighbors, families, lovers, and selves.

To me the more you can go into, I am reluctant to repeat the cliched, "service to others," but the more you open your heart centers to understand the humanity around you and to allow the love energy to flow through you, to put yourself in others' circumstances and allow yourself to love them, even the most horrible creatures, the higher you will rise. It puts you in a higher state. You become untouchable. This is electromagnetic reality. A high frequency field simply repels parasites.

This goes back to creating your own reality—the reality your self creates at that level. We are not talking about addressing evil directly here, but how to rise above it, and to keep it from affecting you. Because at a certain frequency, darkness can't cling to you. It doesn't have the tools or the tether.

## Benevolent Action

Instead of saying service to others, let's say conduct benevolent action. Benevolent action is when you are making sure that every single thing you say and do is not hurtful to someone. Even better than not being hurtful is being helpful in some way. Maybe you're simply serving as a listening device. You know you're there to listen and lend a friendly ear in a supportive way. Maybe you're in a situation where you're being asked to give some direction and guidance.

You don't always know what the other person needs. Maybe they need you to make them understand their self-worth, what their unique skills as a human being are. As soon as you start on this, whoever you're talking to will stop and listen. They will become rapt as you identify the traits unique or wonderful in them. You focus on that, then from there, it blossoms.

You've just fed their soul a nutrient it may have been starving for decades.

Jane: You're talking about how to build a deeper connection to others which in turn wards off evil.

Lane: Yes. In some sense destroys it through starvation. Back to loosh—these negative emotions are not our own. When fear, depression, or rage, etc. are created, the dark side sits back and says, we did this, we created this!

The whole world is upside down. I think most people have realized that by now. The things that we should love and honor have been inverted, and everything that's been told to us is the opposite of truth. Once you realize the world is the opposite of what it should be, it clears up a lot. Understanding the truth of things is an enormous step to eradicating the evil that is all around us. Prayer helps, but sitting in a bubble does not. You're not here to transcend life—you're here to transform it.

## Untouchable by Design

To me, the more you open your heart center, the more you activate something unbreakable. It's not about being a martyr. It's about seeing others clearly, feeling their humanity, even when it's buried beneath layers of distortion. When you allow the current of love to move through you—not sentimental love, but a fierce, truth-based love—you begin to lift.

When you can put yourself in someone else's shoes, even someone who's behaved horribly, and choose to recognize their pain rather than reflect it back, you enter a higher state. You become harder to target. You become energetically untouchable.

This is what it means to rise above evil—not to confront it in hand-to-hand combat, but to make yourself invisible to its grip. To vibrate beyond its reach. That's what we mean when we say you're creating your own reality at a higher frequency—your rebel self starts constructing a reality where the dark can't succeed.

**Whack-a-Shadow**

The whole world is inverted. Everything we should cherish has been mocked or degraded. Everything they told us was "normal" is the very opposite of truth. When you understand that inversion—when it clicks—it changes the game. The fog clears. Truth, in itself, is a form of protection. Understanding is a form of power.

Jane: When you are triggered or are feeling that sadness, depression, anger or frustration—in other words, lower-level emotions—how do you throw them off? How do you raise your vibration?

Lane: Instead of trying to force a higher vibration, I look at it like this: that higher vibration is the natural result of doing the deeper work. It's the byproduct. A damn good byproduct.

But there's a trick. Follow your triggers. Every one of them is a breadcrumb to something hidden. The path to self-realization and ascension runs straight through your pain points. The triggers are your curriculum.

They're fast, slippery, sneaky—like that arcade game where you whack moles with a mallet as they pop up. You think you're done with one and another shows up out of nowhere. Bam! Every time one rises, you follow and dispel it. That's the work.

Sadness. Frustration. Depression... They can all be flipped if you recognize them as messengers, not enemies.

Now, of course, I'm not talking about situations with biochemical imbalance. I'm not minimizing deep physiological conditions. I will say this—I've worked hard to support my system holistically. I don't have those imbalances. If someone does, it may not be easy at first. That's why I go into depth in the section on physical health—because your energetic clarity starts with your nervous system and your gut-brain axis. Remove what clouds your system. You have to work it through.

I don't get depressed anymore. Now, go back thirty years ago? That was another story. When I was being ignored, dismissed, rejected by publishers who wouldn't read my work, I spiraled. Every rejection letter hit like a stone. I would crawl into bed, pull the covers over my head, and disappear. Sometimes for five minutes. Sometimes for far longer.

Sleep was my secret weapon. It was my reset button. Shutting off my mind, even briefly, gave me a chance to bypass the mental loop and ask for clarity. I would call in Source. I'd surrender the noise. I swear, I could feel the presence of spirit teams whispering, You're fine. We've got you. Rest now. When you wake, it will be clear.

It was.

That process gifted me unshakable self-knowledge and authentic self-worth. Eventually, I no longer needed the world to validate me. I validated myself. I saw my own becoming. I wrote through it. I kept sharpening the blade until my words became unbreakable. That part of the process took years. Years of isolation, perseverance, and transformation of ego into self-esteem.

And... it made me.

Sadness, depression, frustration—none of them are pointless. They're invitations. They're signs pointing to what still needs integrating. The adage is true, despite how often it's misused: everything happens for a reason. The trick is to find the origin. Trace it to the source. Because once you do, you're no longer a prisoner to it. You're the one holding the map.

## The Covert Playlist

People in this movement often talk about frequency, and many send out energetic transmissions—sound baths, healing tones, intention-based music. I don't think there's anything wrong with broadcasting positive vibrations, especially when it's done with integrity and clarity. There's a line, though, that must not be crossed: manipulating frequencies or embedding subliminal messages without full disclosure.

That's programming, and it is a tactic of the cabal.

To do this without the listener's consent is a form of psychological warfare. It's brainwashing dressed up in spiritual drag. Doesn't matter if the intention is "love and light" or something nefarious—when you remove conscious awareness, you're tampering with an individual's right to self-determination. That's another form of control.

We've been subjected to this long enough. Frequency manipulation is one of their most insidious tools. The sickness of mind control has infected humanity through sound, language, media, and vibration for decades. It's been weaponized. The damage is deep.

As such, humanity is not operating at full free will capacity. Not even close. We're functioning under a dense fog of suggestion, coercion, and false narratives—programmed to accept illusion as truth. In my observation, we're at about four percent free will. That's it. The rest is conditioned behavior. Automated responses. False assumptions.

Now for some good news: when you start stripping away the layers—eliminating the lies, the trauma, the subliminals—your capacity for true choice explodes. You remember who you are. You remember what it feels like to decide from a place of alignment, not programming.

## The Setup Called Freedom

Free will cannot exist without full information. That's the core of consent. Without the truth, your "choice" isn't really a choice—it's a setup. That's why I'm relentless about getting to the bottom line. Truth isn't optional. It's foundational.

How can we operate with autonomy when we're flying through a thunderstorm at night, and the entire console board has gone dark? That's where most people are: navigating blind, trusting autopilot systems built by the very ones who disabled their instincts.

Jane: You've given your tacit agreement to something because you haven't explored it properly. You don't understand it, and you've given somebody else power over you, and that is unacceptable.

Lane: Completely unacceptable. It gets worse—because by doing this, you're not just compromising your own life. You're affecting your children's lives. Generational harm is being carried forward because of what we're too afraid, too busy, or too conditioned to see.

## Chapter 18
# Meeting the Monster

Triggers aren't random—they're signals. A trigger is any stimulus that jolts your nervous system, stirs a memory, or pulls you into a reaction you didn't consciously choose. It can be a sound, a smell, a phrase, an image, or even a passing look. Triggers are the nervous system's shorthand: messages rising from wounds, unprocessed grief, or deeper lessons asking to be seen.

Sometimes you can trace them easily. Sometimes they need meditation, patience, or guidance to decode. Other times they reveal themselves only after years—or even lifetimes. But nothing you experience is wasted. Every obstacle, every wound, every trigger is part of your path.

The shift comes when you stop seeing obstacles as detours and recognize them as the path itself. That's when frustration loosens its grip. What once felt like it was breaking you is revealed as the very thing forging you.

Sadness may be the hardest forge—especially in loss. Yet even here, you're not as alone as you've been led to believe. Death is not an ending; it's another veil in the great illusion. We've been taught otherwise—that separation is final—but that too is programming. The ones you've loved remain closer than you know, walking with you until you no longer need them. The veil is thinner than you've been told.

But here's the deeper truth: if triggers in your personal life can shape behavior, imagine what happens when they are designed, weaponized, and broadcast at scale. Trauma stops being personal and becomes political. What feels like chaos in your inner world has its mirror in the outer world. That larger pattern isn't coincidence. It's a program.

At the risk of this sounding like a sci-fi script, what follows is not fantasy but record. One of the government's darkest and most pervasive operations shows how trauma was weaponized, scaled, and woven into culture— in plain sight. I debated whether to omit this, but silence is complicity. To understand the manipulation we live under, we must see where it began.

## Weaponized Triggers

If triggers in your own life can carry hidden meaning, imagine what happens when triggers are engineered. That larger pattern is not accidental. It is what I call, The Program.

The Program is engineered triggering on a mass scale. What you experience personally—those jolts that stir old wounds or pull you into reactions—has been studied, mapped, and replicated by those who seek control. Trauma isn't just an unfortunate byproduct of life; it has been weaponized.

Through repetition of tragedy, shock imagery, and symbolic cues, the program fractures attention, manipulates emotion, and reshapes belief. Just as a single person can be broken into fragments, entire societies can be splintered—divided into identities, ideologies, and fears, each triggered on command.

This isn't theory. It's the continuation of MKUltra—the CIA's covert project of psychological torture, trauma research, and mind control. Officially shut down in the 1970s, but only in name, its methods never disappeared. Instead, they increased. The same techniques once used to fracture individuals through drugs, hypnosis, and sensory deprivation now appear in mass form through media cycles, staged crises, and cultural programming.

What MKUltra does to a single child—splintering them into alters, controlling them with cues—has been adapted for whole populations. Public tragedies, political theater, and media rituals serve as triggers. Symbols act like keys, unlocking predictable reactions. Entire nations are conditioned to obey, comply, or despair—without ever realizing they're being programmed.

**The Program**

MKUltra is a mind control program developed in the 1950s by the CIA, a program which ostensibly ended shortly thereafter. Instead, its use grew —not solely by the government, but through ritualistic practices performed by the so called "elite."

Its origins are rooted in Satanic Ritual Abuse (SRA)—black ops torture aimed at control, distortion, and the desecration of innocence. Built on experiments with drugs, hypnosis, sensory deprivation, and psychological manipulation, it lives on today in engineered, large-scale trauma events that shape the core of humanity.

World War II didn't just end with victory parades—it birthed the United Nations, the IMF, the World Bank: global institutions sold as guardians of peace, but designed to centralize power. 9/11 was the doorway to endless war abroad and total surveillance at home, with freedoms traded for the illusion of safety. The financial crash of 2008 initiated a transfer of wealth on a historic scale, bailing out elites while entire populations were chained to debt and dependence. COVID-19 wasn't merely a pandemic—it was the launchpad for medical mandates, digital health passes, and a culture of compliance so deep it rewired how people think about freedom itself. Step by step, each crisis has tightened the leash, breaking spirits, bending wills, and herding humanity into a system where obedience is survival.

## UNLEASHING THE REBEL WITHIN

The abuse endured by true MKUltra victims is beyond most people's imagination—and that's deliberate. Systematic torture begins before birth and continues through childhood and into adulthood, engineered to shatter the psyche and fracture the soul. What emerges is not wholeness but fragments: multiple identities, each carrying a different trauma, skillset, or trigger. The original self is pushed into the shadows, sometimes lost forever.

But this isn't only about individuals with imposed dissociative identity disorder. What happens in the laboratory of one mind becomes a template for mass society. Just as a victim is splintered into parts, entire populations are fractured—divided by propaganda, fear, and engineered crises. Just as one persona is triggered to obey, whole communities are triggered through shock events. What begins as torture in a secret chamber becomes social programming in the open world.

This is the larger operation: not just broken children or controlled celebrities, but a broken humanity—conditioned to live in fragments, to forget its wholeness, and to mistake obedience for survival.

The CIA and its networks provide handlers—lifelong overseers who pull strings, apply pressure, and deepen control. They can be family members, therapists, agents, or spouses. The rabbit hole is long and deep. It is brutal.

The truth? The victims are slaves—mind slaves, soul slaves—cut off from free will, authenticity, and the Infinite Divine, used until they're broken, then discarded.

It's generational. It's widespread, and it's real. Individual MKUltra survivors are speaking—through books, memoirs, documents, and social media. They name names. They reclaim stolen memories. Their stories are raw, shattering, but sacred in their courage.

You may not want to know what they have to say. But once you do, you cannot un-know it. That is the spark of rebellion—not just against a system, but against every lie it ever told you about power, innocence, freedom, and truth.

## State-Sanctioned Psych Warfare

MKUltra has created slaves in many forms, each fractured for a role. Programming is modular—a grotesque operating system running inside the human mind. Some alters are weaponized as spies, assassins, or soldiers. Some are politicians. Some are built for infiltration, blackmail, or seduction. The soul is treated as disposable.

One of the most notorious sub-programs, Beta—or Monarch programming—has produced decades of sex slaves. They become honeytraps, hyper-sexualized entertainers, and public icons. Marilyn Monroe remains the most famous presidential model: a manufactured honey pot, a cog in the system of control.

These same patterns bleed into mainstream culture. Satanic and symbolic programming is broadcast openly in music, film, sports, and celebrity life. Goat heads, one-eye symbols, checkerboards, and surrealist theatrics are not aesthetic—they are ritual signals. Black and white contrasts mirror the split mind. Distortion and dreamlike inversions train the masses to dissociate.

These aren't just set design choices or quirky fashion statements—they're triggers. Ritual signals function like code. When the viewer beholds them, the image bypasses logic and sinks into the subconscious. For the individually programmed, these symbols activate buried alters, summon behaviors, and reinforce obedience. For the collective, they serve to normalize darkness, to desensitize, to make the bizarre feel ordinary.

That's how ritual works: repetition trains the nervous system. A goat head here, a one-eye pose there, checkerboard floors, distorted theatrics—each one is a drip feed into the psyche. Over time, the signal doesn't need explanation. It becomes familiar, even alluring. The audience absorbs it without protest, carrying the programming forward. The power of ritual is not in the single image—but in the constant saturation that shapes what people accept as normal.

## The Programming

At its core, MKUltra is behavioral warfare. Trauma is the tool. The human blueprint is inverted: love is punished, cruelty rewarded, innocence destroyed. A child born of light is reshaped into a vessel of darkness.

When abuse becomes unbearable, the mind fractures. Alters emerge—hundreds if necessary—each compartmentalized, trained, and triggered by cues. A gesture, word, or symbol can summon them. The body becomes a puppet; the spirit is buried alive.

The same system is applied to humanity itself. The collective is fractured into tribes and identities, each one conditioned by trauma events—wars, terror attacks, financial collapses, pandemics. Symbols and slogans become triggers. Media spectacles summon fear or rage on command. Just as an individual alter can be deployed for obedience, entire populations can be activated, divided, and controlled.

The breaking of one child becomes the template for the breaking of the many. What is stolen at the personal level—love, trust, instinct—is stolen at scale. What replaces it is the same: a world where obedience and submission are sold as safety, and where the human spirit is buried beneath layers of programming.

## How This Affects You

You may think this doesn't touch your life. You may believe it belongs only to victims in shadowed rooms or names whispered in survivor accounts. But the blueprint has been magnified. What was once hidden in labs and black sites now plays out in the open, broadcast across screens and headlines.

Every mass tragedy is not only an event but a trigger, aimed straight at the collective nervous system. Shock drops your defenses.

Grief cracks you open. In that raw space, new fears slip in, and with it new systems of control.

Your empathy—your greatest strength—is also your greatest vulnerability. They weaponize it. They don't just want your tears. They want your compliance. They want your consent to systems you would never accept in the calm light of day.

The answer is not to shut down or harden your heart. It's to reclaim your emotional authority. Feel everything—without handing over your discernment. Grieve, but don't surrender. Question every narrative that demands despair. Refuse rage.

Every time you choose clarity over confusion, sovereignty over programming, you weaken the spell. You stop being triggered. You stop being used. And in that moment, you reclaim what was never theirs to take: your sovereign, untouchable human spirit.

## Chapter 19
# The War for Your Heart

Living in an inversion of that which grows the human spirit—and instead being funneled into reactive, fear-based states—keeps us trapped in dense, 3D vibration. That's the point of the trap. To keep you emotionally triggered. Disoriented. Despairing. Because when you're in that state, you stop creating your reality—and start reacting to theirs.

How do you escape this matrix when the world around you seems to be seething with horrors beyond comprehension? How do you avoid falling into despair when evil parades itself proudly in front of your face?

It starts with knowing this: the natural state of humanity is not war, violence, or hatred. We've been lied to.

Left to our own devices, we love each other. We seek connection. We partner up, we make families, we share food, we look after the neighborhood kids whether they're ours or not. Human nature, when uncorrupted, is deeply communal and intrinsically good. That's why we have to be manipulated so viciously—because without manipulation, the plan falls apart.

Every division we've experienced, every bloodshed, every "us vs.

them" conflict has been engineered. We are continuously herded into artificial battles by forces that benefit from chaos. The formula is always the same: incite emotion, inflame identity, divide the people, harvest the fear.

## **Weaponized Compassion**

To see through the trap, sometimes we have to rewind the tape. You can't move forward in an unprogrammed way unless you're willing to admit how badly you've been lied to.

Let's take the Israeli-Palestinian conflict. This isn't a statement of sides—it's a statement of the pattern. It's a headline war. A war staged in pixels, loops, and tweets. One minute, we're told to pick a side. The next, we're hit with dead children, burning cities, terrified mothers. Who benefits? Who profits? The media-industrial complex is never neutral. It's the biggest war machine of them all.

They've been playing this game for decades—whipping up moral outrage, dangling human suffering to justify mass-scale military action. Remember Nayirah al-Ṣabaḥ? This is the Kuwaiti girl who claimed Iraqi soldiers were yanking babies out of incubators. That one speech helped ignite the Gulf War. Later it was revealed she was the Kuwaiti ambassador's daughter—scripted, staged, and coached for the camera. Yet by the time the truth came out, the bombs had fallen. The damage was done. Public opinion had been hijacked. That's how the PSYOP works.

Children have always been their favorite bait. World wars, foreign invasions—the manufactured climate agenda with the infamous Greta Thunberg—none of it gains traction without child imagery to soften your heart and open the gates of consent. Watch the film *Wag the Dog*—not as satire, but as disclosure. It's a blueprint.

Their ritual always ends the same way: bloodshed. Carnage. Trauma on loop. Why? Because this is an energetic war. They feed on loosh. They want your horror, your sorrow, and your grief. The more your frequency drops, the more they have to feast on.

By now we should all understand: the lower our vibration, the more fuel they harvest. The way out isn't just resistance—it's refusal. A total refusal to feed the beast with our pain.

When you see those headlines, those explosions, those sobbing children, remember: your vibration is a weapon. Your discernment is a shield. Your refusal to collapse into fear is a rebellion in and of itself.

Once mass fear was generated through the threat of nuclear war. Now new disasters are in motion. Wildfires rage across regions that were not fire-prone. Rivers suddenly swell into inland tsunamis. Armed combatants, disguised as migrants, hide in urban neighborhoods. Commercial planes fall from the sky—old parts, overlooked warnings, and a media that moves on in hours. Refineries explode. Freight trains derail, spilling chemicals into water supplies. City grids flicker and fail. Through it all, the media spins its web: distraction, distortion, division. The fear is curated. The panic is manufactured. The moment you stop asking why, you've taken the bait.

What they want is panic. Reactive rage. Tribal violence. What we must offer instead is calm, conscious rebellion. Take action. Build community. Train your body. Prepare. Do it without fear. That's how we win this war—by refusing to become its pawns.

**Trust the Vibe, Not the Spin**

While debates and dialogue might nudge us toward truth, they rarely shatter illusions. For that, we need something deeper. Something soul-sourced.

Energetic leaning is a skill—one few of us were taught. It's when you stop outsourcing your discernment to headlines, politicians, or influencers, and start listening to your inner barometer. It's when you learn to trust your instincts without apology.

This is the rebel's gift: the ability to lean into a situation and feel the signal behind the noise. To do that, you must first silence the static.

That means cutting through the emotional fog, the propaganda, and most of all—the projections of others. Even their good intentions can pull you off course. You must anchor into stillness. Pull back from the chaos and enter neutrality. Let go of needing the world to confirm what you already sense. Step into your own knowing.

That's not easy when the media floods your screen with carnage, when mobs are shouting, when death threats fly like confetti and everyone has a flag in one hand and a photo of a dead grandmother in the other. It's not easy to stay unaffected in the face of that kind of emotional drama.

Nonetheless, that is exactly what is being asked of you.

You must master the art of sacred detachment—not because you don't care, but because you care so much, you refuse to let your heart be hijacked.

You are not obligated to feel what they tell you to feel. You are not required to suffer on demand. Your compassion is not a leash.

Your frequency is yours—and it's your responsibility to protect it.

## Refuse to Play

As the chaos intensifies, we're not just being attacked—we're being challenged. Provoked. Called up. The squeeze is on, and every event, every distortion, every fabricated crisis is a test of your discernment and a demand for your evolution.

The timelines are compressing. The lies are louder. The karmic backlash is coming on more quickly than ever before. At times this may seem like punishment, but in face it's opportunity. It's the soul's forge.

Let's go back to a historic example: the war in Yugoslavia. Most people don't understand what happened there. For those who lived it —or studied it honestly—it serves as one of the most obvious plays in the globalist handbook.

## UNLEASHING THE REBEL WITHIN

How does it work? If you're a global puppet-master and you know a certain people were nearly annihilated by a fascist regime a few decades ago, all you have to do is whisper into old wounds. Stoke the pain. Poke the memory. Dangle just enough fear to reactivate generational trauma—and boom. You've awakened the fire.

Suddenly, the targeted group—gripped by ancestral memory and desperate to survive—lashes out. The media seizes it, spins it, reframes it. Now these people are the aggressors. Cue moral condemnation. Cue military response. Bombings. Airstrikes. Occupation. The pattern repeats.

From the Balkans to the Middle East, from Central Africa to Southeast Asia—the playbook stays the same. You provoke, then you blame. You inflame, then you invade. You break the will of a sovereign people. You loot their land—rich in oil, lithium, gas, water, ports, sacred ground. You install puppets. You sign reconstruction contracts. You call it peacekeeping.

Just like that—mission accomplished.

It's always the same war. Just a new border. A new flag. A new lie.

Then? Mass migration. Wide open borders. Refugee floods. These aren't your tired, poor, huddled masses yearning to breathe free. These have been largely foreign fighting-age men, programmed with resentment and primed to detonate. Many of them hate the countries they've entered. Why wouldn't they? They've been conditioned to. They weren't invited to assimilate—they were shipped in to destabilize. The war isn't over there any longer. It's here.

The radical act is this: step back. Zoom out. Peel yourself off the emotional wall and reclaim your objectivity. That's where the power lives.

It takes courage to unplug from propaganda, to ask yourself hard questions, and to admit that both sides of a conflict are controlled. That's the level of lucidity we need now—not to numb ourselves, but to see clearly. Until we do, we will continue to be played.

We are members of the same human family—deliberately fractured by centuries of divide-and-conquer programming. The system is global. The lies are old. Yet so is our spirit. We've got to remember that.

We're at a precipice. A razor's edge. If we don't stand together now—as a species, not as tribes, not as flags—then we will fall apart together.

## Break that Snooze Button

Where does that leave us?

Right here at the crossroads. With one choice: rise or repeat. That's it. No middle ground. No pause button. No more stalling.

You're being asked to evolve into the most crystalline, courageous version of yourself. You're being asked to stop giving your power to fear. To stop identifying with your programming and pretending you're small.

Why is it all getting worse? Why is the pain and chaos amplifying?

Because the alarm clock is going off. You're being shaken awake—spiritually, emotionally, energetically. It's time to become who you came here to be. Not next year. Not when things calm down. Now.

If you meet the lesson—right here, right now—it dissolves. The karmic load lifts. The storm passes. What if you ignore it, defer it, resist it? The lesson gets louder. Sharper. More brutal. While it sounds cruel, it is in actuality the law of soul evolution. Refuse to grow, and the pressure cooker will crank until you crack.

Will we make it? Depends on who you mean by "we."

Some of us will. Some won't. That's the split.

I don't know if everyone is going to awaken. I don't know if everyone will choose clarity over comfort, or courage over obedience. What I do know is this: the ones who rise will carry the next, higher wave of reality within them.

For those who won't? The lessons will keep coming—harder and faster—until something finally breaks through.

# UNLEASHING THE REBEL WITHIN

Better that it be your illusions and not your spirit.

## Mind the Minefield

Respect the laws of karma. We've talked about this—karma isn't punishment. It's a mirror. If you don't look into things and learn from what's staring back at you, it's going to hit harder. Why? Because you're meant to evolve. You're meant to break through—not stall out. The system knows this.

That's why it throws candy-coated grenades at you like power, money, greed, and ego. The need to be right. The thrill of outrage. The seduction of identity politics. These are not harmless distractions—they're weapons of spiritual suppression.

So is war. So is hating your neighbor. That's one of the most indicative traps of all. If you find yourself despising the guy across the street because of what channel he watches or who he voted for, congratulations: the program has succeeded.

The real work? Sidestep the trap and grow anyway.

Jane: Both sides of the camp have fallen hook, line, and sinker for the divide-and-conquer trap. They've walked right into it, and now they're busy feeding the fire. The dark side knows exactly what triggers each culture. They've studied us. Now they're using what they've learned.

Lane: Exactly. They know how to push just the right buttons to get us attacking one another like wind-up toys.

Jane: Because they created the program. They wrote the script.

Lane: That script is designed to override our natural instinct—which is to love. That's the truth. We love each other. Left alone, without propaganda, without engineered fear, we do love each other. They had to write a whole multi-generational operating system to convince us otherwise.

Jane: Because their game is to project their own darkness onto us. To trick us into mirroring it back and then call it "human nature." That's inversion, not human nature.

Lane: It's the Hitler argument. Some people say he triggered rapid-fire spiritual growth and the chance to burn through karma at warp speed. I don't know if that's true, but I do know this: in every manufactured catastrophe you'll find both devastation and awakening. It's all in how you respond.

Jane: Right. It's about contrast. Without contrast, there's no growth. No edge. No pressure. Just spiritual couch potatoes on a mountaintop eating mung beans while watching the sunrise. That's not why we came.

We came here to experience vibrational contrast so we could rise into conscious awareness—not check out. Not float above it all.

Lane: We also came to grow into our oneness with creation, and the Creator—whatever name you give it. We had to do it from the mud. From the mess. That's where real evolution happens.

Jane: You can't evolve without emotion. Without an emotional barometer. You need to feel your way through the distortion. That's how you develop discernment. Through observation of what is.

Lane: Because we do create our own reality. That's not some airy-fairy spiritual slogan. That's a law. Here's the mind-bender: there are infinite realities. That can be a little overwhelming at first.

It used to confuse me too. But now? I've seen too much. I've manifested too many things. I know reality is fluid, and I know we're active participants in shaping it.

Jane: The challenge is, what happens when you're creating peace and clarity—and someone else is creating carnage?

Lane: Exactly. What if my neighbor is slaughtered? Suddenly I am part of that reality. Whether I like it or not, I'm in it. The only question is: How am I going to show up?

Jane: From love or from fear? Because anger's okay. It's part of the human experience. But it can't own you.

Lane: Right. You move through it. Let it give rise to awareness. To new choices. To real action—not just performative rage.

Jane: That's how it works. You feel it, you face it, and then you move differently—in yourself, in your family, in your community. It ripples outward.

Lane: So, the "reality" isn't just what's happening around you. It's how you respond to what's happening. That's the real test.

Jane: That is reality. Perfectly said.

Lane: Sometimes the most radical thing you can do is refuse to participate in their game. Refuse to feed the monster. Just don't plug in to the garbage.

Jane: That's what triggered me at the start of 2020. A lot of spiritual people I knew just checked out. "It's all an illusion," they said. Meanwhile, I was fighting an energetic war 24/7—and they were sipping lattes by the beach.

Lane: Now we see, there are many roles. Some people are holding a peaceful frequency. But others? They're using that as an excuse to avoid the work.

Jane: They're laying grids, yes. They're holding space. Others are spiritually bypassing because they don't want to face their own fear.

Lane: It comes back to choice. To courage. You can't coast on past lives or good vibes anymore. You've got to choose your role.

Jane: I had to accept that—not everyone's going to be a warrior. I didn't want their lectures either. Not when they weren't in the arena.

Lane: The arena is here now. This isn't theoretical anymore. It's not a book club. It's the frontline of human evolution.


## Karma Going Viral

COVID blew the lid off. It was a global Rorschach test. A karmic accelerator. Like every other mass trauma event, it exposed who was awake and who was still sleepwalking.

For some, it was a soft nudge. For others, a spiritual gut punch. For many, it was a full-on existential reckoning. The ones who refused to see it? They felt the ground shift under them.

Because the world they thought was solid—safe, orderly, and

predictable—started cracking. That's karma. That's what happens when truth comes knocking and you pretend not to be home.

Go back to the American Revolution. Speak out and you risked your life. Same thing now. If you're truly in the fight for humanity's freedom, then you've already had to answer this: Are you willing to risk everything?

A lot of us already have. That's what it takes. Not just bumper-sticker activism. Real stakes. Even young parents with kids—especially them—need to find the moral courage to stand up and raise hell when things are wrong. You have to choose your role.

Jane: That's what I keep saying. Everyone can step up—but not everyone has to be a warrior on camera. You don't have to lead the charge.

Lane: You don't have to be one of the doctors giving up their license to tell the truth. You don't have to be a whistleblower risking assassination. You don't have to be a firebrand. But you do have to choose.

Sitting on the sidelines sipping oat milk while tyranny burns through your neighborhood? Not enough. We should all have metaphorical pitchforks in our hands by now.

These people who have been in power? They're not governors. They're invaders. This has been occupation. Unless we stop them, it's going to get a hell of a lot worse. The window's closing.

Yes, this is war. Not just spiritual. Physical, energetic and total.

Most of the world is occupied. You think your country's safe? Think again. The system that owns you is invisible—but it's everywhere.

The crux is that these aren't just bad people. They're not even people anymore. Maybe they were, once. They've long since severed their link to humanity, to Source, to soul. They are husks. Predators. They will not stop unless we stop them.

## Chapter 20
# The Consent Loophole

Many of us now know that those working in the shadows —the ones running the old systems—have made an agreement. It's a cosmic loophole they exploit: they believe they're allowed to inflict their chaos as long as they tell us what they're doing. If they disclose it—even symbolically—they think it lessens their karmic debt.

That's why they hide everything in plain sight.

**The Tell-You-First Game**

They slide news of their coming actions into cartoons, movies and headlines. They cloak it in irony and dismissiveness so that we laugh it off. Still, the disclosure is there, and in their twisted worldview, our silence equals consent.

That's why they love predictive programming. Shows like *The Simpsons* have forecast real-world events with stunning precision for years—not because the writer is a prophetic genius, but because it's strategy. Matt Groening, *The Simpsons* creator, is a multi-millionaire insider worth over $500 million, and he's deeply tied to Hollywood's inner sanctum.

The *Tell You First* game goes deep. Authors like Aldous Huxley and his protégé, George Orwell didn't just imagine dystopia—they reported it. They were part of the Fabian Society, a group that mingled with the architects of the coming totalitarian world. What they wrote —*Brave New World,* and *1984*—wasn't fiction. They were blueprints.

The notorious *Illuminati Card Game* leaked operational plans. What looked like abstract satire turned out to be a coded dossier of future events. Those creators weren't clairvoyant—they were informed. Their cards tell a story of the world we now live in.

What does that mean for us?

It means if we don't say no—if we don't make noise—they count it as yes.

Say it out loud: I DO NOT CONSENT. Say it with force, with clarity, with command.

I do not consent to anything done to me or my loved ones without full knowledge, memory, and my explicit permission.

Not in this life or any other.

Consent isn't a checkbox. It's your spiritual firewall. You must stay alert, because they count your silence as surrender.

## The Language Heist

Now let's talk about language. This one's slippery, because it's been weaponized from both ends. Some say that proper grammar and articulate speech are signs of elitism. That's another inversion. They want you unable to express yourself. They want you stumbling through your limited vocabulary, unable to define or defend your reality. They want you linguistically neutered—disarmed before the fight even begins.

That's the opposite of progress.

What does a society sound like when it loses the power of language? Like a caveman grunt. Like mass confusion. Like gibberish masked as empowerment. When you strip a people of nuance, metaphor, and layered communication, you strip them of shared wisdom.

Instead, the more mastery we have over language—whatever our native tongue—the more precisely we can craft our reality. Words carry power. Intent rides on syllables. Thought takes shape in syntax.

Here's the paradox: the more advanced we become, the less we will rely on language at all.

As we evolve, we turn to telepathy in increasing amounts—in clear, complex transference of meaning, feeling, and memory at once. A single thought will carry volumes. We will talk without speaking. Understand without sound.

Until then, we must reclaim language from the ones who twisted it.

## The Spell of Spelling

Yes, language itself has been corrupted. That's the reality. Letters have been rearranged. Words have been inverted. Vibrational structures have been embedded with traps.

Take the word spelling. It's not just a word—it's a clue. A spell. To spell is to conjure, to encode. Letter placement is ritual. Syntax is incantation. That's how deep it goes.

The dark cabal understands this, which is why they've spent centuries degrading language, promoting slang, and mocking eloquence. They want you incoherent. They want you forgetful. They want your words to betray you.

We combat this by reclaiming intention. We infuse every word we speak with purpose and clarity. No idle talk. No parroting of empty catchphrases. You speak with awareness, or you remain silent. That's the rebel's path.

## Decency Isn't Dead

It's not just language that's been inverted. So have manners, respect and human dignity. Holding a door open, helping someone with a bag, offering your seat—these aren't symbols of "toxic masculinity" or outdated etiquette. They are signals of human decency.

In this upside-down world, they've told us kindness is weakness. They've blurred chivalry with dominance. As a result, society crumbles—not because we've lost civility, but because we've been trained to mock it.

Let me be clear: the elite don't offer courtesy as a kindness—they perform it. It's theater. A mask. Their pleasantries are laced with deceit. That doesn't mean we abandon our standards. We reclaim them. We embody the real version. That's how we win.

Language, respect, frequency—these are tools. You either let them be used against you, or you learn to wield them with discernment.

## Reclaim What's Yours

The system has stolen more than our time and money. It's stolen our clarity. Our command of self. The only way to reclaim that is to self-educate—not through mainstream schooling, but through your own digging, and your own drive.

There are still ancient texts, PDFs, archives online. You'll find the Greeks, the mystics, the mystery schools, the original teachings. You have to look beneath the garbage. Yes, the language can be dense. Archaic. Even confusing.

Nonetheless, keep going. The wisdom is valuable. Once we no longer need the books, we'll begin to retrieve it directly from the ethers.

That's what happens when you rise. The truth doesn't just find you—you become the frequency that attracts it.

. . .

## Sleep Like a Rebel

There is much discussion these days about humanity evolving into crystalline bodies—higher-frequency forms that vibrate beyond the limitations of carbon-based density. Is that possible? I think so. It feels plausible, even probable. I won't claim certainty. What I do know is that we're experiencing waves of incoming energy that can either elevate or flatten us. Sometimes both.

Some of these energy surges feel like light-speed downloads. Others feel like a truck has hit you so hard you're barely able to crawl out of bed. That's the paradox of ascension: it can lift or wipe you depending on what you're integrating.

Jane: When I tap into your energy, I don't have any concerns for you. None at all. I say though, will you just eff-ing rest? That's what I get.

Lane: I'm challenging the narratives—the constant push, the program that says you must earn your rest, hustle to prove your worth. I'm asking if there's another way besides a nonstop outpouring of energy. Because this system glorifies burnout and calls it success.

Jane: You resting is bothering you because mentally you're feeling you're not achieving, not striving. We've got the world to save.

Lane: That's exactly it. I've got this to-do list that taunts me. It just sits there, unmoving, some monolithic sculpture of all the things I haven't done. So, I went back to this low-key exercise class. Nothing extreme. But there are times I can barely move my body. Everyone else is bouncing around, energized, glowing. I'm quietly thinking: Dear God, just get me horizontal. The fatigue comes in waves—cyclical and unpredictable. I'll be fine for a stretch, then boom—I'm wiped.

Jane: I've had a lot of periods like that over the years, a lot. I actually did a podcast on what we feel is laziness years ago. Everybody needs permission to be so called, lazy. Because again, that's just a program.

Lane: It's a brutal one. The programming around laziness is one of the deepest shame triggers in modern culture. What if that so-called laziness is actually something sacred?

Jane: The cohost on that particular show was a psychic medium. Her channeling on laziness said it has to do with spiritual connection, spending more time on rest, giving ourselves permission to stare into space, and so on. This is when souls actually hop out of the body and go on a little adventure.

Lane: Right. For all we know, when you feel like lying down, it's your soul saying, alright, I need to leave this density for a minute. I've got work to do elsewhere—other realms to scout, data to retrieve. I'm heading to another galaxy to check out that situation and I'll be back shortly with intel.

Jane: Do you remember in *Avatar* where they plug in to their conscious thing and take the consciousness out of the body and put it into the big avatars?

Lane: Yes. What a great movie.

Jane: If we were observing those people in the flesh, you'd think they are sleeping. I actually suspect that sleep is where our greatest activity occurs. It makes sense to me that there would be a program from Deep State around sleep where they give us drugs to sleep to stop all of the activity that would be happening otherwise.

Lane: Of course. They do everything they can to interfere with the sleep state. They push sleeping pills that numb rather than nourish. They ensure we've got electronics beside our heads all night. They scramble our circadian rhythms with daylight saving time and keep us working like machines. They rob us of natural rest cycles. Why? Because sleep is the backdoor to truth. That's where real work happens.

When I need to process something big—emotionally, intellectually, energetically—I sleep. Just thirty seconds of sleep sometimes resets everything. I wake up with complete clarity. Like, Poof—done. No more struggle, just integration. I don't always know what occurred during that moment, but I know I'm different on the other side of it.

## UNLEASHING THE REBEL WITHIN

Jane: I don't have them very often now, but when I used to have an upset, I would go straight to sleep to rebalance my body. I think that here we've just flipped a narrative. Sleep is a superpower that they don't want us to know about.

Lane: Exactly. They've turned achievement into a metric of exhaustion. We've got to change our definition of productivity. Listening to your body and saying, yep, I'm going to sleep, without guilt, without mental noise—that's spiritual sovereignty. That's the rebel's version of success.

Jane: It doesn't matter if I'm not paying the bills or writing the next great documentary. As long as the electricity is not getting turned off it's fine. Just don't let the Wi-Fi turn off.

Lane: (laughing) Exactly.

Jane: Priorities. So, because you're in a tired state, you might find it's quite interesting what comes through today for you with the book.

Lane: That's what I'm counting on.

This shift—this radical permission to rest, to trust the unseen, to value sleep as sacred—is not laziness. It's strategy. It's retrieval. It's preparation for the next leap forward. Our so-called fatigue may actually be a sign that our soul is offloading new frequencies, decoding multidimensional truths, preparing our system for what's next.

We don't need more caffeine. We need remembrance.

We need to reclaim sleep as the portal it is.

The rebels of this age won't just fight—they'll rest. They'll sleep when others scramble, and they'll awaken with vision no machine could ever replicate.

Because somewhere deep inside, you already know—your superpower was never about doing more. It was about remembering more.

# Phase IV: Crystalline Rebel

"The greatest service one can offer is the radiance
of the self—no words, no teachings—
just the frequency of being."
— Synthesis of Ra, The Law of One,
Sessions 10–12

## Chapter 21
# Love in the Time of Ascension

People often ask: What is spirituality? Yet there's no single answer. Spirituality is not a one-size-fits-all path, and it was never meant to be. It's the evolving, intimate, often messy journey of developing your own relationship with Supreme Creation, in whatever form that takes for you. That's personal spirituality.

Recently, I went on an outing with a friend who brought along someone new. Before we met, my friend said, "You're going to love him. He's very spiritual." When I was introduced, the man immediately launched into a rundown of the church he used to run, and then asked me bluntly: "What church do you go to?"

Where do I go to be spiritual?

I was caught off guard. Not offended, but surprised. I replied instinctively, "The church of me and God."

It was a reflex—part defense, part truth. I don't go to a physical church. That question jolted me, and I had to sit with it. Was I triggered because I expected more from someone labeled as "very spiritual"? Probably. It reminded me that for many people, spirituality is still equated with religious attendance. For some, to be spiritual is to belong to a structure, a doctrine, a building.

To me, it's the opposite.

Spirituality is a direct connection to God, the Source. No gatekeepers. No robes. No rituals required—unless they're ones you choose. That Source might be called God, Creator, Mother-Father God, Prime Energy, the Universe—is semantics. Some believe there are multiple Godly beings of higher light under one vast originating Source. Others prefer to relate to God as masculine or feminine. For me, Source is genderless. It transcends polarity.

Personal spirituality is about tuning into your highest, clearest self—the part of you that knows who you really are. You don't need to memorize scriptures or sit in pews to access this. You just need a quiet space—internally or externally—to listen. That listening becomes discernment. That discernment becomes inner freedom.

The deeper you go, the more you awaken to your own connection to the Infinite. That's the key: true spirituality is a quest for personal divinity. It's the slow, powerful recognition that you are a creator being—not a usurper of God, but an extension of Source Light, growing in coherence with it. We're not here to dominate or worship blindly—we're here to merge, to remember, and to reclaim our place within the supreme architecture.

What we find on the other side of that quest is this: we are all fragments of the same whole. All divine, all connected, all mirroring one another through different lenses.

## Climbing the Frequency Ladder

Ascension isn't a physical destination. It's a state of being—one that fluctuates from moment to moment. When we talk about moving through dimensions, we're really talking about states of consciousness, degrees of awareness, and levels of energetic coherence.

To deepen our earlier discussion, the "dimensions" aren't places you go; they're frequencies you become.

In the densest reality—3D—we experience separation, ego, material fixation, duality. As you begin to awaken, to shift, to recognize who you really are, you start to move into the realms of higher frequency. You begin to feel into 4D: the bridge between density and light. Eventually, 5D—the frequency of unity, transparency, and divine embodiment—becomes your way of being.

Beyond that? I can't say with certainty. I've heard the stories. I've received glimpses. I don't know which states I've experienced consciously in this body. Still, I believe what lies beyond 5D is radiant, exquisite—a realm of pure coherence, where you no longer perceive yourself as separate from love, from truth, or from each other.

Mark Twain once described what happens when you put red and white fire ants together in a jar. If left alone, they coexist peacefully. Now, shake the jar, and they'll turn on one another—fighting furiously, unaware that it's not the other ant that's the problem, but the one who shook the jar. That's 3D consciousness, plain and simple. We've been provoked, shaken, and manipulated into conflict in an ant jar.

All the same, our natural state—the one we access as we rise—is collaborative, loving, and authentically sovereign. That's what 5D begins to restore.

5D is not perfection or fantasy, but alignment. You are well on your way into shedding trauma and ego. You act not from survival, but from service—not from tribalism, but from truth. You're no longer in this jar for your benefit. You're in it for the whole.

The moment you start seeing through this lens—expanding your heart past your personal wounds—you've stepped into the threshold of ascended being-ness.

## No Robes, No Rules

The basis of real spirituality is to never believe something simply because you're told it's true. Spirituality without discernment is just another cult. Blind faith, especially in this age, is not a virtue—it's a vulnerability.

# UNLEASHING THE REBEL WITHIN

Truth isn't found through dogma. It's uncovered through relentless inquiry.

When I research historical timelines, I know how corrupted the records are. I don't take a single source at face value. I triangulate. I keep digging. I listen to lived accounts, and I cross-examine the distortions. Even people on the same "side" will have completely different versions of events. I look for the patterns beneath the noise. That's how I approximate truth.

Even then—I leave room to be wrong.

## The Hum of Coherence

Everything—everything—must be taken with a grain of salt. Whether it comes from a psychic, a spirit guide, a religious figure, a news anchor, a "truth leader," or an ascended master, no one is exempt. The only real test is your inner resonance.

When you've trained yourself to listen energetically, you start to feel it: the hum of coherence or the static of deception. If something doesn't land, doesn't vibrate in alignment with your system, pause. Don't reject it outright—but don't swallow it either. You can always say: I'll give that one a 70% for now. I'll keep it on the table, but I won't build my house on it.

Most of the time, the information we're being fed is a hybrid. A cocktail of half-truth and hidden spin. It's not just the mainstream media that distorts. The alternative world has caught up fast in the disinformation game.

Eventually, when we emerge from this collective delusion, we'll look back at the narratives we believed and say, wait—I bought that? I followed that? Hopefully, we'll laugh.

Until then, stay on guard. Stay open—but skeptical. Curious—but discerning.

If something resonates, hold it loosely. If it doesn't, don't force it. You'll know in time.

. . .

## Lane Keller

### The Bear Told Me So

Take flat earth. The debate is never-ending, and each side is convinced the other is deluded. There's disinformation on both ends, and that alone tells me one thing: we don't yet have the full picture.

I once received a clairvoyant image of the Earth—clear as day. It's illustrated in my book *A Tale of Running Bear*, published by Arelian Press, a story given to me word-for-word by a visiting bear. Yes, a bear. Yes, I was just as surprised as you might be. I received it in full presence, and the image matched the dome-like descriptions of some flat earth theorists. I don't cling to that image, but I hold it as a possibility.

The point isn't who's right. The point is: don't accept anything outright.

Examine your belief structures. Peel them back. Revisit what you were taught in school, in church, in textbooks. Because nearly all of it is false—or at least incomplete. The historical narrative we've been fed is a hall of mirrors.

Everything deserves scrutiny. Most people don't want to do that work. They want comfort. They want something easy to believe so they can carry on with their day. I get it. Life is hard enough. All the same, when you outsource your discernment, you surrender your integrity. You start walking someone else's path in someone else's shoes.

Truth isn't a luxury—it's a responsibility.

Once you claim that responsibility, you start to see the world not just for what it is—but for what it was meant to be.

There's so much falsity surrounding us that nearly everything must be put under the microscope. Not because we're paranoid—but because we've been so thoroughly lied to. Most people don't want to do that kind of investigation. They want peace, routine, predictability. They want to live their lives, take things as they come, and assume the system is designed to take care of them.

When they hear something on the news—or pronounced by an "expert" or authority figure—they accept it. No questions asked. No deep dive. No spiritual or intellectual discernment. They trust the delivery and never examine the motive. That's where the danger lies.

Jane: Do you think that's because they're worn out from a system that is designed to exhaust them?

Lane: I don't think exhaustion is the full picture. I think it's more about distraction. They're distracted by day jobs, side hustles, digital noise. They're distracted by trying to be the "perfect parent"—whatever that even means. There's this relentless expectation to perform: to get the kids to school, to soccer, to ballet, to tutoring, to birthday parties... all while holding a full-time job, maintaining friendships, managing the household, preparing meals, staying in shape, staying informed, staying sane.

Of course they're tired. More than that—they've been pulled in so many directions that they forget to go inward.

Then comes the financial trap. For many, survival requires two incomes just to keep the lights on. We're still told to "keep up"—with the neighborhood, the school rankings, the cars, the brand of jeans your kid wears. It's a treadmill built by design. A well-oiled machine of distraction.

Is it any wonder that people collapse on the couch at night and zone out to mindless television? They've been conditioned to think that getting off the treadmill equals failure. Maybe what they really need is something to shake themselves awake.

## Straddling Worlds

There are many competing theories about where this planet is heading—and what spiritual ascension really entails. Interdimensional experiencers like Alex Collier, who relays messages from the Andromedans, have said that Earth is moving into 4D. According to his transmission, some of us didn't ascend to 5D at all—we arrived here from higher dimensions like 11D, only to be funneled downward into density.

Others say that those vibrating below 4D won't be able to come along. Dolores Cannon spoke of two Earths—a vibrational split where one Earth continues in 3D consciousness, and the other moves upward into 5D and beyond. There are theories of dimensional divergence, etheric suitcases, and spaceships waiting for the spiritually prepped. I'll refine this into what resonates for me, or maybe it's what any remaining belief structures allows me to grasp.

Dimensional realities are layered, not linear. They co-exist right here on Earth. Your access to them is determined by your vibration. If you're dense—fearful, disconnected, still operating from lack—you can't perceive the others. You'll feel alone. That doesn't mean they aren't there.

What I know with certainty is that we're not all developing at the same pace. We're undergoing a planetary shift—yes. We're simultaneously experiencing personal frequency recalibrations. Some are rising. Some are resisting. Some are waking up slowly, some in a flash. Some... not at all.

I've wondered what this means for the ones we love. Are some of us staying while others go? Are we truly separating into vibrational worlds? If so, can we really leave others behind?

Personally, I can't. Even though I've renounced old contracts, something in me refuses to abandon anyone if I can help it. I'll keep showing up for the stragglers. I'll keep throwing lifelines. Because this awakening is too important to keep to ourselves.

For now, the window is still open.

We're already in the transition. The planetary alignments are signaling radical shifts. The real Age of Aquarius has begun—not just astrologically, but spiritually. It's becoming harder and harder to ignore the split. The illusions are crumbling. The veils are thinning.

The Q phenomenon awakened a lot of people—not just politically, but energetically. It sparked curiosity. It turned people into questioners. With that came a rise in love for humanity and spiritual searching, and a desire for something real.

I believe this momentum will accelerate. More will be revealed.

More will be offered. More souls will be given a clear chance to choose.

As I have said, what it comes down to is the choice. Not a party line. Not a label. Not a role—but a soul-level choice.

A choice between love and fear. Between spiritual courage and numbed-out compliance. Between clarity and comfort. Between living awake or staying in the trance.

We want everyone to come. We're holding the light for that. Not everyone will be able to sustain the frequency. Some won't make the shift—not because they're bad people, but because they're still clinging to what dims them: addictions, ego, victimhood, spiritual bypassing, lies, narcissism, denial, or the refusal to look at truth.

Jane: I think that anybody reading this book without a shadow of a doubt, is on this time space reality as a leader of whatever their gifts are and what brings them joy. So, we're not actually talking about the people who are reading this book, but the people they love. We're talking about the children we love who are not yet consciously aware of the dark and therefore are still being manipulated by things like mainstream media. We're talking about friends who are good people, who are kind and compassionate and funny. They are generous or giving and would give you the shirt off their back.

Lane: I would say that by living in compassion, they've already chosen.

Jane: We've just had a flood and now many of these people are homeless. They're not vibrating any different to us or we're not vibrating any different to them in those moments. They are all for humanity as they share whatever they've got.

Lane: Those people are going to get swept up in this and come along. The people who won't will likely be those who have deliberately chosen to stay on the dark side of things.

Jane: I'm not a fan of segregation. The only thing I can see being good about that is if it's vibrational, is that those who have chosen to deliberately and consciously play for the dark, their vibration won't be swept up in this net of going to somewhere fabulous. It's like a cleaning mechanism.

Lane: Yes. There doesn't need to be any fear. When someone's holding on to victimhood, or self-pity, or unresolved anger, or if they're doing harm—intentionally or not—it doesn't necessarily make them evil. It does mean they're aligning with darkness, however, and not light.

This isn't a binary of good and bad. It's about trajectory. It's about choice. True awakening involves growth, emotional responsibility, joy, discernment, and a willingness to care for others—not from martyrdom, but from coherence. It can't be trauma-based. It can't be ego-based. It has to come from love.

If you're still carrying trauma, it doesn't mean you're doomed—but it does mean you need to heal in whatever form that looks like. Therapy, somatic work, spiritual processing, past life regression, inner child healing—you name it. You need to do whatever helps you release the pain.

Because unhealed trauma leaves you vulnerable to manipulation. It makes you easy to target. Easy to gaslight. Easy to enslave.

When you do the work to transmute your wounds, you begin to access what's already yours: the light, the clarity, the joy, the truth that's been waiting on the other side.

There's a banquet of grace available—but you can't taste it until you drop what's poisoning you.

So, the question becomes: are you ready to let it go?

Are you willing to awaken?

More than that... are you ready to help others rise?

## Chapter 22
# Timeline Outlaws

If you choose to move ahead—to rise in vibration, consciousness, and clarity—the help will be there for you. It always has been. You don't need to have it all figured out in advance. You just need to make the choice. Once you do, the way begins to form. The path reveals itself. People show up —sometimes spiritually, sometimes physically—but the support arrives like clockwork.

Still, the age-old question persists: Do we need darkness in order to recognize the light? Is contrast necessary for evolution? Do we only appreciate goodness because we've seen its absence?

The answer lives inside polarity. Not as a punishment, but as a mechanism of growth.

Choosing is an active state. It moves energy. Remaining in a fog of unknowing—refusing to choose—is passive. Passivity is the signature frequency of the 3D world. The old paradigm was built on inertia, indecision, and obedience.

Yet choosing awareness? Choosing compassion? Choosing truth? Those are radical acts.

They mark the pivot point between bondage and liberation. That leads to the harder questions: what happens to those around you when you begin to rise? When you ascend into an aligned higher frequency free from external controls —will you lose connection to those you love?

If the Earth truly splits into two timelines, two frequencies, or two "realities," what really happens to the ones who don't choose to come along?

## Loving Through the Firewall

Jane: I haven't checked out of the system because I have a daughter living in France and I want to get on a plane and go and see her, and there's no way I can travel from Australia to France out of the system.

Lane: Right. When we talk about multidimensional awareness, we often forget that we still have to operate in 3D at times. You leave a toe in the system—not because you believe in it, but because you love someone enough to walk through it.

Jane: The way I've reconciled it is that I'm staying within the system so I can do the things that I wish to be doing that are important to me.

Lane: So, let's define "the system." What is it, really?

Jane: That's any of their regulation rules, illegal laws, legislation, anything that they tell me that I have to do. Anything that they, being the fat controllers, I mean.

Lane: Yet, you were the one in the airport educating everyone about masks and social distancing as they hauled you off to the clink.

Jane: (laughter) Or tried to. I was going to meet my daughter.

Lane: You took the high road—refusing to comply, but doing it with grace. With explanation. With clarity.

Jane: I pick and choose my battles.

Lane: Exactly. That's the new mastery. We're not here to get arrested for no reason or be forced into silence. We want to keep going. Keep creating. Keep helping others rise. Sometimes that means staying just inside the system's lines—but without letting it define you.

That's how I see it: having one toe in 3D, not because we're asleep, but because we're loving. Our families are still inside. Our children. Our friends. So, we honor their free will. We participate just enough to remain connected—but we remain emotionally, energetically, and spiritually detached.

You can board a plane, deal with TSA, and go through their ridiculous rituals—not because you agree with them, but because your child is on the other side of the world. That's a conscious choice. That's sovereignty.

While the TSA agent is patting you down for refusing the X-ray, you can smile and joke and say, "Hey, I'm grateful for any touch at all." You don't have to suffer through it. You can witness it, even lighten it. You can remain in your higher state, even while they do their job.

We're all just playing roles. You, the traveler. Them, the enforcer. On a soul level—you're one.

So, I go through the line. I let them scan my toiletries. I mourn the loss of my kumquat brandy from Greece, poured down the drain because it didn't meet their liquid ounce requirements. The agent told me I could drink it right there at 8 a.m. Instead, I said, "Enjoy it," and walked on.

That's the paradox: you participate, but you're no longer participating. You comply just enough to keep loving—but you do it without attachment, without allegiance, and without illusion.

## Reverse Engineered Reality

There's something few realize: the entire structure of our communication has been inverted. As mentioned earlier, language, once a sacred harmonic instrument, has been flipped into a mechanism of entrapment. True sacred languages—Hebrew, Aramaic, Cuneiform, Sanskrit—move from right to left. They vibrate at higher frequencies.

Their glyphs, their intention, their cadence—all are encoded with light.

Then came English.

English was engineered as a reversal language—read left to right, severed from its roots, distorted in frequency and form. It wasn't an accident. It was designed to short-circuit resonance. To disconnect us from Source.

It didn't stop with words.

Our music, too, was hijacked. In the early 20th century, the Rockefellers led the charge to re-tune global music from the 432 Hz scale to 440 Hz—a subtle shift that wreaked massive energetic havoc. Baroque music, ancient harmonics, and healing frequencies were all based in 432. The power brokers wanted discord, not harmony.

They brought in Joseph Goebbels—yes, that Goebbels—Hitler's propaganda minister, to sell the idea. Goebbels famously stated: "If you tell a lie big enough and keep repeating it, people will eventually come to believe it." He helped enforce the frequency shift under the guise of modernization.

Thus, almost all music today—your favorite pop songs, your background soundtracks, even classical compositions—have been re-tuned to a scale designed to lower your vibration.

It promotes confusion. Depression. Discord. It keeps you locked into 3D consciousness, even when you think you're relaxing or being entertained.

It is the inverse of what music is meant to be: a portal, a medicine, a memory of the celestial connection.

That's the world we've inherited—a reversed matrix. Once you see the inversion, you can choose to reverse it back to its Source-aligned version. You can re-tune your frequency. Reclaim your authority. Rise from the hypnotic loop.

You can exit the 3D world without abandoning those or the things you love.

You don't need to run away. You need to wake up inside it—and hold the line for others to find you.

Because once you've exited the lie, you become the living frequency of truth.

## Quantum Choice Points

Let's talk about time—and more specifically, timelines. It's one of those topics that can twist your brain into knots if you try to approach it with a strictly linear mindset.

Our spiritual guides often say, there is no past, no future—only the present.

What does that actually mean?

To me, it doesn't mean the past didn't happen. It means that past, present, and future are all accessible from the now. That "now" is a kind of fulcrum. The moment you focus on the future, you're no longer rooted in the present—and yet, paradoxically, that focus begins to call the future into form.

Timelines, like time itself, aren't straight lines. They're not rails we ride once and forever. They're more like braided frequencies—overlapping, shifting, interwoven. You don't travel them in a straight shot; you match their frequency. You align with them.

That's why it helps to think of timelines not as tracks, but as states of being. Each timeline carries its own emotional tone, spiritual texture, and ultimate outcome. Your vibration—your dominant state of being—is the access key.

My state of being is aligned with a timeline where the world does not end in destruction. We are not doomed. I do not subscribe to the idea that evil wins or that the collapse of humanity is inevitable. My timeline is the one where God wins. Love wins. Mother Earth wins. Humanity wins. It's not a hopeful future—it's a vibrational reality that already exists, and which I've chosen to inhabit.

That's the timeline I live on.

We're here for a reason—not to spectate, but to help shape the outcome. We are midwifing a monumental moment in the history of this planet, where good not only triumphs but reclaims its rightful seat. It's not something that might happen—it's something that's already becoming. The shifts are real. The quickenings are undeniable. Yet, the invitation remains constant: stay aligned.

You can slip off into a lower state—a detour, a pocket of darkness—and suddenly feel like you've fallen back into the old world. Fear, anger, despair—they'll try to seduce you, and yet, you can always reclaim your path.

Say it out loud if you need to: I don't choose this. I choose the timeline where good wins. Declare it. Feel it. Return to it.

Some people say we've slipped back onto the dark timeline again. They say we've regressed, or that something shifted and we're back in the mess. I don't buy it. I never left the upper track. I may pass through turbulence, but my compass doesn't waver. I'm not here for doom.

That said, detours are real. We're watching loved ones leave the planet in increasing numbers—cancers, sudden deaths, suicides, accidents. These exits are not meaningless. They're part of the shift. They're not proof that evil is winning—they're evidence of souls making vibrational choices. This doesn't mean we've left the highest timeline. It means we're watching soul contracts at work. For whatever reason, these people chose to leave the planet at this appointed time.

The people left behind get scared. They take the imagery literally. They see every tragedy as a sign that we've been derailed. I say this with full clarity: We are still on the highest trajectory. The most glorious outcome is still in motion.

Jane: I had a very profound vision. I had dropped my husband at work and he unlocked the door to this massive warehouse that houses robotic equipment. As I watched him walk through this tiny door into the huge building, I had a vision of timelines as I thought, I wonder which one he's going into?

It was like the movie *Sliding Doors*, where two timelines were playing out at the same time. It's just choices. Then I got that there's an infinite number of timelines for any moment. Any vibrational being has multiple timelines that are happening simultaneously and you jump them by vibration and literally in any moment you have a choice.

Right now, I'm sitting here speaking with Lane. Am I choosing to speak about something that is low vibration or something that is high vibration? At the same time that I'm having this very high vibrational, intellectual, emotional, spiritual conversation with Lane, there is also the same conversation going on with Lane at exactly the same point in time space reality where we're talking about low vibrational stuff.

Lane: You just touched something big there—those points of connection where timeline jumps occur. That connects directly to what Tesla hinted at: the universe of numbers. There's a brilliant physicist named Nassim Haramein who expanded on Einstein's field theories and tied them back to Tesla's 3-6-9 formula.

You know Tesla's quote— "If you knew the magnificence of 3, 6, and 9, you would have the key to the universe."

Haramein discovered that the toroidal fields—the dynamic energy systems that shape everything from galaxies to atoms—are formed and governed by 3-6-9. Imagine two spinning toruses, one above and one below, forming a full sphere. Where those energetic fields intersect, you find nodes. Points of decision. Inflection points.

At those nodes? That's where we jump timelines.

They're vibrational hinges—moments of choice, encoded in the math of the universe. That's polarity. That's the architecture of freedom. Every moment is a portal. The more conscious you are, the more clearly you see them.

Let me repeat that: Every moment is a portal. The more conscious you are, the more clearly you see them.

Jane: I think that when we jump timelines some people have the perception that they've gotten off one train and got on another that's, let's say, higher and better. That's their perception. But you can keep jumping trains. You can go back to the first train, you can go to this one, you can jump over to this one. It's like we are flying through the air as in dreams of weightlessness where you can scale staircases and mountains.

That's what we're doing. I have dreams where I can run on a hill and then just launch and I fly. I have dreams where I get pulled by magnets up into areas I don't want to be in. That's all we're doing. We're just jumping. When I am sitting here, hoping to write a beautiful book, I am on one timeline.

That is the highest, purist possibility for humanity. When I jump to a timeline where I connect with somebody I love dearly, they might think that right now Lane and I need to be put into a mental asylum. I jump onto another train and another timeline, and I'm choosing to do that because I want to experience all sorts of things.

I didn't come here to just play nice. I want to get dirty. I want to, dare I say it, have my emotions in all sorts of different states. I want the contrast. I want the mud. I want the experiences.

Lane: That's the rebel spirit. We didn't come here for a vanilla life. We came to touch the extremes—to feel the density so we could transcend it. You're right—we're not hopping trains to escape. We're choosing timelines that help us remember, integrate, and expand.

The beauty of this multidimensional reality is that you can hold the highest vibration and still touch the human experience fully. You can choose the mud and still be pure light. You can embrace the shadow without abandoning the mission.

This is the age of vibrational mastery—not detachment, but deliberate navigation. We don't numb out. We choose in. Again, and again.

That's what timeline sovereignty means.

You're not locked into a fate. You're not bound to the train you woke up on. You are a multidimensional being with keys to the whole system.

You just have to remember: you're the one holding the map.

## Atlantis Redux

## UNLEASHING THE REBEL WITHIN

Lane: You deliberately uncovered that Atlantis was one of your past lives, Jane. You know you're not just here to reflect on that lifetime—you're here to recalibrate it. To reclaim it. To fix what went wrong, not only within yourself but within the timeline itself.

Jane: Correct, however, it's all happening simultaneously. There you go, there's the no time, no, no past, no future. This time, am I jumping over to Atlantis and blowing it up? There's a version of me that did do that. Or does do that.

Lane: That's exactly it. That's timeline jumping and time travel, and they're one and the same. That's part of why we say there's no past and no future—because time travel is already happening, right now. Not in theory. Not in a sci-fi novel. In our lived field. This isn't about metaphors anymore. This is about actual shifts in our shared reality.

We've all witnessed it—the Mandela Effect. That eerie disorientation where details from the past change before our eyes. One moment Mandela is alive in prison, the next he's long dead. One day it's Berenstein Bears, the next it's Berenstain. These aren't memory glitches. They're timeline corrections, and they're often the result of someone—or many someones—traveling interdimensionally to alter a thread in time.

So, if you're in Atlantis right now, in another layer of this same moment, correcting what you once set in motion, then that revision is rippling into the now. The field is being updated. The choice you make across timelines feeds back into this one.

Which begs the question: what kind of causality are we creating through multidimensional repair?

It's a mind bender—but it's also a truth we're starting to feel viscerally. That past lives aren't just stories from long ago. They're active currents running parallel to this one, feeding into it, evolving it. Healing one heals many.

As we begin to collapse the illusion of time, we begin to see money the same way. Just as time is not real, money is not real. We've constructed entire systems around scarcity and limitation, but when people begin to experience true abundance, they realize that money was always just an illusion—a placeholder for permission.

That's what's happening now with time.

As the present moment becomes more saturated with meaning, the walls between past and future begin to dissolve. The illusion of linearity begins to fall apart. Suddenly, we're getting it. We're grasping concepts we used to struggle to even conceptualize. We're experiencing time as fluid, memory as elastic, and reality as programmable.

This is the collapse of old paradigms—not in theory, but in real time.

Anyone who says nothing is happening is either still asleep or deliberately looking away. Because everything is happening. The veil is lifting on every level. The illusion that government works for the people? Gone. The illusion that obedience is virtue? Gone. The illusion that religion is the only path to God-connection? Disintegrating.

We are shedding the matrix skin layer by layer.

We are the ones making this possible—collectively, through our vibration, our intention, our choices. We are the ones selecting the higher timeline, refusing the false structures, and grounding the real reality.

We are literally doing this with our consciousness.

## Chapter 23
# Skyrocketing Through 5D

There's one more area I want to touch on—and it's not as high-vibe as the rest of this work, but it's crucial. We've spoken before about energy vampires—how to recognize them, how to expel them, and how not to become one yourself.

Still, what happens when the state itself is the energy vampire?

That's what we're dealing with now. A full-scale assault on the human energy field—through trauma, distraction, deception, and divide-and-conquer tactics. The darkness doesn't just prey on us through obvious evil. It uses movements, media, and false flags to drain the life force of humanity.

We are witnessing the co-opting of our youth. Not just through trafficking and abuse—though that continues behind the curtain—but through social engineering. Through movements that cloak themselves in virtue while stoking emotional volatility and self-righteous separation.

Movements like climate extremism, identity manipulation, and hyper-polarized activism aren't evil. But many have been twisted, infiltrated, and used to fragment our collective field. ANTIFA. Transhumanism. LGBTQIA++. Cultural exploitation. It's not about condemning individuals—it's about recognizing when an energetic hijack is taking place.

What appears to be progressive often carries a subliminal payload of trauma, guilt, shame, or ideological division. These campaigns feed on emotional pain. They separate us. They confuse us. They generate massive waves of loosh, the emotional discharge that dark forces consume.

False flag operations, military escalations, school shootings, gender confusion, and engineered climate hysteria—these are trauma programs. Their function is both physical and energetic. On the surface, they usher in surveillance, legislation, and social compliance. On a deeper level, they are designed to shock your nervous system and implant programmable responses.

This is Trauma Programming 3.0.

You may think trauma is just personal, but it's been weaponized at the societal level. This is why you must heal. Not just to feel better —but because unhealed trauma makes you programmable.

If you are unhealed, you are vulnerable to suggestion. To despair. To manipulation. Trauma isn't just a wound—it's an entry point. That's why the system works so hard to keep you in a state of emotional disrepair. It's not just about surveillance. It's about control of the frequency field.

I've been there. I've lost people I loved. I've had my heart broken in ways that took years to heal. I did the work. I sat with the pain. I metabolized it, and I released it.

Because if you don't, it owns you.

You cannot allow yourself to remain traumatized—not if you want to be free. You must do whatever it takes: therapy, regression, journaling, medicine work, soul retrieval, inner child reconnection— whatever helps you come home to yourself.

Forgiveness is part of it. Not for them—for you. Not because they deserve it, but because you do. You deserve to reclaim your inner authority. To restore your frequency. To cut the tether that binds you to the very systems you're trying to escape.

That's what moves us into the next level. That's the passage point.

## The Real Rocket Fuel

We've all heard it: you must forgive. That's true. Forgiveness is essential. It's a non-negotiable step on the ascension path. What's less talked about is what comes after forgiveness. That's where things really start to take off.

Because it's not just about letting go of pain or releasing resentment. It's about finding gratitude—and not the performative kind. Not, "Oh, I guess that taught me something." No. This is deep, soul-level gratitude. This is standing in front of something that wrecked you, that gutted you, and saying—thank you. Thank you for what you showed me. Thank you for who I became because of you.

Yes, sometimes it's as small as stepping on broken glass in the garage. In that moment, you could curse it, or you could say, Thank you. Because it could've been worse. Now you know—no more barefoot wandering through cluttered boxes.

It sounds silly. The reaction—the energetic orientation—is everything.

When my father died, it was sudden. He seemed healthy. There was no illness, no drawn-out suffering. It was a shock. Yet—there was grace. He left quickly, cleanly. No hospital machines. No prolonged pain. Just a quiet transition. He had been writing a book about the meaning of God before he passed. Maybe, in some way, he's writing it with me now.

I'm grateful—truly, fiercely grateful—that he lived as long and as well as he did. I'm grateful for the way he left. I feel his presence now more than ever. I thank him every time I sit down to write.

This leads us to the level beyond gratitude. It's the real rocket fuel.

You've got to love the experience.

Even the brutal ones. Even the humiliating ones. Even the ones that shattered you.

Love it.

That's what catapults you into the upper frequencies of 5D and beyond. That's what blows open the gates of your higher self. Love it all. Because all of it—every second—is shaping your mastery.

There's no bad karma. There's no wasted time. There's no such thing as a wrong experience. There's only 3D contrast, and what you choose to do with it.

I love this life. I love the mess. The grief. The mistakes. The breakthroughs. The joy. The longing. The resistance. Because this is the proving ground. This is where we remember who we are.

And the more you laugh—really laugh—the faster you rise.

## Recode Yourself

Let's talk about who we really are.

Let's talk about why we came.

This planet—this dense, sticky, polarized playground—isn't for the faint of heart. It's for the brave. The ones who volunteered to leave lighter realms and drop into this chaos for the sake of awakening. Alex Collier says it. Other researchers and experiencers say it too: we are the frontliners of frequency. We came to anchor what others were too afraid to face.

We came to get stuck—so we could learn to rise.

Yes, we've made mistakes. Maybe we did things we came to regret. Maybe we followed kings and rulers when we shouldn't have. Maybe we betrayed loved ones. Hurt others. Gave in to fear. I've seen it. I've remembered it. In one past life I poured boiling oil on someone I loved—because I was following orders.

Jane remembers her role in Atlantis. I remember mine in feudal war. We've all played both light and shadow. What matters now is that we've fought through it. Lifetime after lifetime, we've clawed our way back toward the light. We're still here.

## UNLEASHING THE REBEL WITHIN

That counts for something.

In fact, it counts for everything.

The ones who stayed behind in their comfy galactic lounges? Great. Thank you for the guidance. They're not the ones battling the trenches of 3D polarity. We are. That means we have the clearest perspective on how awakening actually works. Because we're doing it from within.

It's heavy. It's lonely. It's infuriating. Yet— it's also magnificent.

Nietzsche knew this. He wasn't always easy to agree with, but he understood that you must love your fate. Love what life gives you. Love it until it turns into liberation. Love it until it becomes art.

How do you do that?

You laugh.

You laugh so hard you forget what you were afraid of.

Laughter is the frequency that cuts through density like a blade. It's how we alchemize the unbearable. It's how we breathe in the absurdity and exhale freedom.

My family? We laugh at funerals. Not because we're heartless— but because we feel everything, and laughter is how we process the unbearable.

Jane: I used to faint at funerals. You laugh; I faint.

Lane: I do go in the bathroom and cry at times. But my family? We find the humor. I'll share a story. A beloved aunt passed, and my mom, my aunt, and my uncle went to the wake. There were tears, wails, typical Italian mourning when they got there. As their turn came to move to the coffin and say good-bye, something hit them.

This wasn't their aunt.

In fact, they were surrounded by an entirely different family that they didn't know.

That's when my uncle bent over, causing the back of his pants to loudly rip from the crotch to the waist.

Their laughter exploded, rocking the room.

They backed out shaking, eyes streaming, trying to exit without causing more of a scene. They failed.

They then entered the correct room convulsing, holding onto one another in order to stand. It was hilarious. That laughter healed more than silence ever could.

Jane: It is an awful lot of naughty fun to get in a laughing, giggling fit in moments when it's inappropriate, but it's wonderful. Laughter is very powerful.

Lane: I remember in 11th-grade chemistry, I reached back into my purse—because, of course, a teenage girl needs lip gloss at all times—and instead, I grabbed Barb Malone's foot.

I turned and we locked eyes, my hand on her foot. That was it.

I start laughing. She starts laughing. We're gone.

Our teacher, Mr. Friedman, turns red and growls, "You two. Stop it."

The more he says it, the worse it gets. Now the whole class is in it, nearly prostrate with fits of laughter.

Mr. Friedman keeps shouting, "You've got to stop it now. Stop it now!" He's beside himself, purple with rage.

Finally, he explodes. "That's it! Pop quiz. Everyone, put away your notebooks!"

The class groans. They're mad at us and we weren't happy about it either. We still giggled through the quiz. Once the laughter starts? There's no stopping it.

Jane: My memory was Brett Marr, an Australian Olympic basketball player. He's a dear friend, and we were sitting side by side at a sports awards night when someone goes to the podium to make his award speech.

Brett leans in and says, count how many times this guy says, "uhm."

Not everybody's the great public speaker Brett is. As the guy starts saying "uhm," I start laughing. I'm trying to fight it. I'm spitting wine through my nose as Brett counts. I'm trying not to snort. "He's up to 80," says Brett under his breath. My attempts to stifle my laughter grew futile. If I hadn't been sitting next to Brett Maher, I would definitely have been thrown out of that dinner.

## UNLEASHING THE REBEL WITHIN

Lane: That's it, right there.

That's what gets us through. That's what lifts us out of the grid. You can go through 3D with your heart ripped open—but if you can laugh, you transmute the pain.

Forgiveness. Gratitude. Love. Laughter.

These are the keys. These are the weapons. These are the codes that let us rocket through 5D—and beyond.

Because joy, even in the ruins, is rebellion.

Rebellion, when it's grounded in love, becomes ascension.

# Chapter 24
# Mastery or Bust

In the community where I moved, there's a homeowners association composed of 18 townhomes. Many of my neighbors are getting on in years. One by one they came to me, fed up with the HOA president, urging me to run for the board. I tried to put them off—because the one thing I loathe more than almost anything else is politics. Politics, to me, is a distraction engine. A performative maze. A performance of power without truth. Anything that takes me away from the real work—from the soul work I came here to do—feels like theft.

Then the treasurer died. Suddenly there was a vacuum, and once again they turned to me. This time it wasn't about leadership—it was logistics. They needed someone to step in and take over the financials. I laughed. Accounting software? Budgets and spreadsheets? No, siree. That was not where I belonged. I didn't have the time or desire to learn the inner workings of HOA finances. I also didn't want to leave my community hanging.

I took a beat and asked myself a different question: where am I best suited?

The answer came quickly. My real skill lies in communication—

translating complexity into clarity—and in seeing patterns where others see problems. I wouldn't say I "fix" problems, because true solutions don't override another's right to choose. However, I facilitate new paths. I sense what's stuck and I get energy moving again. If I have a superpower, that might be it.

I said no to the treasurer position—but I agreed to be VP. Then I moved into action—not by crunching numbers, but by calling in specialists to assess a current situation. I trusted that someone else would step into the role that fit them best. They did.

This is key: know your gifts. Honor your design. Move from alignment. Serve the whole by staying true to yourself.

Fifteen years ago, I made a decision that still holds. I vowed never to attend another public demonstration. That might seem surprising for someone who's not afraid of a fight for what's right. This decision wasn't about fear. It was about strategy.

At one time, I would have been the one on the front row, waving my sign, yelling for justice. Then I learned they were targeting people. Not metaphorically—literally. Demonstrators on the wrong side of the political spectrum had their license plates photographed. Their taxes audited. Their names added to lists. The Tea Party protests were one such example—those who spoke out found themselves flagged, investigated, erased. For those on the "wrong" side of the narrative, the price was steep. Arrests. Surveillance. Harassment. Even death.

I remembered Charlene Woodard—the actress arrested for demonstrating at the pipeline protests in the Dakotas. Her story was to bring attention to the matter by getting arrested. I realized that isn't mine. Protesting is not my battlefield.

It doesn't mean I don't care. It doesn't mean I'm passive. It means I choose strategy over symbolic action. I do not feel compelled to scream into a megaphone when I know I am better at reshaping thought systems from the inside. I decided my real job is not to march but to influence the frequency grid. My gifts are not signs and slogans. They're narrative re-patterning, soul alchemy, energetic infiltration. I move differently now. Not quietly, but with clarity and precision.

That brings us back to the eternal question: the loaf of bread.

Do you keep it—or do you give it away?

If you're here to help the world, are you meant to sacrifice yourself in the process? Or are you meant to stay alive, stay grounded, stay strong—so you can fulfill your mission?

I still don't know the absolute answer to that question. I suspect there isn't one. I do lean toward the airplane-mask philosophy. You can't help others if you're passed out from lack of oxygen. You secure your own mask first—not from selfishness, but from strategy. Maybe the answer is: give away the bread—but become someone who no longer needs to eat it.

Sometimes the most powerful roles we play are the ones that don't look heroic from the outside. Sometimes we take on positions that don't match our obvious talents, and yet they lead us to where we're supposed to be. Over time, after a lot of misfires and misdirection, I think I've figured out what I am.

Jane: What is that?

Lane: I think I'm an alchemist of the soul.

Jane: Yes, absolutely, that's it. 100%.

Lane: What we've been circling around this whole time—this journey of awakening, purification, release, remembering—it's all alchemy. Soul alchemy. The transmutation of base experience into spiritual gold.

Jane: Yes. I think everybody will become a master of some form of self-alchemy. Hence why injustice and lack of compassion or elitism fire you up. They're the same things that fire me up.

Lane: For a while, I thought I was an energy transmitter. In a past life in Lemuria, I wore long red robes and stood on a high promontory with my arms outstretched, channeling raw energy from the heavens to the people below. I was a human antenna. It didn't end well. My body burned from the inside out. The servant who tended to me as I died? She's my daughter in this lifetime.

## UNLEASHING THE REBEL WITHIN

Before that revelation, I believed I was meant to be a conceptualist—a translator of invisible truths. Someone who sees what others cannot yet articulate and puts it into words that ripple through the collective. For a time, I was. I helped people see the matrix. I gave them language for what they didn't yet know they were feeling. I transmitted energy through my voice and presence—until my guides told me to stop. Not because it wasn't needed, but because it was debilitating me. They told me: You're not here to burn your insides out anymore!

I've had lifetimes of sacrifice. One as a gladiator, fighting for the freedom of the enslaved. I was like Spartacus. Again, I was told: not this time.

The message became clear: you are here to survive this time. Not to suffer. Not to martyr. Not to self-immolate for a cause. You are here to do the work and stay intact.

Jane: You've made it to this point in this incarnation. It doesn't make any sense for you to be a sacrificial lamb now, no sense whatsoever.

Lane: So, do you give the starving person that piece of bread—or do you preserve your life so you can continue awakening others?

Jane: You save yourself. I feel clear on that. It's not an ego or a selfish thing. It's knowing there's a job to be done and it's not saying the other person isn't as important or more important or less important than you, but it is knowing your role to play in this. That must be protected at all costs.

Lane: Yes, that's right. It's not service to self. It's service through self. Through clarity. Through embodiment. Through survival.

Jane: Now in that same action, you could project your intention for that person to have an effortless process of getting bread from the place next door within the next half an hour. That's the win. You visually see them thriving.

Lane: Perfect. That's the magic. Intention is not passive. Intention is influence. Those of us who've been on this path have been working with intention for a long time now. It's at the root of everything. Every prayer, every declaration, every word—these are energetic commands. It starts with your thoughts.

Take Dr. Masaru Emoto's work with water. His experiments can change your life. He showed that water responds to intention. Words, images, sound—all of them shape the crystalline structure of water. Positive intention produces exquisite geometries. Negative intention creates distortions, blackness, chaos.

You are mostly water. What do you think happens when you call yourself beautiful? When you speak lovingly to your reflection? Your cells respond. You literally become what you declare.

It goes deeper. True intention is not a request—it's an acknowledgment. A sacred assumption. It's not begging the Universe to fix something—it's thanking the Universe for what has already occurred. Intention is gratitude for the future as if it's already here. In that moment, time collapses. The illusion breaks.

When you say, I am healed, and mean it—not as a hope, but as a knowing—the Universe adjusts itself to reflect that truth.

Look at yourself in the mirror each morning and say: Hello, beautiful. You're radiant today.

That becomes your reality. Don't say: God, I look so old. I look tired. Look at these wrinkles... or watch what follows. You create your reality with every word.

Speak the future into the present. Appreciate it as if it's already true. You will collapse timelines, activate your own quantum field, and step into mastery.

We are not here to wait for miracles.

We are here to become them.

## **I Am, Not I Will**

Jane: I love that you've mentioned bringing it into a state of it's already having happened. So, it's, I am grateful for my vitality and beauty. The I am statement is more powerful than the I will.

Lane: The word intention, although it sounds right, is not quite correct—because that word still pushes the desired outcome into the future. It creates a gap. An energetic distance. If you're creating a product and your "intent" is to heal people, it's more powerful to move it into present-tense completion. Thank you for healing the masses with this product. That already-happened gratitude creates the field in which the healing becomes real.

Jane: So, it's gratitude. Beautiful.

Regarding Dr. Emoto's work, I wanted to add that Darren Weissman worked with Dr. Emoto and went on to do the experiments with blood. You can see before and after in his book *The Power of Infinite Love and Gratitude*. He's got a stack of before-and-after photos showing intention used on blood work. You can see somebody who's turned up stressed and he's done the blood work before, and then after—with the power of intention, of infinite love and gratitude. What has resulted in the blood work after is fabulous.

Intention is something that is happening regardless of whether people are aware of it or not. Meaning, if people are not aware of their thoughts, their intentions can harm them. The more that we become consciously aware of our thoughts and redirect them toward the positive, the more benefit it is to us.

Lane: Thought is everything. It's the originating code. It begins with the thought—then the word, then the deed. Just like it says in the Bible. They got that right. You have to begin with the root. Direct the thought, and the action follows.

This is where many people miss the mark. We try to change behavior at the surface level, but we never go back and untangle the hijacked thought that created it. We've been programmed in so many directions, from so many angles, that even our thoughts no longer belong to us. They've been injected. Rewired. Weaponized. We've been trained to think small. To think old. To think helpless. We've been trained to misidentify with every passing thought—as if it were truth. It's not.

. . .

## Reclaim the Script

Let's take age as an example.

My mother never wanted her age revealed. Not ever. Partly because she was in the public eye and well aware of the deep prejudice that exists against older women—especially those in the spotlight. It was also because she understood something most people never actualize: if you think your age, your body responds to it.

She knew that the number wasn't neutral. That each age carries with it a host of cultural programming and embedded beliefs. The moment you identify with a number—especially if you believe what that number means—you begin unconsciously living out its story.

We're conditioned to think 62 means something. That 82 means something. That 42, or 22, means something. The body, so beautifully adaptive and intelligent, responds in kind.

Maybe this came from her. Maybe it was my own spirit refusing to be boxed in. As a teenager, I never felt my age. I didn't carry the number. People would ask, "How old are you?" and I'd pause, mentally do the math, and say, "Oh. I'm 16." It always felt distant. Like I was calculating math homework.

Eventually I stopped playing the game. When people asked my age, I'd say simply:

"I don't do age."

I don't.

I do vibrational state. I do coherence. I do mastery. I don't do numbers that come with a script I never agreed to.

Because every story you unconsciously live out was once a thought you didn't catch.

Every thought you catch and reclaim becomes another key to your liberation.

This is the path of the rebel. The infinite sovereign. The alchemist of soul.

It's not about escaping the system. It's about transmuting the code.

It starts, always, with the thought.

## Chapter 25
# Your Superpower

Like I said, I don't do age.

Not in the way the world tells us to do it. Not in the way it's been encoded into society—as a countdown clock, a ticking expiration label, a slow march into irrelevance and decay. I refuse to subscribe to that story.

Part of that is because time itself is a false construct—one of the great engineered illusions used to control perception and limit possibility. They've programmed us to believe in time not as a flowing rhythm but as a hard boundary. A cage. A death sentence wrapped in calendar paper.

My first act of rebellion was simple: Trick myself out of the system.

I stopped mentally participating in time. I quit the age game. I refused the script. I chose—deliberately—not to assign meaning to a number that was never mine to begin with.

Because here's the trap:

When people say they're going to get old and sick and die and get dementia, "just like everyone else," they do. That's exactly what happens. They live out the program.

In my family? We never bought into that. We opted out. We recognized the programming for what it was. A lie. A spell. A projection.

If you want to unleash your superpowers, start here:

Do not let your body buy into the age story.

That's step one.

Then go deeper.

Step two is where the shift really begins. Step two is where you consciously believe—with every cell and every breath—that you are 22 in mind, body, and spirit. Or 33. Or timeless. Or 108. Whatever number feels vibrationally true for you—not the number they handed you at birth and told you to carry like a stone.

Because your body listens to your belief. Your cells believe your inner monologue. Thought is command.

**Refuse the Timeline**

I never felt like I aged in my thirties or forties. Honestly, I just never felt it. It didn't occur to me. It didn't stick.

Now, I'm not saying I look like I'm 22. I hope I do, but that's not the point. I do know that when I get pressed to reveal my so-called "real" age, the reactions are... let's just say, surprising.

There is real truth to the old adage: You are what you think. I've thought myself outside the lines they gave me.

Through some combination of inherited wisdom, deep soul memory, and rebellious instinct, I've mostly mastered the understanding that the age progression program here on Earth has nothing to do with who I am. It's not aligned with my code. It's not a part of my blueprint.

Now, do I fall into it sometimes? Sure. We all do. The system is persuasive. Most of the time I ignore it. I don't feed it.

Jane: That is so unique. I have never heard of another person from such a young age choosing to not engage in any age dialogue. To not know your age when you were young is extraordinary.

## UNLEASHING THE REBEL WITHIN

Lane: I have to credit my mom for that—and also, I think, my weird relationship with time itself.

You know how I can't do time zones very well? It's not that I'm incapable of doing math—I could if I cared—but I honestly think we both have trouble with this because we see through the false construct.

It's not because we're less-than or disorganized or need a better planner. It's because, deep down, something in our spirit is rejecting the lie.

If I'm talking to you right now, we're in the same energetic moment. Whether your clock says 6 p.m. and mine says 6 a.m.—we're here. Together. Now. So, what's with the mechanical labels?

Same thing with daylight savings time. That game is so wrong. It's just more evidence of manipulation—a false recalibration of light, rhythm, and reality. It's all off. It's always been off.

This is key: When you feel yourself inwardly revolting against something—however subtle—that's your higher intelligence pinging you.

That's your soul saying: Hold on. Something isn't right here.

That's how I felt about age. I didn't resonate with it. I couldn't embody it. I didn't see why I had to grow old, get sick, and deteriorate because someone else did or because that's what the numbers said.

I don't take poisons into my body. I don't follow medical dogma. I don't let white coats define me. I sure as hell don't let numbers tell me how to feel.

Once you start down the road of tests and specialists, they'll have you believing all kinds of terrible things. They'll hand you diagnoses you never asked for. They'll name things into existence that would've healed on their own. They'll rob you of your internal compass and replace it with a chart.

I say:

Know your body. Read its signals. Stay in tune.

Don't take pills that numb the wisdom.

Your superpowers live in your discernment.

You cannot discern truth from programming if your senses have been hijacked.

Start where it counts.

Unplug from their timeline.

Reclaim your biological integrity.

Choose the age your soul agrees with.

Because the future is not a place you're going: it's a state you're calling in.

## Reject the Spell

Many friends who've had to deal with cancer have been handed horrifying prognoses by medical professionals who—perhaps unknowingly—cast spells with their words. The worst thing a doctor can do is stand at your bedside and deliver a death sentence in the form of a clinical prediction. The first task becomes spiritual triage:

Don't absorb the prognosis into your cells.

Remember Dr. Emoto's water experiments. We are mostly water. Your body is listening. If someone tells you, "You have a 90 percent chance of dying in the next three months," your cells don't know they're supposed to resist that idea. They take it in. If someone says, "We'll put you on chemotherapy, but you're probably going to die anyway," and you believe it—even just a sliver of it—that vibration infiltrates your field.

That's why I've never, ever wanted to tell anyone my age. Every time you say it, every time you let it live in your mouth, your body hears it. Your body starts to believe the associations the world has given that number. No matter how hard you try to mentally override it, those associations sweep in. They activate the program.

I've done age experiments—not just on myself, but with my pets. I lived in South Florida for a while, surrounded by a community of older people who adored dogs. I had this little fluffy white guy everyone loved to coo over.

They'd ask, "Oh, how old is your dog?" I'd always say, "He's two."

## UNLEASHING THE REBEL WITHIN

The following years, I was still giving the same answer. "He's two."

Eventually, someone would say, "Didn't you say that last time?" And maybe the year before?

Yes. Because I didn't want my dog to think he was old.

You can say what you want, but animals understand. Maybe not the literal words, but the meaning, the intent, the energetic message. They get it. They absorb the vibe behind your words. They feel it when someone leans down and says, "Oh you poor old thing. Is your eyesight going now?" And guess what? My dog's eyesight never did go—even when he was older.

I don't want my animals' cells hearing that kind of prognosis.

I had another dog who lived to 18, and I swear to you, she still thought she was a puppy because we always said to her, "You're a puppy." In her dotage she was probably thinking, But I've lost function in my legs. I'd say, "It's okay. You're still a puppy." I believe—fully—that she thought she was, right up until the day she left this world.

Jane: I find this fascinating because when I started doing radio, I never hid my age and I was really proud when I turned 50. As far as I know, I was the oldest woman in Australia to be given a national radio show. I was proud of that, and I also didn't want to buy into this program of lying about my age and trying to be younger than I am. I wanted to embrace whatever stage I was at. I'm actually really proud that I have never hidden anything like that. Now listening to you, I realized I'm still buying into the bullshit. You were at a much, for want of a better word, a much more advanced, higher level of awareness around the age game than I was.

Lane: Maybe I'm just more stubborn.

There was a moment in time where I stood on the precipice, thinking:

Look, I have quite a number of ambitions that I am going to fulfill in the latter part of my life. Maybe it is a good idea to state my age publicly—to be an example to other women.

The more I thought about it, the clearer it became that—at least for me—the better example would be to defy age entirely. Not talk about it. Not identify with it. Not submit to the illusion.

I realized that if I could embody it—if I could actually live it—then that would be the revolution. Obviously, we're all working on different aspects of ourselves, and I haven't perfected this. This is what I choose to do.

**The Grace Rebellion**

Jane: I wanted to talk about grace because over the last three, nearly four years, we've watched a lot of lack of grace, a lot of hostility from all sorts of people. A lack of respect of allowing others points of view.

I think that grace has a big role to play in the coming years. You are very gracious. I've watched you in millions of zoom meetings in varying conversations, and you are the queen of grace.

Lane: Thank you for saying that.

My mom taught me about grace. She's a very gracious individual. We would talk about it at the dinner table—this idea of grace as a kind of inner nobility. We'd notice when people in our lives lacked it. We'd ask: Why are they so rude? So aggressive? So unkind?

Graciousness, I believe, is allowing someone else to have their opinion without feeling the need to overpower them. Even when you know more than they do, even when you see how incomplete their understanding is, you can either gently offer more context—or gracefully step away.

It's about courtesy. Kindness. You don't attack. You don't put people down. You allow them to exist.

You honor them—not because they've earned it, but because they're human. Humans deserve honor, even when they're still figuring things out.

Maybe they're not offering their light in the way you would. Maybe they haven't developed the kind of awareness you prioritize.

However, if you can show grace in those moments—make them feel seen or appreciated—you change the energy of the room.

Now let's be clear: I'm not talking about the outdated dynamics where women were trained to make everyone else feel good at the expense of themselves. What looks like grace is actually codependence. That's done.

What I'm talking about is intentional elevation—creating a moment where someone feels better about themselves because you saw something in them and named it.

Not empty compliments. Not, "Oh, what a pretty red dress."

Instead offer something true, like how they wear that red dress. How they hold their ground. How they show up. When you do that—when you notice something authentic in another person—it becomes a magical moment.

Jane: That, ladies and gentlemen, is the example of somebody who's done the work, who isn't being triggered, who doesn't need to be heard, seen, felt as the smartest person in the room, even if they are on a particular topic.

That is grace.

Lane: Wow, thank you.

Jane: That really is it. You're not triggered. Most people are triggered with, hang on, I don't agree with that and I need to be heard and seen and felt and validated and I need to convince you all because the world's going to end and blah, blah, blah, blah. You're just not buying into any of it.

You are vibrationally operating at a very high level where you've gone beyond these things. You choose your intention which is to ensure that you have left somebody feeling better about themselves. If we all master that, we're in heaven.

Lane: I assure you—there's no downside to that.

It doesn't diminish your power. It doesn't reduce your worth. Quite the opposite.

When you name something beautiful in someone—something they haven't yet recognized in themselves—and you bring it forward, it lands like grace. Everyone can do that. Even in small ways.

You don't need a deep relationship. You can create a micro-moment with someone in passing—a checkout clerk, a delivery driver, a stranger in a parking lot. A sincere thank-you. A real point of presence. It changes everything.

## Chapter 26
# Being Untouchable

Jane: You touched on an important point. You don't need others to validate yourself. That should be rule Number One on any self-mastery journey. Do not look outside yourself for validation.

Lane: Do not. Period.

Validation comes from within. It's your birthright.

If you're constantly looking for others to recognize your brilliance, you're going to exhaust yourself chasing scraps. Because here is a truth that is difficult to admit—most people don't care. Not really. Most people are too wrapped up in their own stories.

Jane: How do you validate yourself?

Lane: I'm impenetrable.

Jane: I love that. Impenetrable.

Lane: I'm impenetrable because I lived through rejection. For years. Instead of crumbling, I refined. I rewrote. I sharpened. I made my work so clear, so airtight, so undeniably meaningful that I knew—without needing applause—when something I created had real power.

That doesn't mean I never get discouraged. I stopped outsourcing my worth. I know this might sound like ego—but it's not. It's the product of relentless work. I honed my skills in every arena until I became unshakably confident in what I do.

Having worked in the NYC talent agency world, I've seen how arbitrary external approval really is. So much of it is opinion. So much of it is politics. Very little of it is based on merit. It always serves the giver of the compliment.

Furthermore, I've been in entertainment, media, journalism, alternative news—and let me tell you, most people don't even know what they're talking about. Some do, yes. What I found, though, is that true mastery is rare.

Does that sound horribly egotistical?

Jane: No, because it's a program for us too, the tall poppy syndrome. Cut down ourselves and don't brag. That's a program. The more people who confidently speak like this and shine their light, the more it gives others permission to do the same.

Lane: That's the difference. I'm not bragging. I'm owning it.

Also—context matters. If I'm in a CrossFit class, I know I'm the worst one there.

I'm 100 percent confident I'm making a complete fool of myself.

Certainty works both ways.

I also know—without a shred of doubt—who I am, and what I'm capable of.

## Your Powerful Manifestation Ability

For the second time in a short span—maybe a week, two weeks—I manifested something negative. Not catastrophic, but not good either. I thought it, and then it happened. That's the part that got my attention.

The first incident involved a coffee pot. I was on my way to visit my mom, and she mentioned she needed a little one-cup maker. I searched my garage and told her the only one I could find was a big 12-cup machine. She said, "Bring it anyway." As I grabbed it, I had this fleeting thought: If I give her this, then I won't have my backup coffee maker… and what if something happens to mine right before a big meeting?

The next morning, just before leaving, my coffee pot broke.

It was immediate. There was no lag, no delay, no mistaking the link. That's when I knew I had to tighten up my thoughts.

The second time it happened, it was the door from my bedroom to the back deck. I use that door all the time—it's peaceful out there, a great place for the dog. For some reason, whenever the handymen were around, they couldn't get that door open. Still, I always could. I'd touch it and it would glide open, and they'd stare at me like I had some kind of magic. I'd laugh as they asked, "How did you do that?"

For a full year, I had no problem. Then, yesterday, as I opened the door, I caught myself thinking—maybe a little smugly—Funny how they could never open it, but I always can.

This morning, the door wouldn't budge. Completely jammed.

It's uncanny how these manifestations are becoming instantaneous. I realized, the more powerful we get, the more precise and responsible we must be.

Jane: If you flip that and say, "Okay, I can open the door effortlessly and easily," are you forcing that thought, and therefore it's not manifesting?

Lane: Yes, exactly. That's the trap. It's like when I healed the arthritis in my finger. I'd had pain in the tip of my middle finger for a year—couldn't even bend it. One night the pain woke me up, and I'd had enough. I issued a command to my cells: Heal this finger now. Then I went back to sleep.

In the morning, I could bend it. I've been able to ever since.

I haven't yet been able to replicate that result with other parts of my body—not as obviously, anyway. I do know I heal quickly. That moment showed me what's possible.

Jane: I've got similar stories of watching what I manifest with my thoughts. Every time I have a bad thought I quickly bring a shield in. So, if it does happen, I'm still protected.

Lane: It's fascinating. Instant manifestation is real—and it's only going to accelerate. In my experience, it happens most easily when the thought is unconscious, unforced.

Jane: Yes, when it's not a forced one. It seems very difficult to control every single thought that comes to us, but I know that's what we have to do in order to become crystalline, right?

**Your Mighty Self**

The pineal gland sits at the center of your brain. This tiny gland —often called the seat of the soul—is the gateway to your highest connection, your intuition, and your inner knowing. Yet, for most people, it's been shut down, calcified, numbed out. Why? Fluoride. Chemicals. Beyond that, we've been taught to ignore it. To ignore the very sense that helps link us to the higher realms.

Why has there been such a targeted assault on the pineal gland?

Because when you're disconnected from it, you're easier to manipulate. You stop trusting yourself. You doubt your inner guidance. You lose your knowing.

So, what can we do about it?

Start by reclaiming your discernment. Use your intuition as your compass. Strengthen that inner sense until it's louder than the noise around you.

If you want something tangible, try iodine—Edgar Cayce's version, Atomodine, still exists—or zeolite to assist detox. Don't stop there. Speak directly to your pineal. Tell it to awaken. Command it to decalcify. Anchor into your heart's intuition. Make that your baseline.

When you do this, you're not just working on a gland. You're unfreezing your entire being.

You are initiating the crystalline state.

This is where your whole system begins to rewire. Your cells upgrade. Your DNA activates. You begin to dissolve pain—

emotional, physical, spiritual. You shed density. You rise. With that rise comes remembrance.

You remember who you are.

You remember why you came.

You shed the lies and illusions. The traps, the masks, the external approval-seeking. You move into coherence. You become a being of frequency, of resonance, of unshakable clarity. You are no longer prey to this world's distortions. The Creator is no longer a concept—you feel that presence, as one with you. Your love for others flows like a river because there is no blockage anymore.

That is the gift. That is the freedom.

That... is what it means to unleash the rebel within.

# Appendix: The Exit Sequence
## From Awakening to Embodiment

What follows is not self-help.

It is not a set of tips, affirmations, or strategies for feeling better while remaining inside the same structures that made you uneasy in the first place. It will not optimize your productivity, improve your mindset, or help you succeed more comfortably within a system you already sense is misaligned.

It is not advice.

Nothing in the pages ahead asks to be followed blindly or adopted as doctrine. There are no guarantees offered, no promises of ease, no assurances that outcomes will be tidy. What is presented here is orientation — a way of seeing that inevitably alters how you move.

And it is not safe.

Not because it is reckless, sensational, or extreme — but because safety, as it is currently defined, depends on compliance, predictability, and participation. The moment you withdraw unquestioned agreement, safety becomes conditional. The moment you stop optimizing life inside the illusion, you begin to stand outside its protections.

## Appendix: The Exit Sequence

The segments ahead are written for those who have already seen through the illusion — not intellectually, not hypothetically, but viscerally. For those who can no longer pretend not to notice the gap between what is said and what is done. For those who have felt the quiet dissonance grow loud enough that distraction no longer works.

If you are still looking for comfort, reassurance, or validation, stop here.

If you want confirmation that everything will work out neatly.

If you want to feel empowered without being inconvenienced.

If you want awakening without consequence.

This is not the place.

What follows is for those willing to withdraw consent — not dramatically, not publicly, but internally and irreversibly. For those willing to redirect allegiance away from narratives, institutions, and habits that no longer align with truth, even when doing so complicates relationships, choices, and identity.

This is for those prepared to live differently.

Not performatively.

Not perfectly.

But deliberately.

There may be costs: certainty, approval, ease, and the comfort of outsourcing responsibility. There may be moments when you feel less protected than before — not because you are weaker, but because you are no longer hiding inside the crowd.

Awareness is not the revolution.

Awareness can be consumed, discussed, admired, and set aside. Awareness can coexist with the very systems it critiques. Awareness alone changes nothing.

Embodiment is the revolution.

Embodiment means your choices begin to reflect what you know.

Your energy stops feeding what you no longer believe in.

Your life becomes congruent — even when that congruence is inconvenient.

## Appendix: The Exit Sequence

From this point forward, the material is no longer theoretical. It moves into territory where ideas become actions, and actions reshape consequences.

Proceed if you are prepared to act.

# Gate I: Escaping the Theater of Control

Politics is not governance. It's theater. A carefully staged production meant to simulate debate, dramatize dissent, and disguise the machinery of control.

What you've been sold as "democracy" is managed conflict—scripted talking points, scandal cycles, choreographed opposition. You're not watching leadership in action. You're watching actors in a rigged audition, all vying for continued relevance in a game where the rules are hidden, and the winners are preselected.

While the public is baited into partisan brawls, the real deals are made in private. Laws are passed unread. Lobbyists roam unchecked. Politicians grow rich off insider trades while tightening the grip on the people they claim to serve.

If this system were truly about representation or service, we wouldn't need to imagine basic reforms:

- Equal public funding for campaigns—no corporate donations.
- Jail time for lobbying bribes and insider trading.
- Transparent, readable legislation—no bloated, unreadable bills.
- Performance-based audits for Congress.

## Gate I: Escaping the Theater of Control

- Penalties for lying to the public, and lifetime bans on jumping from office to defense contractor.

Yet, none of it exists. It's not for lack of ideas—it's by design.

This isn't a broken system. It's a parasitic one. Built not to serve you, but to extract from you—your labor, your attention, your allegiance. The political class is a revolving mask. The hand behind it rarely changes.

Until you see that clearly—not emotionally, but structurally—you remain trapped in their game. Once the illusion crumbles, something vital shifts. You stop begging to be heard in a rigged arena. You reclaim your agency from the theater.

### Two Wings of the Same Bird

We've been conditioned to pick sides. Red versus blue. Left versus right. Instead, step back far enough, and the illusion of opposition collapses. These sides are funded by the same donors, advised by the same consultants, and kept in line by the same gatekeepers.

For much of modern history, the United States has not operated as a free republic but as a corporate construct—managed by unelected entities, financial syndicates, and entrenched bureaucracies. Elections provided a sense of control, but the outcomes rarely shifted the deeper trajectory. Wars are bipartisan. Surveillance is bipartisan. Bailouts, censorship, and global entanglements—all bipartisan.

Then came a fracture.

A figure emerged who didn't speak the right language, didn't need the money, didn't follow the script. He disrupted the narrative. The backlash has been swift—media hysteria, coordinated investigations, institutional revolt. Not because he was flawless. Not because he was pure. It was because he was unowned.

Is he a savior? A decoy? A disruptor with unknown motives? Time will tell. Regardless, something has changed. The script has cracked. The machinery is now exposed. Millions are beginning to see the stage for what it is.

## Gate I: Escaping the Theater of Control

That alone is a turning point. Because once you glimpse the strings, you stop worshiping the puppets.

At our core, most people want the same things: clean food, good health, safe communities, freedom to speak, and dominion over our lives. These are not political ideals. They are human ones. They are dangerous to the parasite class, which thrives on our division.

**Manufactured Scandal**

In a system this fortified, genuine autonomy is treated like a virus.

Politicians who step out of line are rarely debated—they're discredited, entrapped, or erased. If a headline-friendly scandal doesn't surface, one will be fabricated. If that fails, the person might vanish—silenced by suicide, accident, or family tragedy.

This isn't paranoia. It's precedent.

Whistleblowers are jailed. True journalists disappear. Reformers find themselves under investigation overnight. These tactics aren't new—they're the standard operating procedure of power structures built to protect themselves.

Most so-called leaders aren't governing. They're enforcing. They answer not to you, but to donors, corporations, NGOs, and the unelected operators shaping your reality without consent. The higher the role, the tighter the leash.

When we say "governors," we don't just mean presidents or senators. We mean the whole latticework: royal dynasties, banking families, energy regulators, media figureheads, foundation elites, and public health czars. Any node of control that shapes your environment without transparency belongs to this architecture.

This has never been about being "left" or "right," but about being controlled by those who are bought, blackmailed, or bound by compromise.

This compromise only works as long as people keep believing the story.

**The Illusion Collapses**

## Gate I: Escaping the Theater of Control

What we're witnessing now—especially in the wake of global exposure and digital transparency—is not democracy in action. It's the unraveling of a long-running production.

The public is beginning to see the wires. The soundbites are failing. The patterns are repeating. The cast of characters can no longer hold the illusion together.

Because real leadership is no longer rising from institutions—it's emerging from the edges. From the disobedient. From the truth-tellers and whistleblowers, the healers and hackers, the ones who cannot be bought or banned.

They've been called extremists, conspiracy theorists, traitors. Now look again. These are the ones refusing to kneel to a system that was never designed to serve you.

With every new crack in the facade, more people awaken. Not to chaos—but to clarity.

The revolution isn't televised. It doesn't require violence. It begins when you stop playing your part in their illusion.

That is where power dissolves. This is where freedom begins.

### The Media: Weaponized Perception

If you still believe you're making up your own mind after watching the news, it's time to pause.

Today's media is the Ministry of Narrative. A consolidated, corporate-controlled information web designed to seed confusion, manufacture consent, and reinforce the worldview most beneficial to those in power. What once claimed to serve the public is now a psychological control grid.

As of 2018, six media conglomerates controlled most of what you see, read, and hear globally—across television, publishing, digital content, film, video games, and more. Since then, the grip has deepened. Tech giants like Google, Meta, and Amazon overtook the old gatekeepers, embedding censorship algorithms into every scroll, swipe, and search. Now, those algorithms are being superseded by something even more insidious: artificially intelligent systems

## Gate I: Escaping the Theater of Control

marketed as neutral arbiters of truth. That said, AI is not neutral. It pushes the blind spots, biases, and agendas of its creators—with the illusion of objectivity. Unlike traditional media, which wore its bias on its sleeve, AI cloaks its influence in the language of research, optimization, and efficiency. It doesn't just steer your search results—it rewrites the frame of the question. In doing so, it becomes the next phase of informational control: invisible, unaccountable, and mistaken for omniscience.

These entities possess the power to shape your sense of reality. They are tied into think tanks like the Council on Foreign Relations —home to global policymakers, intelligence veterans, and unelected influencers. They feed both political parties. They shape both sides of every debate. They create the illusion of difference while maintaining control of the entire spectrum.

Propaganda is no longer a wartime relic—it's policy. In 2012, the U.S. repealed the Smith-Mundt Act, effectively legalizing the use of state-sponsored psychological operations on the domestic population. Since then, "fact-checkers" have replaced investigation, dissent has been rebranded as extremism, and the digital town square has become a surveillance trap. Currently, efforts are underway by the administration to reinstate the Act's original protections—though whether this signals genuine reform or narrative control by another name remains to be seen.

Whether it's CNN or Fox, MSNBC or YouTube, if your source is funded by the same hands that steer global policy you're seeing what's permitted or what has been staged.

The media is the battlefield. The war is for your perception. The threat isn't only misinformation; it is also omission. It's the buried search result, the imperfect AI response, the deleted account, the invisible algorithm that decides what never reaches you.

Most don't realize it's happening. They repeat slogans they didn't write, enforce taboos they didn't question, and cheer for wars they never agreed to or truly understand.

## Gate I: Escaping the Theater of Control

Yet—this is the line where rebellion begins. Not with violence. Instead, with discernment.

When you unplug from the screen, when you cross-reference, when you pause before reacting—something radical happens. You reclaim your territorial integrity. You begin to see not just what you were shown, but what was hidden.

**Breaking the Spell**

We are no longer in an age of perfect secrecy. Cracks have formed in the narrative. New whistleblowers are emerging. Classified files are leaking. Testimonies are surfacing—no longer fringe, but vindicated.

Disclosure does not arrive with fanfare. It drips. It fragments. It comes half-coded, wrapped in paradox. Because the full truth would rupture too many illusions at once—and the system knows it.

Even in its unraveling, the machine still tries to steer the story.

This is where your discernment becomes your compass. Not everything revealed is trustworthy. Not every alternative voice is clean. Your task is not to react—but to see.

Ask: Who benefits from this narrative? Who funds this platform? Who gains from my fear, my hope, my outrage?

Learn to hold paradox. Question without spiraling. Seek truth without certainty. Feel what resonates—not in the mind, but in the deeper body where clarity lives.

Because the truth is rising. It's messy. It's raw. It will not be handed to you—you must walk toward it. With courage. With vision. With the refusal to play along.

The spell is breaking. Those who dare to see beyond the veil are building what comes next.

**TOOLKIT**

Awareness is your first weapon, but awareness without method leaves you vulnerable to the same scripts that have always run the

## Gate I: Escaping the Theater of Control

show. If you want to step out of the theater, you need to strip away the illusions and take control of your own stage.

1. **Spot the Script.** Make a mental note of headlines, slogans, and repeated talking points you encounter in media, politics, and advertising. Make sure to ask yourself as each one pops up: "Who benefits if I believe this?"
2. **Decode the Set Pieces.** When a staged crisis appears—complete with symbols, dramatic footage, and celebrity endorsements—pause before reacting. Ask these questions: Is this really urgent or is it manufactured urgency? Is this narrative suspiciously neat? What's missing from the story?
3. **Audit Your Inputs.** Identify 5 or more of your top sources of information. Cut at least two that fail your trust test. Replace them with independent. journalists, primary documents, and direct observation.
4. **Build Your Own Signal.** Create a small network—friends, family, colleagues—who exchange vetted information. Rotate who researches what so no one burns out.
5. **Practice Strategic Withdrawal.** Learn to exit the performance without fanfare. That might mean disengaging from certain conversations, unfollowing emotional triggers, or refusing to give attention to bad actors.

# Gate II: Exit the Currency Trap

It's time for another truth: there is no knight in shining armor coming to fix things. No white hat savior in a suit. No election that will restore your freedom. That's a hard pill. This shouldn't disturb you, because the liberating truth is right behind it: you don't need one.

We've been trained—programmed, really—to believe change comes from the top. That leadership means looking up. That voting is our most powerful tool. History tells a different story. The greatest revolutions, the most meaningful shifts, always begin from below. From the people who finally say, "No more."

In 2012, there was a glimpse of something different. Ron Paul—love him or not—spoke truths that shook the system. End the Fed. Restore liberty. Stop the endless wars. He had crowds that rivaled rock concerts, and a message that crossed political lines. Thus, they buried him. Just like they buried Dennis Kucinich, Cynthia McKinney, JFK, RFK, JFK Jr., Robert F. Kennedy Jr., and others who refused to toe the line. Malcolm X. Martin Luther King Jr. Julian Assange. Edward Snowden. Gary Webb. These weren't perfect people—but they dared to name names, expose corruption, or chal-

## Gate II: Exit the Currency Trap

lenge the machinery. The machine doesn't allow real reformers to rise. They're either smeared, sidelined, or silenced.

The Federal Reserve—still here. Still not federal. Still not a reserve. Still acting as a private banking cartel draining your wealth through inflation, market rigging, and debt slavery. Created in 1913 by design, on the eve of Christmas, while the public was distracted and Congress half-empty, every president who stood against it—Lincoln, Garfield, Kennedy—was taken out. Those who serve it are elevated, protected, and canonized.

What's the answer?

Withdraw your consent.

Not by violence. Not by shouting at a screen. Instead, by reclaiming your energy, your attention, your currency, your choices.

- Stop funding companies that poison your body, your water, your air.
- Stop watching media that lies to you.
- Stop buying food that weakens your system.
- Stop idolizing people who despise you.
- Stop begging institutions for scraps of your own freedom.

Use your wallet like a weapon. Use your mind like a firewall. Use your presence like a frequency disruptor.

Grow your own food if you can. Barter and build local economies. Buy local. Support creators and healers who walk the walk. Unplug from the algorithm. Read banned books. Learn lost skills. Spend less. Waste less. Want less.

Perhaps most importantly: remember who you are.

Are you a political demographic? Are you a left or right puppet? Are you a consumer to be herded or a taxpayer to be bled dry?

No. You are a free, God-connected being. Born with the right to think, to move, to speak, to dream—and to reject the system that feeds on your ignorance.

The act of seeing through it is the first rebellion. The act of choosing differently is what builds the new world.

You don't collapse a system by yelling at it.

## Gate II: Exit the Currency Trap

You collapse it by making it irrelevant.

The good news is: we're already doing it.

The only question now is—will you keep going?

**The Federal Reserve: The Engine of Enslavement**

The cornerstone of modern control isn't war. It's not media. It's not even government.

It's money.

More precisely, debt-based currency controlled by private banking interests—enshrined and enforced through the blood-signed covenant known as the Federal Reserve.

Installed in secret on Christmas Eve in 1913, the Federal Reserve was never a federal institution. It was, and remains, a private banking cartel. Its function? To create money from nothing, lend it at interest, and then bleed the public through inflation, taxation, and debt servitude. It's a system that ensures you are always running—just to stay afloat.

It didn't stop with America. Through the International Monetary Fund (IMF), the same bloodline banking dynasties extended their reach across the world. They offered "help"—loans, restructuring, development funds—and then crushed nations under the weight of repayment, stealing their natural resources and creating internal wars.

They did it to Greece. To Italy. To Portugal. To Argentina. To Yugoslavia. When that wasn't enough, they engineered revolutions under the banner of freedom—only to replace governments with puppet regimes that bowed to the global financial machine.

Make no mistake: what appeared to be a grassroots rebellion in places like Libya, Syria, and Egypt, was orchestrated collapse, designed to destroy infrastructures, plunder resources, destabilize autonomy, and profit from the rebuild. This is war as a business model. It's been repeated over and over.

Weapons of mass destruction? Never found. Instead, oil

contracts, government contracts, and reconstruction deals flowed like gold.

It was all done in your name. By people who call themselves your leaders. Who wrap themselves in flags and smile for cameras while trading lives for capital.

**The Un-human Architects of Control**

Once you understand the financial system is rigged, the next question becomes: who rigged it?

Who benefits from endless war, perpetual debt, social division, and human suffering?

Some say it's the global elite. Others say it's ancient bloodlines. Still others suggest extraterrestrial forces or interdimensional parasites. You don't have to subscribe to any theory. If you observe carefully, you'll see the pattern clearly enough: they don't think like us. They don't feel like us.

Compassion is absent. Empathy is absent. Remorse is absent.

What they possess is ambition. Hunger. Cold, reptilian logic. A relentless obsession with power, control, and—above all—immortality.

Every American president but one can be traced to European royal bloodlines. The same is true for monarchs and prime ministers across the Western world. Coincidence? Maybe. If you think the entire planet just accidentally fell under the control of the same interwoven families—you're not thinking clearly.

What keeps their control alive? Fear.

Fear is the fuel of the matrix. It is the invisible currency of mass obedience. They pump it into your bloodstream every single day.
- Fear of losing your job
- Fear of nuclear war
- Fear of the climate
- Fear of disease
- Fear of dissent
- Fear of freedom itself

## Gate II: Exit the Currency Trap

They will threaten your food, your health, your money, your children, your community—because fear short-circuits the rational mind. It keeps you locked in survival mode. It keeps you begging for the very system that exploits you.

What then, do you do?

You stop believing the fear.

**Paper Shackles**

Why should money accrue interest? Why should we borrow what should be freely available for human growth?

Abraham Lincoln didn't believe we should. He fought to create interest-free currency—money that served the people, not the bankers. That was the real reason he was assassinated. So was Kennedy, who attempted a similar maneuver. So was Garfield. The list goes on.

Every time a leader tries to decouple from the banking elite, they are removed—by scandal, by bullet, or by proxy.

Meanwhile, the illusion persists: that your hard-earned dollars represent wealth. In truth, they represent debt—printed by a private institution and lent back to you with compounding interest. The more you work, the more they own.

J.P. Morgan. Chase. Rockefeller. Rothschild. These names aren't history—they are current, controlling forces. They don't operate on loyalty or patriotism. They operate on profit extraction.

Worse, they're not done.

As for the rebel truth: you are not powerless in this equation.

Yes, you need to pay rent. Yes, you need food and clothes. But you don't have to play their game. You can change the rules by how you live:

- Grow your own where possible.
- Join local co-ops.
- Barter. Trade. Share. Repair.
- Resist the compulsion to consume.
- Buy only what serves you—and starve the beast of your energy.

## Gate II: Exit the Currency Trap

You don't have to go off-grid tonight. You can begin today to divest from the system that enslaves you and re-invest in the one that sustains you: human connection, local resilience, spiritual authenticity, nature and simplicity.

Luxury isn't the enemy. Blind consumption is.

We've been sold a dream that became a trap: bigger houses, faster machines, smarter tech, shinier everything. If you look beneath the glitter, you'll find what we've lost: Peace. Purpose. Time. Truth.

If you look around the world—outside the resort zones—you'll see communities that live with far less, yet feel far more alive. They know their neighbors. They share meals. They watch the sky, not the screen. They remember what matters.

It's not too late to remember, too.

Because once you see that the money is fake you stop worshipping the game and you start building something real.

### The 1%: Manufactured Scarcity, Engineered Obedience

Travel to non-Westernized regions of the world, and something becomes clear: the excess is missing. Not the joy, or community—just the excess. Somehow, the system has convinced the Western world that more equals better. Bigger homes, faster cars, higher status. But at what cost?

It's clear that less than 1% of the population controls nearly all of the world's wealth. That's the rigged game laid bare.

They own the land. They own the banks. They own the patents, the airwaves, the algorithms, the vaccines, the farmland, and the digital platforms. Still, they ask you to donate after every disaster. They ask you to round up your grocery bill for charity. They ask you to feel guilty for not doing enough.

Meanwhile, they hoard.

They offshore their wealth. They build bunkers in New Zealand. They start philanthropic foundations that serve as tax shelters while telling you what's best for your health, your children, your future.

COVID wasn't just a pandemic—it was a wealth transfer on a

## Gate II: Exit the Currency Trap

planetary scale. So was the 2008 housing collapse. So was every so-called humanitarian fundraiser where the money quietly disappeared and the billionaires got richer.

Disaster capitalism is the model now. Create a crisis. Frighten the masses. Transfer wealth upward under the guise of saving them.

The worst part? Most people still clap for it. They repost the slogans. They buy the ribbons. They say, "We're all in this together," while the 1% doubles their net worth behind gated walls and biometric doors.

### The Final Pivot: From Mountaintop to Ground Game

This is the bridge between your inner awakening and your outer rebellion. You are no longer just a seeker on a mountaintop. You are a sovereign being on the ground, in the matrix, breaking the spell from within.

It's not enough to hold light—you must wield it. You must be love and clarity, love and boundaries, love and fire.

The phase you're entering will challenge everything you thought you knew. You are being asked to discern truth in a world built on illusion. You are being asked to stand firm when others flee. You are being asked to see what others cannot—or will not—see.

When the moment of pure clarity comes, you'll realize: your ascension was never just for you. It was for all of us.

The clearer you become, the freer we get. Clarity without embodiment is hollow.

You've seen through the illusion. Now comes the harder part: navigating it.

### TOOLKIT

The spell isn't just about money—it's about belief. Your participation in their system is the current that keeps it alive. To weaken the current, you need clear alternatives and deliberate actions.

## Gate II: Exit the Currency Trap

1. **Track Your Tributaries.** For 30 days, track every dollar you spend and where it flows. Color-code by corporate giant, local business, or self-reliance. This should prove enlightening in and of itself.
2. **Cut the Poisoned Wells.** Replace at least three recurring purchases from corporations tied to harmful practices with local or direct alternatives.
3. **Build a Parallel Economy Map**. List local farmers, artisans, repair shops, barter networks, and skill shares in your area. Keep it offline as well, should systems fail.
4. **Change Your Store of Value.** Learn about physical assets—precious metals, tools, seeds—that hold value outside of fiat currency. Acquire them slowly and discreetly.
5. **Practice Small Sovereignties**. Once a week, make a transaction that bypasses the system entirely—barter, gift economy, cash purchase, or direct trade.

# Gate III: Reclaiming the Body

Many households live with a holistic mindset—eating natural foods, trusting plant medicine, and questioning anything synthetic. When health issues arise, they turn to nature before seeking conventional medical intervention. This approach stands in sharp contrast to the wider Western world, where highly processed foods and synthetic solutions dominate. In school lunchrooms, the standard fare is often nutritionally poor—simple, heavily processed options that reflect a larger shift in society's relationship with food. Viewed from a distance, the pattern is clear: convenience and profit eclipse nourishment and wellbeing.

The average lunchroom is a war zone of engineered food-like substances. Packaged chemical bombs in bright boxes, fluorescent yogurts, and "fruit" snacks that haven't touched a vine, dominate. The cafeteria line is a conveyor belt of compromise—stocked with calorically dense, nutritionally bankrupt meals under the banner of government subsidy. It's not just low-income families relying on these toxic standards. Even in wealthy neighborhoods, McDonald's is handed over like a trophy—an edible gold star for good behavior. "You were good today, so here's your reward: inflammatory oils,

## Gate III: Reclaiming the Body

neurotoxic preservatives, genetically modified buns, hormone-laced meat, and hormone-disrupting packaging."

This isn't food. It's immune sabotage. Gut-destroying seed oils, high-fructose corn syrup, glyphosate residues, synthetic emulsifiers, and artificial dyes—many banned in other countries—are routine fuel for growing bodies. Meanwhile, autoimmune conditions, behavioral disorders, chronic fatigue, and food sensitivities skyrocket. Still, this is normalized and rewarded.

We don't just have a health crisis. We have a cultural one. A generational forgetting of what nourishment is—and who benefits when we forget?

My family? We mostly ate green things. This, of course, made me a target as a child.

Classmates cackled at my lunches. Through the pain of ostracism, I came to learn something powerful: being different wasn't a curse—it was a gift. It forced me to define who I was on my own terms. It showed me the cost of conformity early. It gave me the strength to keep going on a singular if sometimes solitary lifepath.

I grew up hearing about the teachings of Adele Davis, one of the pioneers of the organic, whole-food movement. Meanwhile, my great-grandfather homesteaded in New York before communities were built out there. He maintained a thriving organic farm—not for profit, but for people. He fed his family, the neighbors, the nuns from the local convent, and anyone who came by. Money wasn't the motive. Wisdom and stewardship were.

He was a self-taught inventor. He rigged up his own solar panels before that was cool. He engineered tools and machinery for farm use. One of my favorite childhood memories was his use of an old tennis racket to swat insects off produce—never once did he use a pesticide. He didn't need to. He worked in harmony with the land. He grew up in Manitoba, Canada, where farming was life.

I can only imagine how our ancestors would be rolling in their graves over what we now call agriculture.

### Gate III: Reclaiming the Body

**The Zucchini Rebellion**

I spent summers on Great-Grandpa's farm—not every summer, but enough. He'd point out vegetables and teach me how to grow them. My family had its financial struggles—my father's industry took repeated blows from recession cycles—and many times we relied on the farm to get us through.

We'd bring home bags and bags of cherry tomatoes. My mom would turn them into soups and sauces that tasted like sunlight and soil. The crown jewel of the farm was his zucchini. These were monstrous. I'm talking 6 or 7 inches in diameter, easily 20 inches long. I'm aware that sounds exaggerated, but if you've ever seen the Woody Allen movie Sleeper, you'll understand the visual. One zucchini, mixed with pasta, fed our family for a week.

Great-Grandpa once shared a secret with me. In his younger days, there were horses and cows on the streets. He'd go scavenging for their droppings—manure—which he used as fertilizer. He moved on to store-bought manure at some point, but his produce remained awe-inspiring.

**The Great Seed Heist**

Great-Grandpa generated his own seeds every year. He perfected his own garlic strains, squash, corn, tomatoes, asparagus—you name it. Everything was hand-sown, hand-raised, and hand-harvested. This was not a hobby garden. This was a one-man revolution.

You can imagine the pain and outrage I felt witnessing the rise of Monsanto and the near-eradication of organic farming. Under the guise of progress, they waged war on seed integrity. They poisoned the global supply chain. Mass suicides of farmers in India, forced GMO adoption, and the criminalization of seed saving—all of it was real. All of it was orchestrated.

They strong-armed countries across the globe into adopting genetically modified, pesticide-ridden, sterile seeds that stripped the

## Gate III: Reclaiming the Body

Earth of vitality and stripped our food of nutrition. Most people still don't know.

I do. Because I saw the difference up close.

Back to the lunchroom.

My classmates had their Wonder Bread and Oscar Mayer baloney. Me? I had stone-ground bread, sprouts, dark leafy greens, and odd meats my mom found at the one health food store in the area. We were barely getting by—but she made it work.

That store was run by a woman named Pearl, and I hated going there. Not because of the food, but because I would sit on the floor for what felt like hours while my mom received lessons from Pearl on whole proteins, nutritional synergy, and how to stretch a dollar while still feeding a family of four.

There was no Whole Foods. No organic aisles. No quinoa bowls or packaged "superfoods." We had a few guidebooks, and whatever bulk grains Pearl could spare.

At one point, my family went through a vegetarian phase—back when there were no decent vegetarian options. My mom boiled soybeans and passed them off to us because they were "whole proteins." The taste? Somewhere between a boiled blister and foot fungus. We revolted. We went back to meat.

Still, I marvel at what my mom pulled off. She was a magician. A miracle worker.

**Today's Traps**

Today, families have endless healthy options. You don't need to pull together meals made from soybeans, in fact you can't, because they're all GMO'd now. You do need to watch out for the wolves in lab coats, however.

The "Beyond Meat" products being sold as ethical, healthy choices? Toxic cocktails full of preservatives, unnatural compounds, and heavily processed junk—dreamed up in boardrooms by people who have decided that bio-engineered "food product" grown in a lab should be passed off as a healthy alternative. It doesn't stop there.

## Gate III: Reclaiming the Body

Welcome to the modern health food aisle, where nothing is sacred and everything has a marketing team. Plant-based milks? Mostly water, emulsifiers, and nut residue rebranded as wellness. Add to this inflammatory, fat inducing, seed oils, and you might as well go back to antibiotic-infused cow's milk. Almonds that once crunched now whisper through additives. "Vegan cheese" manages to melt like plastic because it is crafted from oils, modified starch, and whatever lab ingredient they could find that doesn't require an animal.

Protein bars? Candy bars in athletic wear. The label says "20g protein," but the fine print screams sorbitol, maltodextrin, and sweeteners that double as neurotoxins . Don't be fooled by "Greek-style" yogurt—it's often sugar-packed, low-culture, and loaded with thickeners that make it look creamy without offering a shred of gut support.

The crown jewel of deception might be the low-fat scam. Once hailed as the answer to heart disease, it turned entire grocery aisles into carb orgies. What they took out in fat, they replaced with sugar, corn syrup, or chemically engineered mouthfeel. That's before you even get to the "sugar-free" zone—where products hide behind friendly blue or yellow packets while quietly frying your brain with aspartame, sucralose, and other toxins wearing a halo.

But hey, it's all FDA approved. So it must be good, right?

Once you see it, you can't unsee it. Once you taste real food again —like something your great-grandparents would recognize—you realize how deep this rabbit hole goes. This isn't nutrition. It's a war on your body, and it's being waged at the grocery store.

Still, you have a choice. You can opt out of this matrix of manipulated food, nutrient depletion, and synthetic solutions. You can start small, with a single meal, a single habit, a single decision to say: I remember what real food is. I remember who I am.

## Antibodies Over Agendas

This being said, when my own children were born, I was on a

## Gate III: Reclaiming the Body

mission to keep them as vibrantly healthy as possible. This wasn't just about nutrition. It was about survival in a world that was changing fast and not for the better. By now, the medical-industrial complex had grown bolder. Vaccination schedules were ballooning. Parents were being pressured, shamed, and legally coerced. I was one of the few willing to question the system.

What I discovered was alarming: vaccines were not what we were led to believe. The disease eradication charts had been doctored—literally. Historical declines in deadly illnesses had occurred before vaccines were introduced, mostly due to improvements in sanitation, plumbing, and nutrition. The charts were redrawn to create a false narrative: that vaccines had "saved us." No, they hadn't.

Worse still, these injections were filled with toxic ingredients—heavy metals, aborted fetal tissue, lab-created DNA fragments, stealth viruses, and synthetic adjuvants with long-term effects no one wanted to study. There were no reliable long-term safety studies—only industry-funded, manipulated data with built-in deniability. The very foundation of the system was riddled with conflict of interest and hidden harm.

After deep research and soul searching, I made a decision: I would not vaccinate my children.

At the time, it was a terrifying stance to take. Doctors warned me of dire consequences—diphtheria, whooping cough, polio, tetanus! Even my husband wasn't on board initially. Yet my conviction was unshakable, and I hold it tenfold now. Vaccines have gotten worse. The toxicity has escalated, and the coercion has become weaponized.

Today, by the time a child turns two, they're slated to receive upwards of 70 injections—most for diseases that pose little to no serious risk in healthy children. Think rotavirus, chickenpox, Hepatitis B at birth (for a virus typically transmitted through sex or shared needles), and four separate doses of DTaP before age two. The schedule is obscene. No matter what any white coat says, these combinations have never been tested singly, or cumulatively for safety—not in any long-term, placebo-controlled way that compares fully vaccinated

## Gate III: Reclaiming the Body

children to those left unvaccinated. That study doesn't exist. It's been stonewalled for decades.

Meanwhile, your pediatrician isn't just parroting guidelines—he's profiting. For every fully vaccinated child, practices receive bonuses from insurance companies ranging from $400 to $600 per patient—as long as they meet quota. Fall below the threshold (typically 63% fully vaccinated by age two), and they lose the payout. Multiply that by hundreds of patients, and you can see why most doctors don't want to have "the talk." They've got incentives to comply—and absolutely no liability if your child reacts.

Then there's what's actually in the shots. We're talking mercury (still found in multi-dose flu vials as thimerosal), aluminum, polysorbate 80, foreign animal DNA, human fetal cells (MRC-5, WI-38), and various stealth viruses and synthetic adjuvants that bypass natural immune defenses. These aren't trace ingredients. They're biologically active agents that cross the blood-brain barrier, inflame the gut lining, and create lifelong vulnerabilities.

But wait for it...

If you simply delay until your child is past age three, most of those "critical" early vaccines become completely superfluous. Their systems are more developed, the risk of adverse reaction drops dramatically, and in many cases, natural immunity can already be acquired. These shots are no longer even "required."

They don't want you to know this. Because once you start looking, you start questioning. You start noticing things like this: the Amish, who remain largely unvaccinated, are one of the healthiest populations in America. Virtually no autism. No chronic illness. No autoimmune epidemics. No childhood cancer. They're the control group no one dares study. When they're brought up, the medical establishment either dismisses them as irrelevant or pretends they don't exist.

Nonetheless, they do exist. They are living proof.

## Gate III: Reclaiming the Body

This was never about immunity. It was about indoctrination, compliance, profit, and control.

While I refused to play along, I also knew that if we were to bypass this medical gauntlet, we needed to be intentional. If I wasn't going to vaccinate my children, how would I equip them to flourish in a world that thrives on disease?

The answer was actually simple—and ancient.

It went back to Great-Grandpa's farm.

You build the immune system.

You keep it unburdened, unpoisoned, and strong.

That's the secret.

That's the answer no one profits from.

It remains the truest, most essential health truth to this day: strengthen the immune system and you won't need interventions. This doesn't just apply to children. It applies to every person alive.

### CTRL+ALT+INJECT: Rebooting Humanity

Why do people listen to Bill Gates about vaccines?

He is not a doctor. He is not a healer. He is wanted in India for maiming children with his "health shots." He is a eugenicist heir with a monopoly mindset and a disturbing obsession with population control. The fact that this man has even spent five minutes as the face of "public health" should tell you everything you need to know about who controls the narrative.

Time for the rebel truth:

Vaccines don't create immunity. The immune system does.

You build real immunity by being exposed to life. By healing. By recovering. By nourishing your body, your gut, your nervous system, and your soul.

The more recent class of injections—the mRNA gene therapies rushed out under the banner of public safety—changed everything. These aren't vaccines in the traditional sense. They are biological operating systems. Tiny programmable machinery embedded into

## Gate III: Reclaiming the Body

your cells, capable of instructing your body to produce foreign proteins, bypassing the natural immune process entirely.

This isn't medicine. This is software uploaded into flesh.

This is where it flips into surreal territory. Anything genetically modified—by law—can be patented. That includes crops, animals, and yes...humans. Once your cells are altered by synthetic genetic material, you are no longer be considered entirely "natural" in the eyes of the law. The patent holders can lay claim—not just to the product—but to the organism that carries it. This means you.

Still think this is about your health?

There are two vaccine supply chains—one for the elite, and one for the masses. Guess which one contains preservatives, graphene oxide, aluminum salts, aborted fetal cell lines, self-assembling nanostructures, and DNA-hacking lipid nanoparticles?

Do you think your favorite politician's children took the same jab yours did?

No, they didn't. They have private biodynamic farms. They have advanced detox protocols. They have escape plans, underground hideouts, and security teams. Why? Because they know what they've done—and they're preparing for the fallout.

The next time a billionaire technocrat with dead eyes and a computer science habit tells you what to inject into your bloodstream, ask yourself this:

Are you upgrading your immunity—or surrendering your sovereignty?

### The Wellness Exit Plan

You want to opt out of the system?

Start with your health.

Feed your child breastmilk or the closest natural equivalent, like goat colostrum. Reject the lie that formula is just as good. Reclaim ancestral knowledge. Eat whole food, sunlight-fed, soil-grown nutrition—not barcoded poison wrapped in plastic.

Reject pharma dependency, synthetic hormone control, and

## Gate III: Reclaiming the Body

every so-called expert who tells you to trust methods that create profit from your illness.

They've infected us with parasites—literally and energetically. Toxins, heavy metals, emotional suppression, EMFs, GMOs, neurotoxic meds, stress-laden schedules. Their strongest weapon?

Fear.

Fear that if your child misses school, they'll fail.

Fear that if you skip the shot, you or your child will die. Or that child services will come get your child.

Fear that if you question the narrative, you'll be canceled, fired, or disappeared.

Time to face it: fear is the foundation of every illusion. Remove it, and the entire house of cards falls.

Ask yourself: if the end goal is just more money, more status, more things—what happens when you get them?

I once saw the brightest, most idealistic NYU graduates emerge full of passion to change the world only to become cogs in the very machine they swore to dismantle. Wall Street called. Big Tech called. They were seduced by salaries, mortgages, and social ladders they couldn't stop climbing—even when they hated the view.

They were transformed from rebels to regulators.

This is because joy doesn't live at the top of the pyramid, it lives in alignment. In doing what you were born to do. It lives in the part of you that's real, and brave, and unbuyable.

You want money? Great. Make it. First ask yourself: What is it for?

Is it for yachts and name-brand status? Or is it for seed libraries, healing centers, regenerative farms, off-grid shelters, soul-driven missions, and food forests?

You get to decide.

Just don't fall for the trap. Don't let your success cost your soul.

Jesus said, "Give a man a fish and feed him for a day. Teach him to fish and feed him for a lifetime." (Okay, maybe it was about seeds, but you get the drift.)

## Gate III: Reclaiming the Body

If you want to change the world, don't just give. Empower. Plant something real. Teach something true. Build something free. Spend your money where your soul feels most alive.

Because that's the real wealth, and they can't take that from you—unless you give it away.

## TOOLKIT

Health sovereignty begins with the ability to think, choose, and act outside the approved channels. No one is saying to reject all conventional medicine, but rather, to reclaim your right to informed choice.

1. **Map Your Baseline**. Record your current health status: diet, exercise, sleep, stress, known conditions. Keep it private and under your control.
2. **Build a Holistic Library**. Collect books, trusted websites, and contact info for practitioners in nutrition, herbal medicine, bodywork, and energy healing.
3. **Cross-Reference Treatments**. Before accepting any diagnosis or treatment, research at least three independent sources. Compare risks, benefits, and alternatives.
4. **Secure Your Supply Lines.** Source clean food and water. Learn to grow at least one nutrient-dense plant and prepare one natural remedy for common ailments.
5. **Form a Health Circle**. Gather a small group to share knowledge, trade remedies, and support one another during illness or injury without defaulting to the system.

# Gate IV: Sovereign Toolkit

This final segment is a toolkit for taking back control of your health and resilience. Every section is designed to give you actionable steps, practical resources, and strategies to implement right now—covering food, water, and community as the essential foundations of personal sovereignty. It's not theory, and it's not abstract. It's not "woo-woo" and it's not weird. These are methods, systems, and habits that make independence real, sustainable, and immune to the collapse or corruption of external systems.

Of course, I must state that nothing in this book is to be taken as medical advice, and as always, you must consult with a reputable health professional when illness is present.

This final toolkit takes the principles you've uncovered and turns them into tangible steps for reclaiming your physical well-being. These are the foundations that keep you healthy and free no matter what systems rise or fall. Mastering them means you're not just surviving outside the matrix—you're thriving.

You've seen the war. You've traced the poison. You know what's at stake. Now comes the most radical act of all: taking your health into

## Gate IV: Sovereign Toolkit

your own hands. Because no one is coming to save you and no system designed to weaken you will ever hand you the keys to your freedom.

These solutions are not the performative kind, but the kind that change your life from the ground up. It begins with what you feed your family, what you drink, how you grow, and who you gather with. It ends with how you reclaim the clarity, vitality, and sovereign integrity that are your birthrights.

If you're serious about reclaiming your health and stepping off the toxic treadmill that passes for modern wellness, then you're going to have to take matters into your own hands. That means sourcing clean food, safe water, and nutrient-rich options for your family that aren't poisoned by the corporate supply chain.

Start local. You'll need to find a small farm—ideally one that still honors regenerative, organic practices. Don't take their word for it. The label "natural" means nothing. Ask questions. Ask what they use on their soil. Ask whether their animals are given hormones or antibiotics. Ask if they rotate crops, use cover composting, and save their own seeds. If they hesitate to answer, that's your answer.

Next: connect with others. The lone wolf model doesn't work here. Start a co-op with neighbors or friends. It sounds daunting, but once it's in motion, a buying co-op becomes one of the simplest, most cost-effective ways to feed your family well. If no one around you seems ready, don't underestimate your leadership. Your example might be the spark someone else is waiting for.

Still stuck? Consider a community garden. Better yet, build your own vertical garden in your basement, spare room, or garage. Hydroponics can produce massive yields in small spaces. Add aquaponics—fish raised in a closed-loop system—and you've got protein and produce in a self-sustaining garden. Of course, there's always the humble fishing rod. Protein doesn't need to come from a box.

Whatever system you choose, you'll need two essentials: heirloom seeds and clean water.

Find a seed distributor with a proven track record—one that hasn't sold out to corporate interests or jumped on the panic-profit

## Gate IV: Sovereign Toolkit

bandwagon. These companies are out there, but you have to dig, pardon the pun. As for water, reverse osmosis remains a reliable purification method. Yes, there are many theories about how to "charge" or structure water, and you're free to explore them—but clean, contaminant-free water is non-negotiable.

Here's where it gets serious.

If you live in the United States, odds are you're on or near a shale formation—which means fracking chemicals like benzene, mercury, lead, strontium, and others may be seeping into your groundwater. If you're on a well, get your water tested. If you're in a city, check the reports. They're public, though not always complete. Many don't mention fluoride—which, contrary to everything you've been told, does not prevent cavities. In fact, it does something much darker.

Fluoride is a toxic waste byproduct. It calcifies your pineal gland—your body's intuitive antenna. Your spiritual signal. Your connection to higher guidance. Studies show that remote villages without fluoridated water have stronger, healthier teeth and far clearer minds than those who've had it forced into their water supply.

Ask yourself: if fluoride has been distributed in order to help your teeth resist cavities why are they forcing you to drink it? It is much more easily, effectively, and inexpensively delivered via small packets or by others means—if indeed it is for your dental health.

Do not take this lightly.

Fluoride is linked to lowered IQ, dementia, cognitive disorders, and tumor growth. It is unnecessary and deliberately harmful. If you do nothing else, invest in a water filter that eliminates fluoride at no less than 99%. This is not the time to cut corners.

Don't ignore frequency exposure. At minimum, turn off your Wi-Fi router at night, hardwire devices when you can, and consider shielding high-exposure zones—especially bedrooms and nurseries. EMF isn't theory. It's disruption at the cellular level.

While we're pulling the thread, let's revisit food.

If you're eating processed food—even if it says "organic"—you're still filling your body with allergens, endocrine disruptors, and toxic

## Gate IV: Sovereign Toolkit

residue. Your immune system grows weaker by the day fending off wheat, dairy, seed oils, and refined sugar. That constant low-level inflammation is the gateway to real illness.

You want sweetness? Reach for raw, unheated honey or true maple syrup from untreated trees. Never heat your honey—it turns into a toxin when exposed to high temperatures. Forget what the shelves are telling you. Stevia is fine, that is as long as you're not trying to conceive, because it is a natural birth control substance. I mean the real stevia, not Truvia, which is a synthetic masquerade. Organic stevia has no glycemic impact and can be a smart alternative. I used it in baking for years, and my kids never knew the difference.

That said, not every sweetener is created equal. Erythritol can wreck your digestion. Xylitol carries more question marks. Monk fruit has an aftertaste that some tolerate, others don't. Allulose appears to be a possible contender. Choose wisely, and consciously.

Let's not forget the worst offenders: artificial sweeteners and sodas, otherwise known as biochemical warfare in a bottle. They leach calcium from bones, disrupt gut bacteria, and introduce phosphates, neurotoxins, and hidden allergens your child's system was never meant to endure. Agave? Don't be fooled. Most of it is processed with high-fructose corn syrup. Labels lie.

Remember: toxins don't just need to stop entering. They need to exit.

Support your drainage pathways—sweat, lymph, liver, and bowels—through infrared saunas, dry brushing, and daily movement. Add natural binders like activated charcoal or zeolite to help escort toxins out of your system, not just stir them up. Detox these systems regularly, and don't forget detox from parasites.

Parasites are far more common than most people realize. Whether you eat sushi, travel internationally, walk barefoot outdoors, or simply own a pet—you likely have them. Not just one kind. Tapeworms, liver flukes, rope worms, microscopic protozoa—some lodge in the gut, others migrate through the brain, lungs, and liver. That chronic fatigue you've normalized? That unexplained bloating, itch-

## Gate IV: Sovereign Toolkit

ing, brain fog, weight gain or mood instability? Often, it's parasitic in origin.

Natural health practitioners are beginning to agree: parasites may be the root cause behind all – yes, you read that right – behind all chronic disease. There are dozens of parasite cleanse protocols out there—from herbs like wormwood, black walnut, and clove, to timed anti-parasitic rotations with castor oil packs and biofilm busters. The key is not just killing them, but eliminating them completely. If you don't open the exit pathways first, you'll only reabsorb what you've disturbed.

Get real light. Morning sun calibrates your circadian rhythm, boosts melatonin at night, and fuels your mitochondria. Block blue light after sunset. Your biology isn't artificial—it runs on nature's code.

Don't just stop at morning light. Your body needs full-spectrum, unfiltered sunlight for at least 20 minutes a day to synthesize natural vitamin D—one of the most critical hormones for immune function, mood regulation, calcium absorption, hormone balance, and cancer prevention. This means no sunscreen. Commercial sunscreens are one of the most insidious health scams of our era. Not only do they block your body's ability to generate vitamin D naturally, they also contain endocrine disruptors, hormone mimickers, and carcinogenic chemicals like oxybenzone and avobenzone. Slathering them on daily is like shrink-wrapping your skin in poison while telling yourself you're protected.

The truth? Vitamin D deficiency is directly linked to a higher risk of autoimmune disease, depression, and nearly every form of chronic illness—including the very cancers sunscreens claim to prevent. Real protection comes from building a solar callus gradually —exposing your skin wisely, not avoiding the sun altogether. Your skin was designed to meet the sun. It's the chemical industry that told you otherwise.

What's the bottom line?

## Gate IV: Sovereign Toolkit

This is about discernment. About remembering that your body is not a chemistry lab for synthetic shortcuts. It is a living temple.

If you want to rebel against the system that's profiting off your sickness, try this major step:

Stop feeding it.

**Reclaim Your Spark**

Let's return to the question of immune system stressors—the ones that sabotage our health at the deepest level.

If you will permit one last mention of vaccines, it is important to note that it is within your legal right—as a parent, as a free being—to refuse vaccinations for your children. At the time of this writing, 46 states in the U.S. offer a religious exemption, which can be claimed by submitting a simple form stating that vaccination violates your spiritual or religious beliefs. That form remains valid through grade school and can often follow your child into college.

This isn't about ideology. It's about informed consent. If informed consent is not free, uncoerced, and fully transparent—it is not consent at all.

Now let's widen the lens.

As I've already stated, we are besieged by environmental toxins at an unprecedented scale: mercury, cadmium, barium, fluoride, strontium, lead, and other heavy metals that have no place in the human body. These are not minor irritants—they are biological disruptors, neurologic poisons, and mitochondrial saboteurs. They are being introduced through multiple delivery mechanisms: polluted water, fracking runoff, contaminated soil, food additives, cleaning supplies, industrial fallout, and yes, chemtrails.

I understand the hesitation. Many recoil at that word—chemtrails—as if it immediately marks one as delusional. Florida has made them illegal. So have other states. This isn't theory. It's observation. It's whistleblower testimony. It's international patent filings, Department of Defense budgets, and weather modification contracts hiding in plain sight.

## Gate IV: Sovereign Toolkit

What many still dismiss as harmless white streaks in the sky—those daily plumes crisscrossing the atmosphere—are not the benign condensation trails (contrails) of commercial jets. They are deliberate chemical dispersals. They alter the air we breathe and contribute to contaminating the soil.

The implications are enormous. There is growing evidence that chemtrail particulates carry nanotechnology, genetically disruptive agents, and disease-causing compounds. Chronic illnesses such as Epstein-Barr, Morgellons, Lyme, Lupus and AIDS are increasingly being traced back to environmental bioengineering—spreading not merely through ticks or physical contact, but through aerosolized delivery systems that bypass every layer of informed consent.

You are not imagining things. The rise in autoimmune disorders, unexplained neurological conditions, chronic fatigue, fibromyalgia, infertility, autism, and so many "mystery illnesses" is not coincidental. The terrain is being attacked from the outside in.

What can you do?

First, protect your internal terrain. You can't stop the sky—but you can fortify your body. That means daily detox practices: binders like zeolite, fulvic acid, and activated charcoal to trap and escort heavy metals out; glutathione to support liver function; and chlorella to magnetize toxins for safe removal. Consider nascent iodine to displace halogens like bromide and fluorine, which weaken your defenses. Get adequate silica—it helps detox aluminum, a major chemtrail component. Don't forget: sweating is sacred. Whether it's sauna, movement, or hot baths with magnesium salts—your skin is a drainage pathway. Use it.

Second, neutralize what you can. EMF exposure amplifies the effects of these particulates, especially the nano components. Ground yourself daily—bare feet on earth is vital. Use EMF-shielding paint or fabrics where possible. Unplug Wi-Fi at night. Install dirty electricity filters. These steps won't eliminate the problem, but they lower the body's total burden.

Third, build local pressure. This isn't conspiracy—it's evidence.

## Gate IV: Sovereign Toolkit

Organize screenings. Share patents. Ask questions at city councils. Contact weather modification offices in your state—yes, they exist. Demand transparency. Awareness breaks the spell.

Finally, elevate your frequency. No matter how advanced their tech becomes, consciousness remains the ultimate shield. Fear feeds the system. Coherence breaks it. Detox your body, clear your mind, fortify your field—and become the kind of human their algorithms can't predict.

### Spirit Unleashed

While we're fighting on the physical front, another war rages silently within: emotional stress.

Of course, we all experience stress. It's a normal part of life. Tools like breathwork, meditation, and movement can support us in transmuting it. The kind of stress I'm referring to here is not natural. It is engineered. It is weaponized. It is fear—deliberately manufactured, socially programmed, and pumped into our systems 24/7 by a media machine that thrives on your submission.

We are not meant to live in fear. That state of prolonged hypervigilance is not native to the human soul. It is a distortion. A form of spiritual poisoning. It is the final immune system killer.

You've heard me say this throughout these pages for a reason: Fear is the control mechanism.

They've learned how to induce it. How to monetize it. How to engineer it into every breaking news alert, every pharmaceutical ad, every narrative of doom that scrolls across your screen. If fear is their frequency, love is your counter-force.

I don't claim to have every answer. However, I do know this:

When you send unconditional love to even the darkest circumstance, the alchemy begins. The body relaxes. The nervous system recalibrates. The immune system returns to truth.

Love dissolves fear.

This isn't just an abstract sentiment. Love changes your biology. It lowers cortisol. It reduces systemic inflammation. It activates

## Gate IV: Sovereign Toolkit

the vagus nerve, rebalances the nervous system, boosts heart rate variability, and strengthens immune function at the cellular level. T-cells multiply. The endocrine system calms. Your biochemistry becomes coherent again.

Where fear fractures the field, love restores it. It is a biological counterattack.

Yes, rejecting their poisons matters. So does rejecting their programming. Because even if you eat clean, filter your water, and detox your cells—if your mind is still captive to fear, you are not free. You are not whole.

Choosing love—fierce love, discerning love—is how you reclaim that wholeness. Not the sentimental kind, but the kind that says: I will not comply with sickness. I will not surrender my sovereignty. I will not live under threat.

When you send unconditional love into even the darkest circumstance, the alchemy begins. The body relaxes. The nervous system recalibrates. The immune system remembers truth.

Love dissolves fear.

In this world—where the toxins are not just in the food and water, but in the stories we're fed daily—that is no small act.

# Glossary Of Terms

5G: The fifth generation of wireless technology, often associated with faster data speeds and concerns about health and surveillance.

**A**

Adaptogens: Natural herbs or substances believed to help the body adapt to stress and restore balance.

Algorithmic control: The use of computer algorithms to shape behavior, decisions, and access to information.

Algorithmic nudging: Subtle manipulation of choices or perceptions through algorithm-driven suggestions and prompts.

Alternative exchange: Non-traditional systems of trade, such as barter or community currencies, outside mainstream money.

Ancestral healing: Practices aimed at addressing unresolved trauma and patterns inherited from one's ancestors.

Ancestral memory: The idea that lived experiences and wisdom from ancestors can be carried within us.

Aquaponics: A system of food production combining fish farming with hydroponic plant growth in a closed loop.

# Glossary Of Terms

Archetypal imprinting: The influence of universal symbolic patterns (archetypes) on human behavior and belief.

Archetypes: Universal symbols or roles that represent recurring patterns in human stories and psychology.

Ascendence: The process of rising to higher levels of awareness, consciousness, or spiritual development.

Ascension seal: A symbolic marker representing the completion of a stage of spiritual awakening.

Ascension window: A period believed to be favorable for rapid spiritual growth and collective awakening.

Astral gate: An energetic entry point to non-physical planes of consciousness, often accessed in dreams or meditation.

Astral layers: Different vibrational levels within the astral plane or non-physical realms.

Astral travel: The experience of consciousness leaving the body and traveling in non-physical dimensions.

Astrological portals: Specific alignments of celestial bodies believed to open gateways for transformation or insight.

Aura integrity: The state of maintaining a strong, healthy personal energy field that resists intrusion or imbalance.

Authentic self: One's true, unconditioned identity, free from external programming or false masks.

Authentic will: The inner drive or intention that comes from one's true self rather than societal conditioning.

Autonomy practices: Practical methods of living independently of centralized systems and external control.

Awakening completion: The full realization and embodiment of spiritual awakening.

Awakening process: The gradual journey of becoming more conscious, aware, and spiritually aligned.

## B

Banishing: A ritual or practice to remove negative energies, influences, or entities from one's space or self.

## Glossary Of Terms

Barter networks: Community-based systems where goods and services are exchanged without the use of money.

Behavioral economics: The study of how psychological factors influence economic decision-making, often used to guide or manipulate consumer behavior.

Belief deconstruction: The process of breaking down inherited or conditioned beliefs to examine their truth or usefulness.

Belief hacking: The intentional reshaping of beliefs to empower new outcomes and perspectives.

Belief loops: Repetitive cycles of thought that reinforce the same perception or reality.

Bio-hacking: The practice of using science, technology, and lifestyle changes to optimize the body and mind.

Bio-surveillance: Monitoring of human biological data (such as health or movement) by governments or corporations.

Blueprint activation: Awakening or unlocking latent spiritual or genetic potential within the human body.

Body of light: A subtle, energetic body believed to develop through spiritual practice, associated with higher consciousness.

Body sovereignty: Full authority over one's own body, health, and choices, free from external control.

Bread and circuses: Distractions provided by entertainment or trivial pleasures that keep people from questioning authority.

Bread and circuses redux: A modern return to using entertainment and consumer culture to pacify the masses.

Breaking consent loops: Ending cycles of unconscious agreement with systems of control or manipulation.

## C

Cabal: A secretive group believed to hold hidden power and influence over society.

Celebrity programming: The use of celebrity culture to shape public opinion, values, and behaviors.

Celestial guidance: Wisdom or direction believed to come from

## Glossary Of Terms

the stars, planets, or cosmic forces.

Cellular memory: The idea that experiences, traumas, and patterns are stored not only in the brain but in every cell of the body.

Chaos magic: A form of magic focused on belief as a tool, using symbols and rituals flexibly for personal empowerment.

Circadian alignment: Living in harmony with the body's natural sleep-wake cycles to support health and energy.

Clean water sovereignty: The ability to source and protect one's own safe, uncontaminated water supply.

Coded narratives: Stories or media designed with hidden meanings or symbols that shape perception subconsciously.

Collapse cycles: Patterns of decline and renewal that occur in civilizations, systems, or personal lives.

Collective awakening: A widespread rise in consciousness and awareness across society.

Collective field: The shared energetic or psychological space influenced by the thoughts and emotions of many people.

Collective timeline: The path of humanity's shared experience, shaped by collective decisions and energies.

Command of vibration: The ability to consciously direct one's own energetic frequency and presence.

Community resilience: The strength of a group to withstand, adapt, and thrive despite crisis or disruption.

Conscious abeyance: A state of holding back immediate reaction, allowing awareness to guide response.

Conscious dreaming: The practice of being aware within dreams and directing them intentionally.

Conscious navigation: Moving deliberately through different states of consciousness or awareness.

Conscious nutrition: Eating with awareness of how food affects body, mind, and spirit.

Contracts of silence: Unspoken or hidden agreements to remain quiet about corruption or abuse.

## Glossary Of Terms

Control grid: The invisible network of systems, technologies, and institutions designed to monitor and control people.

Control systems: Mechanisms of social, political, or technological power used to maintain dominance.

Controlled narratives: Official or mainstream stories that conceal truth while shaping belief.

Controlled opposition: A person or group presented as resisting authority but actually working to maintain the system.

Controlled outcomes: Results engineered in advance by those with influence, regardless of apparent choice.

Controlled demolition: The intentional collapse of a structure, system, or institution disguised as natural failure.

Cultural engineering: The shaping of collective beliefs and values through media, institutions, and propaganda.

Currency trap: Dependence on centralized money systems that keep individuals bound to debt and control.

## D

Dark entities: Non-physical beings believed to feed on fear or manipulate human behavior.

Data harvesting: The large-scale collection of personal information for profit or surveillance.

Debt slavery: A condition in which individuals or nations are trapped in endless cycles of borrowing and repayment.

Decentralized networks: Systems that operate without a central authority, often peer-to-peer or blockchain-based.

Death-rebirth pattern: Cycles of transformation involving endings followed by renewal and growth.

Discernment: The skill of distinguishing truth from falsehood, especially in spiritual or social matters.

Dimensions: Levels of reality or consciousness beyond the physical three-dimensional world.

Divine feminine: The archetype of nurturing, intuitive, receptive, and creative energy.

## Glossary Of Terms

Divine masculine: The archetype of active, protective, logical, and initiating energy.

DNA activation: The process of unlocking latent codes within human DNA for spiritual or evolutionary growth.

Dream seeding: The practice of planting intentions or questions into the subconscious before sleep to influence dreams.

Dreamscape: The symbolic or energetic landscape experienced while dreaming.

## E

Ego traps: Mental pitfalls where the ego distorts spiritual growth into pride, superiority, or avoidance.

Elite illusion: The appearance of freedom or choice created by those in power to mask deeper control.

Elite signaling: Symbols or codes used by powerful groups to communicate hidden agendas.

EMF (Electromagnetic fields): Invisible radiation from electronic devices and networks, sometimes linked to health concerns.

Empirical truth: Facts that can be directly observed or experienced, independent of opinion or belief.

Energy imprinting: The lasting effect of energetic patterns on people, spaces, or objects.

Energetic consent: The agreement, conscious or unconscious, to allow energy exchange or influence.

Energetic contracts: Subtle agreements, often unseen, that bind individuals to relationships, systems, or patterns.

Energetic portals: Openings to other dimensions or states of consciousness.

Energetic shielding: Practices used to protect one's personal energy from intrusion or harm.

Entities: Non-physical beings, sometimes seen as guides, spirits, or parasites.

Esoteric coding: The use of hidden, symbolic messages to convey deeper spiritual or occult meaning.

## Glossary Of Terms

Exit currency trap: The process of moving away from reliance on centralized money into independent systems.

Exit strategies: Practical plans for leaving unhealthy relationships, systems, or environments.

## F

False flag: An event staged to appear as if caused by an enemy or outsider, used to justify control or war.

False gurus: Spiritual teachers who manipulate followers or distort truth for personal gain.

False idols: People or symbols elevated to worshipful status that distract from authentic spiritual connection.

False matrix: The artificial layer of reality created by manipulation and control systems.

False narratives: Stories promoted to mislead or distract the public from truth.

Fear porn: Media or messages designed to generate fear and keep people disempowered.

Federal Reserve: The central banking system of the United States, often criticized for creating debt cycles.

Fiat currency: Government-issued money not backed by physical assets, valued only by trust.

Filtered through the ego: The distortion of truth or experience when interpreted only through personal bias.

Final initiation: The last stage of a spiritual or transformative journey, marking full integration.

Flow state: A heightened state of focus and creativity where actions feel effortless.

Food system trap: The cycle of dependence on processed and industrial foods that undermine health.

Freedom codes: Energetic or symbolic patterns that support liberation and sovereignty.

Frequency: The vibrational rate of energy, often linked to mood, health, or consciousness.

## Glossary Of Terms

Frequency alignment: Bringing one's energy into harmony with higher or desired frequencies.

Frequency coding: Embedding vibrational information into the body, mind, or environment.

Frequency pollution: Disruptive or harmful frequencies from technology or environments that disturb balance.

Frequency shift: A change in vibrational state that alters perception, energy, or awareness.

## G

Gaslighting: A manipulation tactic that causes someone to doubt their own memory, perception, or sanity.

Galactic heritage: The belief in spiritual or genetic connections to other star systems or civilizations.

Goodbye fear: A call to release fear as a controlling force in life.

Gratitude practice: A daily or intentional focus on appreciation as a tool for shifting perspective.

Group field: The shared energy created by people gathering with intention.

## H

Heirloom seeds: Seeds passed down through generations, free from genetic modification.

Health machine: The system of industrialized medicine driven by profit rather than true wellness.

Health sovereignty: Full control and responsibility over one's health choices, practices, and resources.

Hidden elite: Powerful groups operating behind the scenes of politics and society.

Hidden programming: Subconscious conditioning introduced through culture, media, or institutions.

Hidden in plain sight: A tactic where truths are concealed within obvious places, unnoticed by most.

## Glossary Of Terms

Higher planes: Subtle dimensions of consciousness beyond ordinary physical reality.

Higher alignment: Living in harmony with one's soul or higher aspect of being.

Higher vibration: A state of elevated energy associated with love, clarity, and awareness.

Holistic medicine: Approaches to healing that consider the whole person—body, mind, and spirit.

Hopium: False hope promoted to pacify or distract from taking real action.

Hydroponics: Growing plants without soil, using nutrient-rich water solutions.

## I

Illusion maintenance: The constant reinforcement of false realities by systems of control.

Illusion of choice: The perception of freedom when all options are still controlled by the same powers.

Inverted symbols: Sacred or cultural symbols used in reversed or distorted ways to manipulate meaning.

I AM: A phrase signifying divine identity and self-realization.

Initiation rites: Ceremonial or symbolic acts marking transition into a new stage of awareness.

Inner barometer, Emotional barometer: The internal sense of discernment that detects lies, manipulation, or falsehoods.

Inner child healing: The practice of addressing wounds or unmet needs from childhood.

Inner reframe: Shifting perspective from within to alter one's reality.

Integration: The process of embodying insights and changes into everyday life.

## K

## Glossary Of Terms

Karmic loops: Repetitive cycles of action and consequence carried across lifetimes.

## L

Last threshold: The final barrier before full awakening or transformation.

Light codes: Vibrational information carried in energy, often described as activating DNA or consciousness.

Localism: A movement toward sourcing food, goods, and governance locally rather than globally.

Loosh: Energetic output (often fear or suffering) believed to be harvested by parasitic forces.

Lucid dreaming: The ability to realize one is dreaming and consciously direct the dream.

## M

Magnetism: The personal energy that attracts people, opportunities, or experiences.

Managed collapse: The deliberate steering of societal or economic breakdown for hidden agendas.

Manufactured consent: Public agreement shaped through propaganda and media influence.

Manufactured urgency: The creation of artificial crises to force decisions or compliance.

Mass entrainment: The synchronization of people's emotions or actions through shared rhythms or stimuli.

Mass hypnosis: Large-scale influence of people's perception through repetition and suggestion.

Mass psychology: The study or exploitation of collective behavior and decision-making.

Mass resonance: Shared energetic alignment across groups that amplifies effect or outcome.

Matrix: The artificial construct of reality created by programming and control.

## Glossary Of Terms

Media puppetry: The manipulation of narratives and perceptions through controlled media figures or outlets.

Media symbolism: The use of images, logos, and cultural cues in media to encode hidden meaning.

Medical sovereignty: The right and responsibility to make independent decisions about one's health and treatments.

Method of control: Any deliberate strategy used to manipulate or dominate populations.

Mind flip: A sudden reversal in perception that reveals a hidden truth or new perspective.

MindFlips: A practice of deliberately shifting thought patterns to break conditioning and expand awareness.

Mirror neurons: Brain cells that fire in response to seeing others act, believed to link empathy and learning.

Money spell: The perceived enchantment or illusion of debt-based currency systems.

Morphic resonance: The idea that fields of information influence species' behavior and collective memory.

Multi-dimensional self: The concept of one's consciousness existing simultaneously across multiple planes of reality.

Mutual aid web: Community networks formed to provide support, resources, and resilience outside mainstream systems.

## N

Narrative control: The power to shape how events are understood by managing stories around them.

Narrative management: The active steering of cultural and political discourse by media or elites.

Neuro-linguistic triggers: Words or patterns of speech that reprogram beliefs and behavior.

Neuroplasticity: The brain's ability to reorganize itself by forming new neural connections.

Night work: Spiritual or energetic practices believed to happen during sleep or dreams.

## Glossary Of Terms

Nootropics: Substances that enhance cognitive function, memory, or focus.

Nothing is set in stone: A reminder that reality is flexible and subject to change.

Nutrient resilience: The ability to maintain health and vitality through diverse, sustainable nutrition.

## O

Occult symbology: The use of mystical or hidden symbols in rituals, culture, or control systems.

Oneness: The awareness of unity and interconnectedness with all beings.

Out-of-body experience: The sensation of consciousness separating from the physical body.

Override: Choosing to step out of conditioned reactions and reassert conscious choice.

## P

Parasocial control: Influence exerted by celebrities or influencers through one-sided relationships.

Parallel economies: Alternative systems of trade and currency that function outside mainstream finance.

Parallel economy map: A framework for building or navigating such independent systems.

Parallel society: A self-organized community operating outside dominant structures.

Parallel systems: Networks that mirror existing institutions but operate with autonomy.

Paradigm: A model or worldview that shapes how reality is understood.

Perception filter: A lens through which experiences are interpreted, often limiting awareness.

Perception management: Strategies for controlling how people interpret events and information.

## Glossary Of Terms

Phoenix archetype: A symbol of death and rebirth, resilience, and transformation.

Pharma spell: The entrancing influence of pharmaceutical culture and dependence.

Pineal gland: A small gland in the brain often linked to intuition, dreams, and spiritual vision.

Plant medicine: The use of herbs or natural substances for physical, emotional, and spiritual healing.

Planned scarcity: The deliberate restriction of resources to create dependency.

Polarity balance: The harmonizing of opposing forces such as masculine/feminine or light/dark.

Pop culture spell: The influence of entertainment and trends on mass consciousness.

Possession states: Conditions where an external entity or influence temporarily takes control of a person.

Power scripts: Pre-determined strategies elites use to maintain authority.

Predictive analytics: Data-driven forecasting used to predict and influence human behavior.

Predictive programming: The seeding of ideas in culture or media to normalize future events.

Presence: A state of full awareness and being grounded in the current moment.

Processed food: Industrially altered foods that are stripped of natural nutrients and integrity.

Programmed trends: Social fads manufactured to direct collective behavior.

Propaganda filter: A critical lens to identify and reject manipulative information.

Psyops: Psychological operations intended to manipulate perception and morale.

# Q

## Glossary Of Terms

Quantum biology: The study of biological processes influenced by quantum mechanics, a branch of physics where the usual rules of classical physics no longer apply.

Quantum choice: The recognition that choices at any moment shape reality.

Quantum choice points: Critical decision moments where reality can shift in dramatically different directions.

## R

Radiate: To emit energy or presence outward, influencing others and the environment.

Radical Karma: A concept of accelerated karmic return, where actions bring swift and powerful consequences.

Reality pivot: A sudden shift in perspective that redefines one's understanding of reality.

Rebirth codes: Symbolic or energetic patterns associated with renewal after collapse or transformation.

Rebel archetype: The symbolic figure who challenges norms and defies systems of control.

Rebel's ascension: The process of achieving liberation and spiritual rise by resisting false systems.

Regenerative farming: Agricultural methods that restore soil, ecosystems, and biodiversity.

Relationship programming: Cultural or psychological conditioning that dictates how relationships are formed and maintained.

Renewal path: The direction of growth and transformation following collapse or breakdown.

Resilience mapping: The practice of identifying and strengthening resources to withstand disruption.

Revelation of the method: The tactic of revealing truth in plain sight to diminish its impact.

Ritual inversion: The deliberate reversal of sacred or cultural rituals for manipulation or control.

## Glossary Of Terms

Ritual theater: The use of ceremony or staged acts to influence collective consciousness.

## S

Sacred economics: Systems of exchange based on values of fairness, reciprocity, and community.

Sacred union: The spiritual integration of masculine and feminine energies within or between partners.

Scripted reality: Events orchestrated to appear spontaneous but actually planned in advance.

Scripted reveal: A controlled disclosure of hidden truth at a chosen time.

Seed saving: The act of preserving seeds from crops for future planting, ensuring independence and biodiversity.

Self-knowing: Deep awareness of one's own true nature and purpose.

Self-mastery: The ability to direct thoughts, emotions, and actions consciously.

Semiotics: The study of signs and symbols and how they create meaning.

Service to other: A path of spiritual growth focused on compassion, giving, and cooperation.

Service to self: A path of spiritual growth centered on personal power, control, or self-interest.

Shared vision: A collective sense of direction or purpose held by a group.

Shadow government: A hidden power structure that influences or controls official governments.

Shadow integration: The process of acknowledging and transforming hidden or denied aspects of the self.

Shadow projections: Attributing one's denied traits or fears onto others.

Shock doctrine: A strategy of exploiting crises to push through unpopular policies.

## Glossary Of Terms

Shamanic journeying: A spiritual practice of traveling into non-ordinary realities for healing or insight.

Signal hijacking: The redirection of attention or energy away from truth toward manipulation.

Sleepers: People unaware of deeper truths, living entirely within the illusion of control systems.

Smart grid: A digital energy network designed for efficiency but also capable of surveillance and control.

Social engineering: The manipulation of human behavior and decisions through psychological tactics.

Social hypnosis: The widespread entrainment of society into collective belief or behavior patterns.

Soul contracts: Agreements made before birth believed to shape life lessons and relationships.

Soul fragmentation: The splitting off of aspects of self due to trauma or manipulation.

Soul mission: The higher purpose or calling of an individual's life.

Soul retrieval: The healing practice of reclaiming fragmented parts of the self.

Soul sovereignty: The ultimate authority and freedom of one's soul beyond external control.

Soul triumph: The victory of authentic self and spirit over manipulation or fear.

Spectacle economy: An economy driven by appearances, events, and distractions rather than substance.

Spectacle politics: Political theater designed to entertain or distract rather than inform.

Spell loops: Repetitive thought or behavior cycles reinforced by cultural or energetic programming.

Spiritual bypassing: Using spirituality to avoid facing uncomfortable truths or emotions.

Stagecraft of Power: The manipulation of public perception through carefully orchestrated events.

## Glossary Of Terms

Stagecraft: The art of creating illusions or appearances to control audiences.

State theater: Political or social performances staged to manipulate belief.

Strategic withdrawal: A conscious retreat from harmful systems, environments, or relationships.

Strength of will: The ability to remain committed to truth and self-sovereignty under pressure.

Supply chain audit: A review of where goods and resources come from to ensure independence and resilience.

Supplement stack: A combination of vitamins, herbs, or nootropics used to optimize health and performance.

Symbolic disclosure: The act of revealing truth through symbols, often hidden in media or culture.

Synthetic solutions: Artificial or chemically derived fixes that ignore natural or holistic approaches.

## T

Tavistock: A research institute often cited as influential in mass psychology and social engineering.

Telepathic field: The energetic web of thought or communication shared beyond spoken language.

The Great Channeling Debacle: A cautionary reference to failed or misleading spiritual communications.

The Matrix: The metaphorical construct of control that limits perception of true reality.

Theater of control: The orchestrated spectacle of power designed to maintain illusions of order.

Threshold crossings: Key points of transition where individuals or societies move into new states of being.

Timeline hopping: The practice of shifting one's awareness or life path onto different potential realities.

Twin flames: A spiritual concept of two souls mirroring each other's growth and lessons.

## Glossary Of Terms

Truth anchoring: Grounding insights and revelations into everyday reality.

Truth frequency: The vibrational state aligned with honesty, authenticity, and higher awareness.

Truth veil: The thin barrier that separates illusion from deeper reality.

## U

Unity consciousness: The awareness of being part of one universal whole.

Universal Synchronicity: The experience of meaningful coincidences that reflect deeper order.

Unmasked: The act of revealing one's true identity or exposing deception.

## V

Vibrational integrity: The consistency of living in alignment with one's highest values and frequency.

Vibrational resonance: The energetic harmony that allows beings or systems to align with each other.

## W

Warding: A protective practice to keep out harmful energies or influences.

War profiteering: The act of making financial gain from warfare and conflict.

Wellness autonomy: The ability to make one's own informed choices about health and well-being.

# Afterword

Welcome to the world of independent thinkers. If you haven't already, you're in the process of shedding the programming which tells you how to think, act, and live your life. At the end of this process is complete freedom.

The books which excite you may not conform to an "accepted" way of thinking. The author may have broken through some barriers. A book may be revolutionary in how it changes your thinking.

You are joining with others who are rebelling against what is wrong in this world by adopting the biggest revolutionary act of all: standing in your own truth and authenticity.

See more at https://LaneKeller.com

To learn more about Jane Donovan:
https://www.janedonovan.com.au/

# I Hope You Enjoyed This

I hope you enjoyed this book and that you found the information presented here valuable. I sincerely hope it has provided enough information to speed you on your journey to a beautiful, blissful life.

I ask once more for a favor, and that is to take a moment to write an honest, sincere review of this book on Amazon. Reviews help authors like me out more than you can imagine.

To leave a review, please use this link:
https://kdp.amazon.com/en_US/bookshelf?publishedId=A1XITKUE4S5MW1

If the link doesn't work, copy and paste into Amazon: "Lane Keller, Unleashing the Rebel Within."

I truly appreciate your effort!

# About the Author

An undeterred seeker of truth who combines a mix of an advanced professional writing career with the development of empowerment strategies, Lane Keller is the voice and motor behind Bright Mind Media and its subsidiary organizations.

Keller writes in many genres including alternative health, the truth of the world, history and politics, the New World Order, personal spirituality, and more. As an experienced public speaker, Keller has spoken out about the subterfuges afflicting our planet on various radio shows and podcasts.

Keller is a true proponent of empowerment from within, believing that the way for society to break its enslavement is through education and revibration, without dogma, brainwashing, or hero worship. Keller is committed to unleashing humanity from the control system that binds it through education and the lifting of consciousness.

See more at Lanekeller.com

# Other Works by Lane Keller

For news of upcoming releases:
https://lanekeller.substack.com
Or go to my website:
Https://Lanekeller.com
More of my work can be found at the following links.
*Alice in Pedoland* (2-part docuseries)
https://linktr.ee/aliceinpedoland
*Lane Explains, Down the Rabbit Hole in Two Minutes*
https://linktr.ee/lslaneexplains
*Light Your Fire: The Ayurveda Diet for Weight Loss: Boost Metabolism, Regain Health & Lose Weight.* A unique and simple system based on the ancient science of Ayurveda
https://amzn.to/4b9NNkq
*Why Am I Here? A Concise Guide to Your Purpose and Potential* Written with Joyce Keller
https://amzn.to/49TobHr
*Tale of Running Bear, A Picture Book for Adult-Minded Young People*
https://amzn.to/4b2MuUs

www.ingramcontent.com/pod-product-compliance
Lightning Source LLC
Chambersburg PA
CBHW050508240426
43673CB00004B/156